AF521648

The Origins of the Common Core

The Origins of the Common Core

How the Free Market Became Public Education Policy

Deborah Duncan Owens

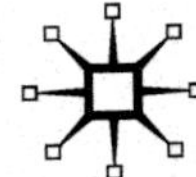

THE ORIGINS OF THE COMMON CORE

First published in 2015 by PALGRAVE MACMILLAN® in the United States—a division of St. Martin's Press LLC, 175 Fifth Avenue, New York, NY 10010.

Where this book is distributed in the UK, Europe and the rest of the world, this is by Palgrave Macmillan, a division of Macmillan Publishers Limited, registered in England, company number 785998, of Houndmills, Basingstoke, Hampshire RG21 6XS.

Palgrave Macmillan is the global academic imprint of the above companies and has companies and representatives throughout the world.

ISBN: 978-1-137-48267-9

Library of Congress Cataloging-in-Publication Data

Owens, Deborah Duncan.
The origins of the common core : how the free market became public education policy / by Deborah Duncan Owens.
pages cm
Includes bibliographical references and index.
ISBN 978-1-137-48267-9
1. Education and state—United States. 2. Education—Standards—United States. 3. School improvement programs—United States. I. Title.
LB89.O93 2015
379.73—dc23

2014028535

A catalogue record of the book is available from the British Library.

Design by Amnet

First edition: January 2015

10 9 8 7 6 5 4 3 2 1

Transferred to Digital Printing in 2015

Contents

Foreword

By Thomas J. Fiala, PhD

For a growing number of Americans, the Common Core State Standards (CCSS), and the educational ramifications of these standards, have become the most contentious education reform initiative in American history. For some, the creation of these standards reflects the ominous hand of the federal government that intends to dominate locally controlled public schools. For others, these standards are connected to a corporate assault on America's public school system. One thing is certain, however. There is a war now being fought over the very existence of America's public school system, a system that has played an essential role in helping make America become not only a preeminent world power, but that has also been a democratic means to increased individual improvement and opportunity, overall social betterment, and another reason why so many diverse groups have always come to the United States in order to help make their hopes and aspirations become reality.

There is, however, a nagging two-part question that is being asked by a vast number of Americans. How did the Common Core State Standards come to be, and how did America and its public schools become entangled in the plethora of educational initiatives that have made the public school system a feeding ground for profit. Until now, it seems that no single coherent in-depth analysis is available that begins to unpack the historically complex social, political, and ideological influences that are at the root of the CCSS phenomenon. Without this type of in-depth rigorous analysis, Americans will only continue to ask, "How did the CCSS come to be?" While there exist short, fragmented answers to this question that are partially correct, and there are many fine books that address this question in an indirect manner, no single well-researched narrative exists that begins to explain the long and complex origins of the CCSS and the current assault on America's public school system.

Stepping forward to take on this daunting challenge is Dr. Deborah Duncan Owens, without a doubt a defender of America's democratic system of public education. What the reader will discover in this book is a story that will fortify the beliefs of many Americans who cherish their locally controlled public schools, while also arming these public school supporters with the needed knowledge to understand, and then disarm, those who see the free market as the solution to solving the complex educational challenges confronting the United States. What Owens has been able to accomplish is an explanation of how, as the title of the book boldly states, the free market became public school policy. Most important, as Owens points out, within this process, America's public school system has once again become a scapegoat for all that ails American society, while heralding all the ramifications of free market systemic education reform as the means of saving the United States from its supposed enemy—the public school system writ large.

For those who see the numerous reform initiatives such as high-stakes testing, charter schools, vouchers, value-added measurement, student-data collecting, and the disempowerment of citizens in decision making when it comes to their public schools as the wrong approach to meeting the education challenges confronting the United States, this is an empowering book. By helping parents, teachers, and other stakeholders who support America's public school system to not only understand how these initiatives came to be, but also understand the weaknesses within these initiatives, this book has the potential to not only further unite supporters of the public school system in order to save this system, but also add clarity and validation to their efforts to maintain control over their public schools and guide future education policy making. For those who support current reform initiatives, the book has the potential to change some minds regarding these initiatives.

For those individuals on the political and ideological right or left who are militantly wedded to their ideas, however, this book will not provide safe haven. This is because, as the book makes clear, both political parties have found common ground in a unified allegiance to a free market approach to systemic education reform that has created an educational sea of profit at the expense of America's most important resource—its children. That being the case, the book is more than an academic exercise, although that in itself is obviously worthwhile. It is also a book that challenges fundamental beliefs and creates ideological dissonance, which can reenergize democratic discourse.

In the end, readers will gain important insight into the current state of education reform. They will get a better understanding of how and why the current state of education reform came to be, while also understanding that there is a good deal that needs to be done, particularly for those marginalized groups and individuals who need a better education. Very importantly, however, this book will challenge the notion that a free market approach to systemic education reform is the proper way to positively improve public schools. Clearly, Owens believes that it is a misguided attempt to destroy, and not merely reform, America's historically beneficial public school system. Perhaps after reading this book, others will agree as well.

Chapter 1

The Nation Was at Risk and the Public Schools Did It

It was "morning again in America" in 1984. The credibility of President Ronald Reagan's economic policies had been bolstered during his first term in office by lower inflation rates, higher employment, and an increase in new home purchases. Indeed, many of the issues that had dampened prospects in America during the 1970s were over. The government turmoil associated with Watergate was history, the Vietnam War and the draft had ended, the Iranian hostage crisis was resolved, the oil embargo ended, and, in spite of the higher cost for gasoline, America seemed to be on the road to an economic recovery. The free market ideals that Reagan espoused seemed to be working, and, for many, his assertion that government was not the solution to the country's problems, but that government was the problem, seemed to be correct.[1]

During Reagan's 1980 presidential campaign, he affixed blame for the economic distress of the country on the big-government policies of Democratic President Jimmy Carter, vowing to shrink the size of an unwieldy, overly bureaucratic federal government.[2] One of the government entities targeted for elimination was the newly formed federal Department of Education (DOE), established by President Carter in 1979. When Jimmy Carter took office, the governance of federal education policies was primarily overseen by the Department of Health, Education, and Welfare (HEW). But with the creation of the DOE, education policy makers would gain credibility and power by making the secretary of the department a cabinet-level position with a seat at the table when all federal policies were being made.

The Creation of the Department of Education

Efforts to create a federal DOE date back to as early as the turn of the twentieth-century. Between the years 1908 and 1975, more than 130 bills to create a cabinet-level position for a separate federal DOE, which would provide power and autonomy for education policy makers, were unsuccessfully introduced. In 1972, the National Education Association (NEA) formed a political action committee, and, in 1975, they joined forces with eight other unions to form the Labor Coalition Clearinghouse (LCC) for the purpose of supporting and endorsing political candidates. Of the eight unions that coordinated their efforts through the LCC, all but three were members of the American Federation of Labor and Congress of Industrial Organizations (AFL-CIO). Missing from the list was the American Federation of Teachers (AFT), a teachers' union affiliated with the AFL-CIO. With the support of other members of the LCC, the NEA released the document, "Needed: A Cabinet Department of Education" in 1975. Additionally, for the first time in the history of the NEA, the organization endorsed a presidential candidate—the Democratic candidate Jimmy Carter.[3]

While campaigning for the Democratic nomination for president in 1976, Carter made a commitment to the creation of a federal department of education in an address before an NEA convention. However, he would not officially declare his position on this matter until he had secured his nomination by the Democratic Party. In spite of the fact that he had campaigned on a platform of streamlining the federal government, he would honor his promise to the NEA. Among his strongest supporters for the creation of the department was Senator Abraham Ribicoff, who had previously served as Secretary of HEW under President John Kennedy. After Carter was elected president, Ribicoff, along with four other Democratic senators, crafted the Department of Education Organization Act. The proposal to create a federal DOE was hotly debated through two sessions of Congress. Opposition to the department came from both the political right and the political left. It isn't surprising that many Republicans opposed the creation of another arm of the federal government, attempting to stall passage of the bill by adding amendments that would restrict school busing, affirmative action, abortion rights, and limits on school prayer. However, opposition also came from some of the more liberal allies of the Democratic Party. Generally, those concerns had to do with the transferring of smaller departments to the DOE, resulting in the weakening of their influence. For example, the Children's Defense Fund lobbied in favor of maintaining its office within the Department of Health and Human Services, fearing that some of the components of the Head Start program, such as nutrition, health, and family participation, would be lost under the governance of a newly created DOE. Likewise, other program administrators argued against their program's proposed transfer to the DOE. The Department of Agriculture wanted to maintain control over school nutrition programs, and the Department of Interior wanted to maintain control of Indian schools.

The AFT, a competitor of the NEA, opposed the creation of the DOE because the union claimed that their affiliation with the AFL-CIO gave them powerful and influential allies on the House Education and Labor Committee, and a new department would actually weaken the influence of the union on education issues. A coalition of civil rights and education groups also opposed the creation of a separate DOE because they feared that the enforcement of civil rights laws would be weakened. Joseph Califano, who had been appointed by President Carter to serve as the secretary of HEW, actively lobbied against the creation of the DOE and was subsequently fired.

After two years of contentious debate and political wrangling, the bill was finally sent to the Congressional Conference Committee. All the issues had been resolved. Liberal concerns had been resolved, with programs such as Head Start, school nutrition programs, and Indian schooling remaining in their existing departments. All the amendments added by the conservatives had been removed by the Conference Committee and the bill passed with a narrow margin, making way for the creation of the DOE. President Carter signed the Department of Education Organization Act into law on October 17, 1979, thus creating the thirteenth Cabinet department.[4]

In President Carter's November 17, 1979, statement following the signing of the Department of Education Organization law, he provided his rationale for the creation of the DOE and reconciled the need for the department with his efforts to streamline federal government bureaucracy. Carter acknowledged that the primary responsibility for education should rest with the states, localities, and private institutions "that have made our Nation's educational system the best in the world." The federal government, however, had failed to effectively support education and had "confused its role of junior partner" with that of silent partner, providing only part-time support for America's schools while increasing added burdens to schools through regulations. The newly formed DOE would "allow the federal government to meet its responsibilities in education more effectively, more efficiently, and more responsively." The American people, stated Carter, "should receive a better return on their investment in education."[5]

Carter explained the benefits of the DOE within the federal government: (1) the DOE would increase the nation's attention in education, giving educational issues the top priority they deserve with a cabinet-level position; (2) federal education programs would become more accountable; (3) administration of aid-to-education programs would be more streamlined; (4) tax dollars would be saved through the elimination of bureaucratic layers; (5) federal education programs would be more responsive, giving the American people the ability to decide what "the government should and should not be doing in education." Finally, and most important, Carter explained that the DOE would ensure that local communities would retain control of their schools and education programs. The DOE would prohibit the federal government from making decisions about education policies that are best made at the local level by those who are better able to make decisions about the students they serve.[6]

In 1979, President Carter appointed Shirley Hufstedler as the first secretary of education. Hufstedler, who had a distinguished legal career and had been appointed associate justice of the California Court of Appeals in 1966 by President Johnson, went to work quickly to establish the DOE's agenda. Her first set of goals included the reduction of regulatory red tape associated with student aid to schools; a second set of goals supported the notion that the DOE would not supersede local control over schools through the imposition of regulations; and a third set of goals focused on educational equity. Hufstedler then committed herself to spending time traveling around the country to "elevate the consciousness of Americans about the good work classroom teachers do."[7]

Hufstedler's tenure as DOE secretary was short lived, however, when President Carter lost his bid for a second term in office and the newly elected President Ronald Reagan would pursue his educational goals of abolishing the DOE, returning control over education to states, providing vouchers and tax credits for students to attend private schools, and restricting limitations on school prayer. Reagan would learn, however, that abolishing a federal department and a cabinet-level position would not be a simple task.

In order to fulfill his campaign promise to abolish the DOE, Reagan would have to appoint a secretary of education to oversee the project. Terrel Bell, who had formerly served as commissioner of education within HEW under Presidents Nixon and Ford, was appointed by Reagan to return to Washington to oversee the process.[8] Interestingly, Bell had supported the creation of a DOE during the Carter administration and had even testified before a senate committee in support of the legislation.[9] However, he understood the charge he was given by Reagan and he tried to resolve the disconnect between his own support of the department and the new administration's intention to abolish it. Early in his tenure as secretary of the DOE, Bell worked with Reagan's administration to draft a bill that would abolish his department and replace it with a foundation that would maintain authority and governance over public education at the federal level. In spite of his concern that such a move would eliminate the cabinet-level position the new department had created and reduce the power of education policy makers, Bell understood his tenuous role within a conservative administration intent on downsizing the federal government. He was surprised, however, when, one by one, conservative members of Congress who supported Reagan's conservative economic and social policies refused to support a bill to abolish the DOE.[10] Bell, a conservative himself, was frustrated when trying to reconcile the factions that existed among conservatives in Washington in the early 1980s as right-wing conservatives working closely with the president used their power and influence to stifle the voices of more moderate conservatives.[11] Throughout his first two years at the DOE, Bell had to muster up all of his administrative skills to keep his department functional. It was clear to him as well that the conservative administration was sharply divided among themselves, and conservative members of Congress did not have the will to join the Reagan administration's efforts to abolish the DOE.

In spite of the internal wrangling taking place within the Reagan administration, Bell had to carry on the business of overseeing the DOE. In 1981, he proposed the formation of a presidentially appointed commission to study the current state of education in America and prepare a report for the government. His proposal was met with "diffidence and scorn" and summarily rejected by the White House.[12] Nevertheless, Bell steadfastly proceeded with his plan, circumventing the White House's approval and obtaining a federal charter through the Office of Management and Budget (OMB) to establish the commission that would later be named the National Commission on Excellence in Education (NCEE). According to Bell, the appointment of this commission was considered by some White House administrators and OMB staffers to be an act of insubordination.[13] Bell imagined that the commission's report that would be produced by the NCEE could be the final task for the DOE.

Instead, however, the commission's report, later named *A Nation at Risk: The Imperative for Educational Reform* (*ANAR*), set off an educational firestorm that would radically change America's educational landscape, increasing the power and influence of the federal government over education in all 50 states while ensuring the department's continued existence.

The National Commission on Excellence in Education

Terrel Bell called upon David Pierpont Gardner, president of the University of Utah and president-elect of the University of California, to chair the national commission. Seventeen other commission members would eventually be appointed from across the country, representing what Bell considered to be a balanced group of "liberals and conservatives, Republicans and Democrats, males and females, minorities, educators and noneducators."[14] Three of these appointees, like Gardner, served as presidents at institutions of higher education: Norman C. Francis, president of Xavier University of Louisiana in New Orleans; A. Bartlett Giamatti, president of Yale University; and Shirley Gordon, president of Highline Community College. Three members of the commission were affiliated with school boards: the vice-chair of the commission, Yvonne W. Larsen, had served as the president of the school board for San Diego City Schools; Margaret S. Marston was currently serving as a member of Virginia's Board of Education; and Robert V. Haderlein was the past president of the National School Board Association. Anne Campbell was the former commissioner of education for the State of Nebraska. Two school principals served on the commission: Emeral A. Crosby, from a public school, Northern High School in Detroit, Michigan; and Richard Wallace, from a private school, Lutheran High School East in Cleveland Heights, Ohio. One superintendent of a public school district served on the commission: Francisco D. Sanchez, Jr., from Albuquerque Public Schools in New Mexico. The interests of the science community were served by Gerald Holton, a professor of physics and the history of science at Harvard University; and Glenn T. Seaborg, Nobel laureate and professor of chemistry at the University of California, Berkeley. Business interests, with a strong emphasis on science, were served by William O. Baker, former chairman of the board for Bell Telephone Laboratories in New Jersey. Also serving on the commission were Charles A. Foster, Jr., past president of the Foundation for Teaching Economics in San Francisco, and former governor of Minnesota, Albert H. Quie.

The only teacher on the commission was Jay Sommer, a foreign language teacher who had been honored as National Teacher of the Year for 1981–82.[15]

Possibly the most interesting appointment to the commission was Annette Y. Kirk. While her affiliation was simply listed as Kirk Associates of Mecosta, Michigan, she was the person who, as Gardner later explained, represented the views of parents. Kirk was the only person Reagan personally nominated for the commission.[16] A onetime New York City schoolteacher, she was the wife of Russell Kirk, one of the founders of the modern conservative movement and a man who fundamentally opposed the institution of public schools. Russell Kirk has been called one of President Reagan's favorite philosophers.[17] All 18 commission members shared the common perspective that public schools were failing to meet the needs of America's students, with three members, Yvonne Larsen, Albert Quie, and Annette Kirk, actively promoting one of Reagan's most controversial education reform proposals—tuition tax credits and vouchers.[18]

A NATION AT RISK: THE EVIDENCE

The NCEE asked Secretary Bell for, and was granted, full autonomy in their work analyzing the state of education in the country. He also pledged the full support and resources from the DOE and unlimited access to the department's data. The commission met for the first time October 9, 1981, and for the next 18 months held hearings across the country and considered evidence that would help them formulate an opinion about the status of education in America.[19] The hearings held by the NCEE were hosted by various luminaries in education, such as the president of Stanford University, the State Commissioners of Education, and the president of the Exxon Education Foundation, on various topics such as "Education for a Productive Role in a Productive Society" and "Education for the Gifted and Talented." Information learned at these hearings provided evidence for the commission's findings.[20] However, the question is, what empirical data was used by the NCEE in their evaluation of schools in America? In the current era of data-driven decision making in education and a focus on testing data, this is a fair question to consider.

Since 1969, the state of public education has been measured by the National Assessment of Educational Progress (NAEP).[21] For many years, statistics derived from NAEP scores have been the source of numerous alarming headlines decrying the failure of public schools. Understanding the NAEP testing program is essential when considering the data it provides as a means of assessing the state of schools in America and judging the validity of claims that the schools are failing.

The NAEP program began testing America's students in 1969. NAEP is not designed to be a high-stakes test, examine a particular curriculum, measure the adequacy of a particular school or district, or assess individual student success. Furthermore, NAEP is not administered to all students in America. It is administered to samples of students and, of the students sampled, no one takes the entire test. Students never receive a test score. As a matter of fact, children will most likely never take a NAEP test and, if they do take this test once, will probably never take it again. The test is designed to measure what a sampling of students from across the nation either know or don't know, not what is taught in school or to measure the effectiveness of teachers. Test items range in difficulty from easy to very difficult. It is expected that 90 percent of students will answer some of the questions correctly, 50 percent of students will answer other questions correctly, and some questions are so difficult that only 10 percent of students will answer them correctly.[22] While NAEP procedures and reporting methods have changed over the years, NAEP does provide a way of examining trends across America over time.

At the time when the NCEE was conducting its extensive evaluation of America's schools, NAEP data had been available since 1969; therefore, it would seem that this data could provide important information when judging the health of American schools at that time. However, no mention of NAEP data appears in *ANAR*. According to Bell, NAEP data was inconsistent, with some states participating and others refusing. Of the states that participated, some left it up to local school districts to make decisions about participation in the national testing program.[23] Therefore, the NAEP testing program prior to 1983 did not provide the type of data that could be used to assess teachers or the state of public schools in America.

As a matter of fact, when NAEP was first proposed, its critics were concerned that it would lead to national standards and a national curriculum, undermine state and local control over schools, and impose large-scale federal control over education. The creators of NAEP, therefore, recognized the danger of "unwittingly establishing standards" and gave control of the testing program to the Education Commission of the States (ECS) instead of the federal government and purposefully did not design a test that would measure individual schools, districts, or states. The earliest NAEP tests measured a wide range of subjects like citizenship, writing, science, music, social studies, math, art, career and occupational development, health awareness, consumer skills, basic life skills, and energy awareness and attitudes. NAEP was originally designed to be an innovative way to examine what people know and can do, favoring constructed-response items over multiple-choice answers, and was not designed merely to measure the knowledge of school children.[24] The nature of NAEP testing would dramatically change in 1983, however, as a result of the publication of *ANAR*. Administration for the national testing program would no longer be overseen by the ECS when Educational Testing Services (ETS) was awarded a federal grant to assume responsibility for administering the NAEP program. As a result, the test was revamped, paving the way for state accountability in the form of the "Nation's Report Card."[25]

It is hard today to imagine a country in which standardized test scores of elementary and high school students were not the driving force behind education policy decisions. However, in the years prior to 1983, standardized testing was actually de-emphasized and certainly was not universal in its use across the country.[26] In his memoir, Bell described the lack of data for determining student achievement through test scores in 1983:

> Putting together accurate assessments of each state's educational standing proved to be much more complex and controversial than I had anticipated. Gathering academic achievement test scores state by state turned out to be an utter impossibility.[27]

Prior to 1983, and, in particular, during the years after the *Brown v. Board of Education* decision, much of the impetus for reforming education had to do with addressing the disparities associated with racial segregation and unequal access to quality education.[28] Arguably, during the years of resistance to federal desegregation laws, there was little desire to administer standardized tests to all students across the country if the end result would be to demonstrate the vastly unequal educational experiences of white middle-class students and minority students. Beginning in 1967 with the book *Death at an Early Age*, Jonathan Kozol would provide an alarming chronicle for the next 30-plus years of the vast inequities in American public schools.[29]

In 1983, there was longitudinal standardized statewide test data available from only two states, Iowa and Minnesota, that supported the assertion that test scores increased for elementary and high school students during the post-Sputnik years (1959–66), followed by a steady decline.[30] Both of these states had been administering standardized tests to elementary and secondary students for a number of years and, therefore, trends in scores on those tests are well documented. While an analysis of the states' respective testing data could yield interesting information about their students' achievement over time, any comparison between states would be invalid because the states used different tests. Iowa administered the Iowa Test of Education Development and Minnesota administered the Minnesota Scholastic Aptitude Test.

In an analysis of student performance on the standardized tests administered by Iowa and Minnesota, L. A. Munday cites three possible explanations for the decline in test scores for these two states:

1. Testing was de-emphasized during this era. There were no high-stakes attached to the tests, and, therefore, students were not motivated to perform well.
2. The curriculum did not require students to know as much. (As will be discussed later in this chapter, there had been a curricular shift during the 1960s and 1970s as a result of efforts to retain more students in school through high school.)
3. Standardized tests were designed by psychometrists to be statistically sound over time and, therefore, were not intended to be closely aligned with the curriculum.[31]

Munday, however, provides an interesting caveat. During the years leading up to 1983, when standardized testing was not a routine part of schooling in America and testing data was not enshrined as the measure of school success, he argues that "no factual information was collected that showed what kind of schools, teachers, or instruction were most potent in bringing about the gains" during the post-Sputnik years.[32] During the years when the test scores were reported to be in decline, educators were required to explain lagging test scores but in the absence of factual information about what actually produced the higher test scores earlier. This was a difficult question to answer. In reality, according to Munday, the academic achievement of elementary students in 1976 was greater than that of their parents 20 to 25 years earlier.[33]

Without an adequate, reliable, and valid storehouse of data for public schools to use in their analysis of the state of education in 1983, the NCEE felt they had only one means of empirically examining student achievement. The Scholastic Aptitude Test (SAT) was first administered to American students in 1926, and, therefore, the commission had a longitudinal set of data to use in their examination of student achievement across decades. The SAT, however, was designed to be very different from the College Board Exams (CBE) that it would eventually replace. The CBE had been used to test content knowledge and, therefore, favored students who spent considerable time studying and preparing for the exam. For elite universities, this was seen as problematic as some ethnic groups, in particular some black and Jewish children in public schools, were scoring high enough on the CBE to attend exclusive universities. The SAT, therefore, was designed to be a psychological test of aptitude and qualities in much the same way as an IQ test. In an era in which eugenics was considered to be real science, this test was appealing because of supposed connections between ethnicity and intelligence. As a result, SATs could be used as a way to limit the admission of certain ethnic groups to elite universities.[34]

The SAT was normed in 1941 and thus became a standardized test. An important point in the standardization of the SAT is that the population used to establish scoring ranges was 10,654 students from the northeastern region of the United States. These students were overwhelmingly white (98 percent), male (61 percent), and many attended private, college-preparatory high schools (41 percent). In other words, they were elite. In spite of the changing demographics of high school and college-bound students in the coming decades, the norm established by this elite group remained in place until 1996.[35]

In the years prior to the NCEE's examination of public schools, there had been a consistent drop in SAT scores since 1963. Public school critics jumped on these reports to solidify their position that public schools were failing to meet the needs of America's school children. In 1975, the College Board established a panel to examine the decline in SAT scores and, after an exhaustive analysis, published their findings in 1977.[36] The panel concluded that declines in SAT scores were due to two different types of changes taking place in schools since 1963: compositional changes and pervasive changes. The compositional changes cited by the panel reflected: (1) a dramatic increase in the population of school-aged children in America as a result of the post–WW II baby boom; (2) increased efforts to reduce the dropout rate; and (3) judicial and legislative efforts to eliminate discrimination and provide educational equity for all Americans.

Between 1960 and 1970, the number of high school graduates in America had increased by a million and the number of students taking the SAT had tripled.[37] Furthermore, the increase in the number of students taking the SAT reflected a much broader array of students. In the 1950s, the panel reported that SAT takers had been "students enroute to relatively prestigious and selective four-year, liberal arts colleges and universities."[38] By the late 1960s, however, more women and minorities were taking the SAT and there was a precipitous increase in the number of SAT takers who were less economically privileged and planning to attend colleges and universities with less selective admission policies, two-year colleges, or vocational schools. These compositional changes in SAT takers, according to the panel, coincided with the beginning of declines in SAT scores. The panel further found that 25 years earlier, only one-half of all Americans remained in school through the twelfth grade. By 1970, however, three-fourths of all Americans were completing twelfth grade, with almost half of those students going on to college. The panel also suggested that the decline in SAT scores may reflect the nation's "tardy legislative decision to attack previous discrimination based on race, sex, and family income."[39] Very few minority students were taking the SAT in the early 1960s or attending college. According to the panel, in the early 1960s, an estimated one to 2 percent of all SAT takers were black and that was probably high. By 1970, that percentage had risen to approximately eight percent. The panel found:

> Score differences between blacks and whites parallel closely with differences in averages between students from low- and high-income families and between those whose parents have differing levels of education. Beyond this, two centuries of racial bigotry have unquestionably left an educational system that serves blacks and other minority groups less well than whites, particularly when it comes to meeting traditionally accepted "majority" standards. The contributing cause of the score decline is not that more minority group members now take the SAT, but that despite statutory guarantees of equal opportunity the society has not yet developed either the educational means or mores that will bring children with different racial roots to a parity of aptitude.[40]

Moreover, the panel found that although "women score lower than men on the mathematical sections of the SAT," this "almost unquestionably reflects more than anything else the traditional stereotyping of career opportunities and expectations."[41] Most telling, the panel stated:

> It would be pleasant to think that as increased percentages of vastly larger numbers of young people stay in school longer and go on to college, the college entrance examination averages achieved before by a favored fraction of students could be held constant. Yet any such expectation would be ruefully unrealistic. The major move toward equality of

> opportunity in the 1960s will be judged unfairly unless it is recognized that an increasing school retention rate is bound to mean, at least at first, some drop in the average developed ability level.[42]

Compositional changes, according to the panel's findings accounted for the decline in SAT scores between 1963 and 1970. The declines following 1970, however, were attributable to other factors that the panel identified as pervasive changes.[43] These pervasive changes were actually quite diverse and included both school-related and non-school-related factors. School-related changes included fewer basic courses and more electives; less emphasis on writing; more emphasis on objective, multiple-choice tests; grade inflation and lower standards; automatic promotion from one grade to the next; and increased absenteeism. Other factors were beyond the reach of schools, such as more time watching television, the decline of parental influence, and "a decade of distraction."[44] Additional factors, probably related to both in school and out of school responsibilities, were cited as well, such as less time doing homework and less motivation to learn.

Interestingly, the panel did not cite public school teachers, teacher quality, or administrators as a reason for the decline in SAT scores. A sharp increase in the demand for teachers because of the large influx of students during the 1960s and early 1970s resulted in a greater reliance on substitute teachers and less experienced teachers. Between 1961 and 1971, the average number of years of experience for elementary teachers dropped from 13.3 years to only 8 years. Public school teachers and administrators may have been guilty of tolerating excessive absenteeism, adopting less demanding textbooks, or not requiring enough reading and writing in the classroom. However, the panel conceded that these are issues that may not have been entirely within the power of teachers and administrators to control due to the vast compositional changes taking place in schools.[45]

After the publication of *ANAR*, in 1985 William W. Turnbull, who served as president of the Educational Testing Services (the agency responsible for the administration of the SAT) from 1970 to 1981, completed his own analysis of the decline in SAT scores. According to Turnbull, the report by the panel was actually a negative report card on the nation, not on the schools, since "the SATs are neither specific nor sufficient measures of school effectiveness."[46] Turnbull further asserted:

> The SAT was never intended to represent all of the important areas of understanding, knowledge, or skill—not to mention constructive attitudes, values, and other noncognitive characteristics—in which

> schools aim to bring about student growth. Moreover, the scores are not affected only by formal schooling: they measure abilities that are developed both in and out of school.[47]

Turnbull proposed what he called "the reciprocal score declines" hypothesis to explain the SAT score declines. This theory argues that both the compositional and pervasive changes, cited by the College Board panel as the causes of declining test scores, were a "reflection of the same phenomenon: the new composition of the upper high school students."[48] According to Turnbull's hypothesis, the new student body evolving in the 1960s required modified pedagogical strategies. These strategies were geared to the reality that there was an ever-increasing number of students who were finding the traditional program of study too difficult. In order to retain and give them some hopeful level of success, the curriculum was attenuated and expectations were lowered. Textbooks, too, were revised by publishers to meet the needs of the growing numbers of students less prepared for rigorous course content.

These changes in the curriculum and textbooks also impacted higher ability students. Not only were they bored and unchallenged, but they also knew less at the end of their high school years. Course offerings also changed during the 1960s. Watered-down elective courses designed to meet the future practical needs of students were made available to all students. The greater choices in classes made available to all high school students had a great deal of impact on SAT scores. If you were a student who chose to take courses such as "consumer education," for example, your SAT scores would be much lower than those of students who took traditional academic courses. During the 1960s there was a movement in which high school students gravitated away from academic courses toward vocational nonacademic courses. Turnbull suggests that this shift might reflect "an increasingly pragmatic or materialistic attitude" among students during the 1970s.[49] Grade inflation also became rampant and the number of hours demanded for homework dropped considerably. This might have happened because of relaxed curricular demands or perhaps teachers were discouraged because homework assignments were often not done. All of this, according to Turnbull, resulted in a downward spiral in SAT scores.

Turnbull cites another of the College Board's findings that is unrelated to compositional or pervasive changes as a cause of declining SAT scores: the decline in the number of high-scoring students taking the test. This point was not fully explored by the panel, according to

Turnbull, because it seemed "discordant with the compositional shift hypothesis."[50] In a telling statement, the College Board asserted:

> An inordinately extended analysis of the drop in the number of these "high scorers" indicates, however, that the decline probably results almost entirely from the reduction in the number of students taking the SAT and from the impact at the top of the same pervasive influences that have been affecting the scores of the test-takers as a whole.[51]

According to Turnbull, while the panel did not pursue the issue of high scorers further, "the decline in high scores has continued to and remains a source of concern."[52] Not mentioned by the College Board or Turnbull, however, is the fact that by 1977, a large number of states had turned to American College Testing Program (ACT, begun in 1959) as the test that would be used to indicate academic success and the gatekeeper for entrance into a university. This fact alone may have explained, at least in part, some of the decline in the SAT scores overall, as more students began taking the ACT and not the SAT.[53]

With SAT scores as the only usable longitudinal test score data available to the NCEE in their analysis, the commission based their analysis on the following sources:

- Papers commissioned from experts on a variety of education issues;
- Opinions of administrators, teachers, students, representatives of professional and public groups, parents, business leaders, public officials, and scholars who testified at eight meetings of the full commission, six public hearings, two panel discussions, a symposium, and a series of meetings organized by the DOE's Regional Offices;
- Existing analyses of problems in education;
- Letters from concerned parents, teachers, and administrators who volunteered extensive comments on problems and possibilities in American education; and
- Descriptions of notable programs and promising approaches in education.[54]

The commission's work took 18 months to complete. Every few weeks the NCEE would gather together to conduct their work at various locations. Seven of their meetings were held in Washington DC for two-day sessions. They held six one-day hearings across the country in the following locations: Stanford City (Bay Area), California; Houston, Texas; Atlanta, Georgia; Chicago, Illinois; Denver, Colorado; and Cambridge, Massachusetts. Commission members attended two panel discussions: one at the University of Pennsylvania focusing on performance expectations in American education and the other at the University of Rhode Island focusing on issues related to the college curriculum. Two other gatherings of the NCEE were at San Diego State University in California for a symposium on the student's role in learning and in New York City for a meeting hosted by the Exxon Education Foundation.[55]

While traveling to cities across the United States, commission members visited exemplary schools and programs. For example, while conducting the hearing in Houston in April 16, 1982, the commission visited two elementary schools, one middle school, and four high schools. In addition, they heard testimony from over 25 hearing participants representing different segments of the local and national education community. Attendees of the Houston event included teachers and administrators from area schools, representatives from various universities across the country, and representatives from national and state education associations.[56] In addition to the various meetings, hearings, panel discussions, and symposium, the NCEE commissioned forty different papers by respected researchers from a wide range of universities across the country, with topics ranging from "Educational Excellence—The Secondary School–College Connection and Other Matters: An Historical Assessment" to "Motivational Factors in School Achievement."[57]

The analytical data that resulted from the NCEE's investigation was vast. The original draft of the report, therefore, was 225 pages in length. Some commission members were concerned that the lengthy report would be relegated to the fate of so many other governmental documents that end up being merely archived among the thousands of reports generated over the decades. Therefore, they were concerned that the American public would never know the conclusions they reached or be awakened to the crisis the commissioners perceived existed in education in 1983. The final report would be shortened to a mere 36 pages, plus appendices. It is important to bear in mind, however, that the many people who provided testimony at the hearings and wrote papers and analyses for the commission were evaluating the level of excellence in education in America, not the status of the United States as being "at risk." During the months of the commission's investigative process, the idea of attaching the work of teachers and schools to the economic health and security of the nation was not the subject of the hearings or papers. One has to wonder if the tone and substance of the testimony provided by the participants would have been different if they had known the conclusions of the final report that would be presented to the president in April 1983. It is one thing for an educator to participate in a discussion about excellence in education and how to improve the educational system; it is quite another thing to provide evidence that what you are doing as a teacher is leading to the downfall of America and putting the nation at risk.

THE IMPERATIVE FOR EDUCATIONAL REFORM: THE NATION WAS AT RISK

The final report published by the NCEE packed a powerful punch, beginning with the following two paragraphs:

> Our Nation is at risk. Our once unchallenged preeminence in commerce, industry, science, and technological innovation is being overtaken by competitors throughout the world. This report is concerned with only one of the many causes and dimensions of the problem, but it is the one that undergirds American prosperity, security, and civility. We report to the American people that while we can take justifiable pride in what our schools and colleges have historically accomplished and contributed to the United States and the well-being of its people, the educational foundations of our society are presently being eroded by a rising tide of mediocrity that threatens our very future as a Nation and a people. What was unimaginable a generation ago has begun to occur—others are matching and surpassing our educational attainments.
>
> If an unfriendly foreign power had attempted to impose on America the mediocre educational performance that exists today, we might well have viewed it as an act of war. As it stands, we have allowed this to happen to ourselves. We have even squandered the gains in student achievement made in the wake of the Sputnik challenge. Moreover, we have dismantled essential support systems which helped make those gains possible. We have, in effect, been committing an act of unthinking, unilateral educational disarmament.[58]

If the commission's intention in revising their original report was to create a firestorm across the country, then they were certainly rewarded for their effort by the reaction of the press. Historians would debate the extreme alarmist tone of *A Nation at Risk*, however. Over the years, commission members would defend the language employed in the document as necessary.

In a 1998 interview, NCEE Chair David Gardner provided the rationale for the brevity of the document and the incendiary tone the commission employed. According to Gardner, the original 225 page draft was boring. "It read like a Master's thesis," and put him immediately to sleep after the first few pages.[59] Several other commissioners had a similar reaction and the decision was made to radically change the entire character of the report. While the commission's original charge was to write a report to the government, they decided that the impact of their work would be greater if they approached the project in a much different way. According to Gardner, he told NCEE members:

> Look, we're asked to make a report to the government. Well, we will do that. But let's **pretend** [emphasis added] we're making a report to government. What we really want to do is write an open letter to the American people because we need their understanding, we need their support, we need their involvement. And moreover it will change the whole character of the report. We'll write it in plain English. It'll be brief. It'll be to the point.[60]

While commissioner Glenn Seaborg agreed with Gardner's approach in reformulating the report, he conceded in 1993 that the commission "went through a period of contentious argument" before agreeing on the dramatic language of the opening paragraphs of *ANAR*.[61] In the end, however, the commission would agree to the inflammatory language of the report, citing the need for a "clarion call" to the public about the alarming state of education.

Perhaps the most contentious language used by the commission was the assertion that the educational performance of American students, as a result of the inferior education they were receiving, was tantamount to a declaration of war on the nation. This language would be defended over the years by commission members. In 2009, Norman Francis would acknowledge that the rhetoric used in *ANAR* was hyperbolic, but stated, "If somebody else had done this to us we would have declared an act of war to treat us like this [*sic*]."[62] Albert Quie overtly defended the employment of a war metaphor, stating in 1998 at a summit marking the fifteenth anniversary of the publication of *ANAR*, "We did intend to start the war," and Emeral Crosby reported, "We were trying to electrify the community. We used terms that were as negative as we could think of, so we used war."[63] In 2009, Jay Sommer, the lone teacher on the commission, defended the use of the alarmist tone in the final report. He further asserted, however, that for the commission, the choice to use hyperbole was more important than the facts. According to Sommer, "In order to be more effective some alarming language had to be used. That was immediately there, it was understood that we have to say things in an alarming kind of way—even to the point where the statistics may not have been quite correct."[64]

Nevertheless, Sommer would call into question the portrayal by the commission of all American schools as failures, stating:

> We were talking about inner-city schools, . . . we left out the successes and that was deliberate. I mean there is no comparison between an inner city school anyplace, in Chicago and let's say New Rochelle High School where I taught. So things were sort of obscured and covered up, but there were many schools that produced wonderful students and students who went on to colleges and careers. That too was an element of emphasizing things in such a way an element (of failure) would be created . . . mainly, America was not falling apart educationally, there was a segment of American student that was and that is almost a natural consequence of things.[65]

Interestingly, as early as 1985, Sommer seemed to be having second thoughts about how *ANAR* was being promulgated to the nation. While the commission had discovered some very bad schools, it had also discovered many good schools; and even within these schools, there were sometimes both "effective" and "inferior" educational practices taking place. According to Sommer, "This posed a dilemma for the commission." Most importantly, as Sommer explains, "The commission never intended its recommendations to be taken as dogma for every school or school system in America."[66]

Unfortunately, for the next thirty years, the report became an example of dogmatism on a national scale, leading to the notion that the American public school system was an utter failure. One thing was certain—the final version of the commission's report was not boring. It did get the attention of the American public, even though, if Sommer's assertion is correct, they were less than accurate in their use of empirical data.

"History is not kind to idlers," the commission wrote in the sixth paragraph of their report.[67] America had become a nation of idlers, unable to compete in the world market. The Japanese were overtaking the American markets for automobiles, South Koreans were producing steel more efficiently, and the Germans were surpassing Americans in the production of machine tools. The commission included a quote from the controversial education critic, Paul Copperman: "For the first time in the history of our country, the educational skills of one generation will not surpass, will not be equal, will not even approach, those of their parents."[68]

The commission had satisfied their goal in firmly establishing that the public schools were failing and the nation was at risk because of this failure. Of course, for the members of the commission this was a foregone conclusion since the one common characteristic shared by all of the NCEE members was their belief that public schools were failing. What they wanted to do was to convince the American public that public schools were failing. The NCEE cited their findings about the causes of school failure in four categories: content, expectations, time, and teaching:

Findings Regarding Content: High school curricula had become "homogenized, diluted, and diffused to the point that they no longer have a central purpose." Students were offered a "curricular smorgasbord" complete with appetizers and desserts that could "easily be mistaken for main courses."[69]

Findings Regarding Expectations: Academic expectations for American students were lower than ever before. Less homework was assigned in high school and, in spite of declining achievement, grades were inflated. High school students in America were expected to take far fewer higher level math and science classes or foreign languages than their counterparts in other industrialized nations. Rather, American students were given the choice of low level electives, such as classes in "bachelor living" to take during high school. Minimum standard exams, required in 37 states in 1983, were lowering educational standards for all schools and students. Colleges and universities had lowered their standards for admission. Textbooks had become easier and less challenging and schools were not even purchasing as many textbooks for their students as they had in past years.[70]

Findings Regarding Time: American high school students spent a great deal less time in school than their counterparts in other industrialized nations. For students in many schools "the time spent learning how to cook and drive" counted as much toward a high school diploma as the time spent studying mathematics, English, chemistry, U.S. history, or biology. "In most schools, the teaching of study skills is haphazard and unplanned. Consequently, many students complete high school and enter college without disciplined and systematic study habits."[71]

Findings Regarding Teaching: Too many teachers enter the profession from the bottom quartile of high school and college students. Teacher preparation programs spend too much time on methods courses and not enough time is devoted to subject matter courses. Teacher salaries are too low and teachers have "little influence on critical professional decisions as, for example, textbook selection." There is a critical shortage of high quality teachers in some fields such as mathematics, science, foreign languages, and in fields such as education for the gifted and talented, special education, and teachers of English language learners.[72]

Based on their findings, the commission outlined a set of recommendations they believed could result in sustainable education reform:

Recommendation A—Content: Education in the "New Basics" should form the foundation of the high school curriculum. The commission offered recommendations for strengthening English, Mathematics, Science, Social Studies, and Computer Science curricula (the "New Basics") and further recommended the inclusion of foreign languages, the arts, and vocational education in secondary education programs of study.[73]

Recommendation B—Standards and Expectations: Grades should adequately reflect the performance level of students, and colleges and universities should raise admission requirements. Standardized tests of achievement "should be administered at major transition points from one level of schooling to another and particularly from high school to college or work." Textbooks and other school materials should be upgraded to assure more rigorous content. Instructional materials used in schools should "reflect the most current applications of technology in appropriate curriculum areas."[74]

Recommendation C—Time: More homework should be assigned. Effective study and work skills should be taught, beginning in the early grades. Longer school days and a longer school year should be considered and the school day should be better organized in order to expand the time available for learning. Schools should address discipline problems by disruptive students by considering alternative classrooms, programs, and schools. Absenteeism and tardiness should be reduced through the implementation of attendance policies with clear incentives and sanctions. "Administrative burdens on the teacher and related intrusions into the school day should be reduced to add time for teaching and learning." Promotion and graduation policies, as well as student placement and grouping policies, should be guided by the "academic progress of students and their instructional needs, rather than by rigid adherence to age."[75]

Recommendation D—Teaching: Standards should be raised for students enrolled in teacher education programs. Students should be required to demonstrate their aptitude for teaching and their competence in an academic discipline. Colleges and universities with teacher education programs should be judged by "how well their graduates meet these criteria." Salaries for teachers should be raised and teacher salaries should be tied to an effective evaluation system that includes peer review. Superior teachers should be rewarded, average teachers encouraged, and poor teachers improved or terminated. Eleven month contracts should be adopted for teachers to provide time for professional development and to provide programs for students with special needs. A system of "career ladders" for teachers should be implemented to distinguish between new teachers, experienced teachers, and master teachers. Critical shortages in mathematics and science teachers should be addressed through the engagement of non-certified personnel who have expertise in this area. Grants and loans should be made available to attract outstanding students to the teaching profession, "particularly in areas of critical shortage." Master teachers should be engaged in the development and design of teacher education programs and the supervision of novice teachers during their probationary period.[76]

Recommendation E—Leadership and Fiscal Support: Principals and superintendents should garner support from the school and community for the school reforms recommended by the commission and school boards should assist these efforts by providing administrators with professional development and other support. State and local officials, school board members, governors, and legislators should incorporate proposed reforms in educational policies and fiscal planning. The federal government, with the cooperation of state and local governments, should help meet the needs of diverse students, such as the gifted and talented, the socio-economically disadvantaged, minority, English language learners, and special needs students. The federal government should fulfill its role to: 1) ensure that the constitutional and civil rights of students and personnel are protected; 2) collect data and statistical information related to education; 3) support curriculum improvement and research; 4) support teacher preparation in critical shortage areas; and 5) provide financial assistance in research and graduate training. "The federal government has *the primary responsibility* to identify the national interest in education."[77]

Once the reader gets beyond the hyperbolic language of the first few pages of *ANAR*, the commission's recommendations are less than sensational. American high school students needed to get back to the basics, spend more time in school, do more homework, have higher expectations, take standardized tests, and read harder textbooks. America also needed smarter teachers who made more money and were better prepared through more rigorous college and university teacher preparation programs. School administrators, school boards, and federal, state, and local governments needed to make sure that the NCEE's recommendations for education reform are implemented. And the federal government should continue to fulfill its responsibilities, although this would depend on the continued existence of the federal DOE.

It is interesting to note the commission's recommendations regarding disruptive students: "The burden on teachers for maintaining discipline should be reduced through the development of firm and fair codes of student conduct that are enforced consistently, and by considering alternative classrooms, programs, and schools to meet the needs of continually disruptive students."[78] However, it isn't the content of this recommendation that is interesting. As any teacher knows, disruptive students have always been a problem and finding solutions for dealing with the behavior problems has always been a hot topic for teachers and administrators. What is interesting is that this is the first mention in *ANAR* of disruptive students as being a confounding issue in educational achievement. The burden of maintaining discipline in a class with disruptive students was not cited at all by the NCEE in their findings as one of the causes for the decline in academic achievement. Nor is there any indication in the findings that absenteeism or tardiness were contributing factors in lower achievement. Yet, they made the recommendation for stronger attendance policies. The commission also recommended reducing "administrative burdens on the teacher and related intrusions into the school day" because these took time away from the teacher that could be used for teaching and learning.[79] This, too, is not mentioned in their findings as a possible contributing cause for lower academic achievement.

The NCEE's findings can be distilled into two categories. One is that the nation was at risk because of the curriculum. There was not enough academic rigor and students spent too little time in school. The other was that the nation was at risk because of those who taught the curriculum. The smartest college students didn't choose teaching as a profession. A lot of teachers were actually the weakest students in high school and college, and, not only that, they didn't get a very good education in their teacher preparation programs. They took too many methods classes and not enough content classes. Oddly enough, the NCEE did find that teachers needed to make more money. Of course, if teachers made more money, the profession might attract more smart people.

What seems to be missing from the NCEE's findings is any explanatory factor that may have given teachers credit for doing a very difficult job in light of the many societal factors that impact the academic lives of their students. Much of the decline in SAT scores had been found by the College Board to be attributable to the changing demographics of those taking the test, and, according to Turnbull, changes in the curriculum and other factors were likewise associated with the changing population of students remaining in high school.[80] America's growing commitment to ensuring that most students graduate from high school, a prerequisite for earning a living wage, was actually a noble goal for a country that for too many decades had segregated students by race and class. To be clear, there was widespread agreement in America, on both the political left and the political right, that there was a need both for education reform and to think about how we could better meet the needs of our students. The commission, however, in its zeal to get the nation's attention and explain the complexities of education in America as something that could be summarized in a few short pages, ignored the many factors that contributed to the decline in achievement of American students.

In the introduction of *ANAR*, the commission briefly explained that they had been directed by Secretary of Education Terrel Bell to "examine the quality of education in the United States."[81] What has been lost in many discussions of *ANAR* is that the commission did not examine American schools in their entirety.[82] The focus of the commission's report was the status of *high schools* in America and, clearly, as their findings and recommendations reflect, all of their data, analyses, and hearings focused on issues related to high schools. Arguably, the report should have been entitled *A Nation at Risk: The Imperative for Reforming High Schools.* In spite of this, in the 30 years since its publication, *ANAR* has served as an indictment of all public schools, kindergarten through twelfth grade.

Commissioner Jay Sommer made it clear in 2009 that he certainly never considered all schools to be failures and that the commission obscured facts in order to promote the notion that all schools were failing.[83] Within the report there is a nod to the fact that there were, indeed, at least some outstanding schools and programs in the country. However, according to the NCEE, their "distinction stands out against a vast mass shaped by tensions and pressures that inhibit systematic academic and vocational achievement for the majority of students."[84] As noted in Appendix F (Notable Programs), the commission conducted four searches for examples of notable programs and "promising approaches to specific problems in American education."[85] The commission, however, did not evaluate the validity of the claims made by the more than two hundred schools, school districts, colleges, or other educational organizations that responded to their call and submitted profiles, most of which came from postsecondary institutions.

Blue Ribbon Schools

As the NCEE was conducting its assessment of public schools in America, the DOE, under the leadership of Terrel Bell, instituted the Blue Ribbon Schools Program in 1982 as a way to identify and honor excellent schools. In order to be recognized by the U.S. DOE as a Blue Ribbon school, a school had to "demonstrate a strong commitment to educational excellence for all students."[86] According to Bell, the DOE wanted to feature public and private schools with "large concentrations of low-income and minority students who were defying the odds and swimming successfully against 'the rising tide of mediocrity.'"[87] Shortly after the publication of *ANAR* in April 1983, 126 middle and high schools were awarded the honor of being Blue Ribbon Schools for the 1982–83 school year. The following year, the number of Blue Ribbon Schools increased to 201. The fact that the Blue Ribbon School Program predates the publication *ANAR* and continues to this day, seems to call into question the assertion that all public schools were (or are) failing. Of the 327 middle and high schools who applied for and were subsequently awarded the distinction as Blue Ribbon Schools in the 1982–83 and 1983–84 school years, over 90 percent were public schools. Were there more than 327 in the nation that could have been awarded this honor if they had applied? Most likely, yes.

Regardless of any flaws in the federal program for identifying Blue Ribbon schools, the fact is that excellent schools did exist in 1983 and still do today. Yet the commission relegated any examples of excellence to a one or two sentence comment in an appendix that basically stated that they were "in no position to validate these programs or claim any of them to be 'exemplary.'"[88] However, wasn't that the entire point of the National Commission on Excellence in Education? It would seem that the commission was singularly the best group to decide what an exemplary program should be. If the commission's intention in writing *ANAR* was to start a war over education reform, then any discussion of excellent schools in America might have gotten in the way of their declaration.

The Politics of a Nation at Risk

Bell's initial reading of *ANAR* left him "surprised, elated, and apprehensive all at the same time." He was concerned that the education community would reject the report and their reaction could "bring down its wrath upon us."[89] The title and language of the report was explosive, and, regardless of the education community's reaction, he was confident that the short report would not be relegated to the fate of many other governmental reports gathering dust on a shelf. He immediately sent a copy of the report to Reagan, hoping that the brevity of the document would prompt the president to read the entire report and not simply rely on an assistant to interpret it for him, and he was hopeful that the president would support the NCEE's report.

Bell was told later that the president did read the entire document and was pleased with it. A ceremony was arranged in the State Dining Room with President Reagan to publicly release *ANAR* before the full press corps. Given the tensions Bell had experienced over the previous couple of years, he was concerned about how *ANAR* would be presented to the press and the public. Clearly, the report did not address Reagan's own education agenda of school tax credits, vouchers, or prayer in schools The day before the official release of the report, Bell learned that his concerns were justified. A group of NCEE members had met with administration officials privately to discuss the report.

Almost three decades later, in 2010, NCEE member Annette Kirk, while speaking at a luncheon at Grand Valley State University, revealed for the first time that she was a member of that group, along with the vice-chair, Yvonne Larsen, and Albert Quie, and that their motivation for meeting with the president's administration was concern that their own educational agenda had not been included within the final report. More specifically, according to Kirk, they had been unable to "convince the commission to adopt a recommendation supporting school tax credits and vouchers."[90] Apparently this was quite a contentious issue, and, as a compromise, the commission permitted the inclusion of wording in the document that, according to Kirk, "would imply the policy" of school tax credits and vouchers. Kirk told the attendees of the luncheon that the omission of a recommendation for vouchers and tax credits from the report was grave enough to warrant a suggestion by a Reagan staffer that the disgruntled commission members should publicly resign from the commission at the press conference announcing the report. According to Kirk, however, the statement in the report about "parents as the primary educators of their children" opened the door for a discussion by President Reagan about school tax credits and vouchers.[91] This was the subject of the meeting she, Larsen, and Quie had with Reagan administrators on the eve of the release of *ANAR*.

President Reagan would begin his speech on April 26, 1983, by lauding the commission's work and reiterating their findings that the educational system in America was failing. He supported their recommendations. A little over halfway into his speech, however, his focus shifted sharply from the actual content of the NCEE's report:

> Your report emphasizes that the federal role in education should be limited to specific areas, and any assistance should be provided with a minimum of administrative burdens on our schools, colleges, and teachers.
>
> Your call for an end to federal intrusion is consistent with our task of redefining the federal role in education. I believe that parents, not government, have the primary responsibility for the education of their children. Parental authority is not a right conveyed by the state; rather, parents delegate to their elected school board representatives and state legislators the responsibility for their children's schooling.
>
> In a 1982 Gallup poll, the majority of those surveyed thought Washington should exert less influence in determining the educational program of the public schools. So, we'll continue to work in the months ahead for passage of tuition tax credits, vouchers, educational savings accounts, voluntary school prayer, and abolishing the Department of Education. Our agenda is to restore quality to education by increasing competition and by strengthening parental choice and local control.[92]

According to Patricia Albjerg Graham, the commission feared that the White House would use the release of their report to reaffirm their own conservative agenda of prayer in schools, tuition tax credits, vouchers, and the abolition of the DOE. Gerald Holton would later report that, upon hearing the president's comments, one of his fellow commissioners remarked "We have been had."[93] When the president began discussing school prayer in his speech, Bell looked over at the group of Reagan staff members gathered in the foyer to see one member of the group give a congratulatory gesture and victory sign to another staff member. They had successfully used the occasion to reaffirm Reagan's commitment to their own cause.[94]

A Nation at Risk was a sensational hit across America, featured in headlines in all major newspapers. Terrel Bell's life dramatically changed and he became an instant celebrity. While vacationing with Vice President George H. W. Bush in Kennebunkport, Maine, Bell was asked to attend an annual meeting of the nation's governors in Portland, Maine, to discuss *ANAR* and push for implementation of the reforms recommended by the commission. In attendance at this meeting was then Governor William Clinton of Arkansas, and, as will be discussed later in this book, his presence at this meeting with Secretary Bell would have a profound impact on education reform in the coming years.[95]

After the publication of *ANAR*, Bell would enjoy his new status within the Reagan administration, becoming a frequent flier on Air Force One as he traveled around the country promoting the report. *The San Diego Union* published a story about Bell with the headline, "My, How the Humble Has Risen," describing his newfound popularity among the top-level hierarchy of the White House. As a cabinet member, Bell campaigned for the reelection of President Reagan in 1984. During the Republican Convention, Bell was intent on trying to prevent party leaders from renewing their 1980 pledge to abolish the DOE.[96] According to Bell,

> *A Nation at Risk* placed educational reform high on the public opinion agenda, and this had its political payoff for the president. He stole the issue from Walter Mondale, and it cost us nothing in the budget. It was simply a splendid issue to use in the domestic affairs arena, for it obscured concern about cuts in welfare, aid to dependent children, Medicaid, and other social program reductions. It has such broad-based national and popular support that by the time the Republican Platform Committee addressed the issue, it was clear that any move that even hinted it might be anti-education, was doomed.[97]

The Republican Party now owned education reform. For those dedicated to free market ideals, the actual findings and recommendations made by the NCEE in *ANAR* would be inconsequential. The inflammatory language of the report that served as a clarion call for education reform, however, would become an invaluable tool in refashioning education in line with not only the ideologues who had inspired President Reagan and the increasingly conservative standard bearers of the Republican Party, but Democrats as well.

CHAPTER 2

PUBLIC SCHOOLS: CONSERVATIVE COALESCENCE AND THE SOCIALIST THREAT

For conservatives in America, their long crusade over many decades to gain the power they needed to change the United States had finally been won when Ronald Reagan was elected president. For President Reagan it was a time of personal triumph. He had turned away from his allegiance to the Democratic Party during his early years as an actor, and now his long dedication to conservative ideals had reaped the ultimate political reward. President Reagan, however, was not a man who ignored history, and, in particular, the efforts of past conservatives who helped create his path to the White House. In 1981, at a large victory dinner hosted by the Conservative Political Action Conference (CPAC), he reminisced about the late 1940s and 1950s when real conservatism seemed like a cause with little hope of success—these were the "dark days." But he also knew that there were conservative giants who had always helped keep the cause alive against all odds. At the dinner Reagan stated that, in the early 1960s, "had there not been a Barry Goldwater willing to take the lonely walk, we would not be talking of celebration tonight."[1]

Reagan was also well aware of the essential contributions to the conservative movement that had been made by conservative social, political, and economic theorists. Reagan, as Peter Robinson of the Hoover Institution explains, was an intellectual. He was, therefore, familiar with the works of conservative intellectuals such as Friedrich A. Hayek and Milton Friedman. He was particularly "thankful for their intellectual acuity in dark times" when Reagan's brand of conservatism seemed to be fading from the American political, social, and economic landscape.[2] Reagan was also very familiar with the writings of Russell Kirk, for many conservatives the most important philosopher, political theorist, and moralist in American history. Speaking at a 1981 testimonial dinner in Kirk's honor, newly elected President Ronald Reagan proclaimed: "Dr. Kirk helped renew a generation's interest and knowledge of 'permanent things,' which are the underpinnings and the intellectual infrastructure of the conservative revival of our nation." In 1989, Reagan awarded Kirk the Presidential Citizens Medal for his achievements.[3]

The number of conservative intellectuals that played an important role in the conservative cause, however, goes beyond those lauded by President Reagan at conservative dinners and testimonials. These intellectuals helped crystalize and fortify conservative thought during the almost 50 years leading to the election of President Reagan. In the process, they acted as standard bearers who articulated their perspectives to other conservatives on topics that generally focused on their notion of proper political, social, and economic order—and education. During the 1930s and the decades that followed, conservative intellectuals consistently criticized the institution of public schools and traditional teacher education programs. Conservative intellectuals as a group would be comprised of political, economic, social, and educational theorists. Their criticism of public schools would be one of the bonds that consistently helped unite disparate conservative groups such as southern segregationists, free market capitalists, libertarians, the Moral Majority, and the more traditional conservative establishment. A powerful conservative movement required the creation of a spontaneous attitude among disparate conservative factions that helped bond them together as the conservative base was expanded during the decades following WWII. A conservative disdain for public schools would be part of helping to create that spontaneous attitude. In 1980, this newfound unity was able to elect their president, and in the process help America on its way to the education reform initiatives of the twenty-first century and the Common Core State Standards.

Who were some of those conservative intellectuals and what were their attitudes toward America's system of public education? Very importantly, how did America's public schools help bring together disparate conservative groups and expand the conservative base? While the list of important conservative intellectuals is a long one, the views of a few individuals stand out as particularly indicative of how conservatives felt about the institution of public schools. Included in this list are Albert Nock, Friedrich A. Hayek, Frank Chodorov, Russell Kirk, William F. Buckley, Murray Rothbard, and Milton Friedman. Other individuals such as Mortimer Smith, Bernard Iddings Bell, and Arthur Bestor during the years immediately after WWII would help further the conservative cause by writing books that specifically focused on their criticism of America's public schools. Conservative blood, however, really began to boil during the 1930s.

The 1930s was a watershed decade for conservatives in America, and in many ways the nadir of a unified multifaceted conservative movement. The New Deal, a series of domestic programs enacted in the United States between 1933 and 1938 under President Franklin Delano Roosevelt's administration, was put in place to help ameliorate the harsh economic and social effects of the Great Depression. The administration's approach to eliminating these effects was based on the liberal economic ideas of John Maynard Keynes. Keynesian economics called for direct and increased government intervention in the economy, which conservatives believed was a fundamentally flawed approach that not only violated their allegiance to conservative free market principles, but was tantamount to the actions that were being taken by Communist and Fascist governments at the time. New Deal policies were perceived by conservatives as a liberal attack on political, economic, social, and individual freedom, and state supported public schools, under the influence of progressive education, would be seen as a troubling weapon being used in this attack.

Public schools, however, were being given the awesome task of trying to help meet the social and economic challenges facing America. Within the education establishment, progressive education would be seen as the educational means to this end. On the other hand, during the 1930s, the public school system and its teachers would come under increasing scrutiny by conservative ideologues who criticized the institution for being socialistic, communistic, authoritarian, and professionally and academically incompetent. As a result, for many conservative Americans this decade would be seen as a time of educational deterioration. For example, Kevin Ryan states, "Since the early 1930s, when the federal and state government became more aggressively involved in education, control has become more centralized." He goes on to claim that in spite of massive school consolidation to improve education and the many millions of dollars spent on public schools by federal, state, and local governments, "the result . . . has only been to diminish the quality of their output."[4]

For conservatives the liberal gauntlet was thrown down during the 1930s. Most troubling for conservatives was their belief that the coercive nature of state-supported public education influenced by progressive education ideals was a subversive attempt to corrupt American youth and undermine conservative notions of proper social order, economic principles, freedom, and republicanism in America. As a result, the public school system and its teachers would be caught up in some of the earliest efforts to accuse these schools of becoming progressive, liberal, socialistic, and even communistic, any of which for conservatives threatened America's security.

ALBERT JAY NOCK: THE PROBLEM WITH EDUCATION

Arguably, no single document during the 1930s better represents conservative disdain for the state-supported institution of public schools and progressive educational ideas that were impacting these schools than does Albert Jay Nock's 1931 book *The Theory of Education in the United States*. For most teachers and citizens in general, Nock is an unknown figure, particularly when it comes to education in America. But for many conservative elites, then and now, Nock's libertarian ideas about state authority and education reflect a conservative ideal that would be used to attract a wider populist base to the conservative cause. Russell Kirk, for example, would later call Nock's book "one of the most manly and timely protests against the conquest of American education by the pragmatic and collectivist ideas of John Dewey." He goes on to explain that "it was the precursor of a larger body of conservative writings on education" that resulted "in a popular agitation for conservative reform in American schools."[5]

So what did Nock, as an important conservative educational theorist, believe about the institution of public schools? By looking a little more carefully at what he said in 1931, one can begin to enter the conservative mind about not only public education and progressive educational theory, but his notion of proper political and social order. It is important to know that Nock saw the use of centralized collectivist state power, which for conservatives beginning in 1933 was personified in Roosevelt's New Deal policies, as the wrong approach for solving America's problems. Nock summed up the New Deal by comparing it to Fascism and Communism. He believed that centralized state power was the enemy of individual freedom, and state institutions such as public schools were the facilitators of state power over that freedom. According to Nock, the progressive educational approach taken within public schools was wrong because of three misguided theoretical flaws: (1) the educational theory of equality,

(2) the educational theory of democracy, and (3) the educational theory of the literate citizen.

Nock believed that the progressive theory of "educational equality" that undergirded America's education system was particularly troubling because he felt it was based on a socialist model that created a "perverse" popular doctrine leading people to believe that "everybody is educable."[6] Nock based this conclusion on his elitist definition of education versus training. Training, whether it was for becoming a plumber, lawyer, or chemist required a set of skills backed by a specific kind of knowledge related to those skills. Education, on the other hand, consisted of a curriculum derived through the Great Traditions.[7] For example, in 2011 Richard Gamble was explicit in his list of books that reflected the Great Traditions, books that included those written by ancient Greeks and Romans like Plato and Tacitus; Christian authors like St. Augustine, St. Thomas Aquinas, and John Calvin; political theorists such as Edmund Burke; and educational theorists such as Erasmus and John Milton. Interestingly enough, by 2011 Nock's *Theory of Education in the United States* had made the list![8]

Nock further believed that knowledge within these types of books could be understood by only an educable elite. Nock proclaimed, "The educable person, in contrast to the ineducable, is one who gives promise of someday being able to think; and the object of educating him, of subjecting him to the Great Tradition's discipline, is to put him in the way of right thinking, clear thinking, mature and profound thinking." Nock believed that while "educable persons are relatively few . . . their social value is great" since they preserved civilization.[9] But what was an educated person supposed to look like? For Nock, their appearance became almost spiritual in nature. An educated person showed a "disciplined and experienced mind, was capable of maintaining mature and informed disinterestedness," and had "the patrician fineness of taste."[10] This was one reason why he felt America's educational system, now under the influence of progressive ideals, was wrong. Progressive education was based on the idea that everyone could be educated and an education system needed to meet the complex and multifaceted needs of both the individual and a modern society. According to Nock, this view of education was dumbing down America and was allowing the use of progressive, modern pedagogical approaches in schools that had become a "hunting-ground of quackery."[11]

If the progressive educational idea of equality was a perversion, as Nock claimed, then the educational theory of democracy that was also undergirding education was a "perversion upon a perversion."[12] According to Nock, the American school system was based on a misguided popular notion of democracy. He believed that the notion of democracy first became perverted because of popular uprisings such as the French Revolution. As a result of these uprisings, eighteenth-century political theory interpreted democracy as a means to self-expression in politics. By 1931, Nock felt that the notion of democracy had changed from one that referred to political status to one that was about economic status. He argued that this was the result of the Russian Revolution that instilled this idea into the minds of too many individuals, including those in the United States.[13]

Democracy was now wrongfully being interpreted "in some kind of economic terms" because the manifestation of democratic equality was being connected to a person's economic status. For Nock, democracy had nothing to do with extending the right to vote to all members of society, nor did it have to do with economic status. Instead, he explained that it was "a matter of the diffusion of ownership; a true doctrine of democracy is a doctrine of public property."[14] He felt America had a big problem because "the popular idea of democracy is animated by a very strong resentment of superiority." Nock further explained,

> It resents the thought of an elite—the thought that there are practicable ranges of intelligence and spiritual existence, achievement and enjoyment, which by nature are open to some and not to all. It deprecates and disallows this thought, and discourages it by every available means. The whole institutional life organized under the popular idea of democracy, then, must reflect this resentment. It must aim at no ideals above those of the average man; that is to say, it must regulate itself by the lowest common denominator of intelligence, taste and character in the society which it represents.[15]

The problem with locally controlled schools, therefore, was that they reflected the will of the common person through their elected representatives and thus "the business of the school is not to be good," but rather "to give the people what they want."[16]

But there was a third misguided theory of education that Nock felt was influencing America's public school system at the time. According the Nock, it was wrongheaded to believe "the idea that good government and a generally wholesome order are conditioned upon a literate citizenry."[17] In fact, Nock did not believe the majority of citizens could become truly literate. Nock did make the valid point that there was a difference between being able to read and being literate.

In America this idea would be analyzed and discussed for the next 80 years by a vast array of liberal and conservative scholars, educators, educational policy experts, and social theorists, all of whom recognized that there was a difference between reading and literacy, but not necessarily agreeing on what it meant to actually be literate.[18]

However, supposedly there was a problem when progressive educators engaged in creating a literate citizenry. First, Nock posited "that in general the mere ability to read raises no very extravagant presumptions upon the person who has it." Second, while he admitted that most people had the ability to read, only an intellectual elite could actually become literate and the literature that would make this happen was only accessible by these superior people. He felt that America's school system, now increasingly influenced by the equalitarian beliefs of progressive educators and their pedagogical methods, was based on a "perverted" theory of equality and democracy that now had created a perverted equalitarian notion of literacy. Nock believed these three theories had created a school system that did not recognize that certain subject matter was not "manageable by everybody." Therefore, he was critical of America's educational system because it was "disallowing and disregarding" the fact that most American citizens were "ineducable," based on his definition of education, while ignoring the needs of the few who were truly educable.[19]

Nock also agreed with a number of university academicians, one of whom lamented, "The type of education offered in our new million-dollar high schools is about one-twentieth as valuable as the kind given in the traditional little red schoolhouse of a generation ago." Nock further believed that other nations, in contrast, such as Holland, Belgium, Germany, France, and the Scandinavian countries Denmark, Norway, Sweden, and Finland, with little resources were producing a "moderately acceptable product." On the other hand, in "more rich and well-equipped" public schools, America was not.[20]

Nock passed away in 1945 but his legacy would impact conservative thought in many ways, not the least of which were his views on public education in America. The conservative Ludwig von Mises Institute calls Nock "an influential American libertarian author, educational theorist, and social critic of the early and middle 20th century." The institute goes on to say that "Murray Rothbard was deeply influenced by him, and so was the whole generation of free-market thinkers of the 1950s."[21] George H. Nash perhaps best sums up Nock's appeal to so many conservatives during the post-WWII era. He explains that Nock "articulated their thoughts so fully and so well" because his "passionate anti-statism, his stern educational traditionalism (with its disdain for "progressive" education), his scorn for the masses, and his pre-war isolationism were likely to attract people whose hopes for the future differed from those of Franklin Delano Roosevelt or John Dewey."[22]

The Progressive Educators

During the 1930s, the conservative right began to increasingly claim that the public school system was a socialist institution under the influence of progressive education and the educational ideas of progressives like John Dewey. The role and scope of public schools continued to expand as progressive educators called on schools to create learning environments that went beyond academics. For these progressives, learning meant that a school needed to address the entire spectrum of a child's social, psychological, and educational development, something they began endorsing in the 1890s. For example, vocational courses increased as well as extracurricular activities such as sports, music, and assorted student organizations and clubs. A differentiated curriculum was now in place, which progressive educators believed was needed to meet the needs of individual learners. Educational objectives included the self-realization of a student's individuality, the development of proper human relationships, the ability to be more economically efficient, and the awareness of civic responsibility. But how was an educated person supposed to act, what were they supposed to know, and, very importantly, what were they supposed to be able to do according to these progressive educators? The following are some examples of broad educational goals according to the progressive Educational Policies Commission, a group first appointed by the National Education Association (NEA) and the Department of Superintendence in 1936:

Self-realization—The educated person:

- has an appetite for learning;
- can speak the mother tongue clearly;
- writes the mother tongue effectively;
- solves his problems of counting and calculating;
- is skilled in listening and observing; and
- is participant and spectator in many sports and other pastimes.

Human relationships—The educated person:

- puts human relationships first;
- enjoys a rich, sincere, and varied social life;
- can work and play with others;
- observes the amenities of social behavior;

- appreciates the family as a social institution; and
- conserves family ideals.

Economic efficiency—The educated producer:

- knows the satisfaction of good workmanship;
- understands the requirements and opportunities for various jobs;
- has selected his occupation;
- succeeds in his chosen vocation; and
- maintains and improves his efficiency.

The educated consumer:

- plans the economics of his own life;
- develops standards for guiding his own expenditures; and
- is an informed and skillful buyer.

Civic responsibility—The educated citizen:

- is sensitive to the disparities of human circumstance;
- acts to correct unsatisfactory conditions;
- seeks to understand social structures and social processes;
- has defenses against propaganda; and
- respects differences of opinion.[23]

Conservatives felt that a curriculum with these kinds of goals not only marginalized rigorous academic study in schools, but also reflected socialist teachings. But it was the social and educational ideas of a certain type of progressive educator that caused conservatives to react most strongly against progressive education in general.[24] When some progressives called for schools to engage in complete social reconstruction in America, employing either socialist or Marxist rhetoric, such as George Counts, in his socialistic *Dare the schools build a new social order*, or Theodore Brameld, in books titled *Karl Marx and the American Teacher* and *American Education and Class Struggle,* the obsessive and continual hunt by conservatives for socialists and communists within the ranks of progressive educational theorists and teachers was on. Counts was no communist, however, and he along with others like John Dewey, played an essential role in an attempt to eliminate the communist faction within New York's Local No. 5, the largest local of the AFT during the 1930s.[25]

Nevertheless, John Dewey would also be caught up in the search to find Communists and socialists within the ranks of progressive educators. Dewey was particularly critical of the revolutionary tone of Counts' and Brameld's more radical books. According to Lawrence Cremin, Dewey wanted "an education system that would produce intelligent men and women sensitive to social issues and able to act on them." In his response to Counts, Dewey explained that in a democratic industrial society, schools could "never be the main determinant of political, intellectual, and moral change."[26] Dewey also criticized Brameld's Marxist take on education. As Clarence Karier points out, Dewey was critical of Brameld's educational ideas because its "Marxian position substituted class struggle and conflict for our democratic traditions and its methods."[27] It is important to understand, therefore, how Dewey's notion of democracy and democratic equality, and their essential role in the educational process, stands in stark contrast to the beliefs held by Albert Nock. For example, in *Democracy and Education*, Dewey stated,

> The superficial explanation [of democracy] is that a government resting upon popular suffrage cannot be successful unless those who elect and obey their governors are educated. Since a democratic society repudiates the principle of external authority, it must find a substitute in voluntary disposition and interest; these can be created only by education. But there is a deeper explanation. A democracy is more than a form of government; it is primarily a mode of associated living, of conjoint communicated experience. The extension of space of the number of individuals who participate in an interest so that each has to refer his own action to that of others, and to consider the action of others to give point and direction to his own, is equivalent to the breaking down of those barriers of class, race, and national territory which kept men from perceiving the full import of their activity.[28]

According to Dewey, education and democracy needed to become a symbiotic experience in that one facilitated the actions of the other. He further explained that a democratic educational experience is a "liberation of power" that must be varied and must result in action. "If citizens are only limited or partially encouraged to act in an educational setting, the citizen must be placed in a group, and because of its exclusionary and elitist nature, education becomes designed to shut out many interests." Then, in a statement that rings truer today than ever before, Dewey, as the champion of progressive education, proclaimed, "A society which is mobile, which is full of channels for the distribution of a change occurring anywhere, must see to it that its members are educated to personal initiative and adaptability. Otherwise, they will be overwhelmed by the changes in which they are caught and whose significance or connections they do not perceive."[29]

According to conservatives, Dewey's words reflected the socialist menace they felt was permeating America's public school system. For liberal progressives, Dewey's words captured the true essence of the appropriate role of education in a democratic society. Regardless, by the end of WWII conservatives believed that the socialist threat to America was now stronger than ever. The 1940s would be troubling times for conservatives. For many Americans, and particularly those millions in the working and lower classes, government programs and the Roosevelt administration had saved their families, given them jobs, saved family farms including those in the dust bowl states, and had helped bring America out of the Great Depression. Conservatives, both agitated and invigorated by the threat of a new powerful Soviet Union, steadfastly opposed what they believed were these misplaced and ill-informed notions held by many Americans. In addition, for many Americans, public schools were now viewed as important places to help solve the nation's complex social and economic ills and in the process improve their lives.

From the end of WWII to the present, public schools would indeed be called upon to address the complex and never-ending social challenges of America, even when these challenges went far beyond academic and even vocational education per se. During the 1940s, however, conservatives would never lose their voice as they militantly assailed New Deal policies and the increased government intervention that they believed was putting America on the path to becoming a socialist state. For conservatives, public schools would be increasingly seen as an appendage of this socialist threat. In many ways, the years immediately after WWII were, indeed, the "dark days" of conservatism. The conservative electorate was still too small to control America's political and social agenda, and Democrats would continue their 16-year control of the presidency with the election of Harry S. Truman in 1948. Nevertheless, conservatives were resolute and steadfast to their cause, and public schools would become an important pawn in an eventual conservative resurgence.

What is often overlooked, however, is that Dewey was also a critic of Roosevelt's New Deal policies. This criticism was based on Dewey's notion of democratic socialism, which connected individual equality to democracy. According to Robert Westbrook, Dewey believed that democracy, as a form of liberatory power, needed to facilitate the maximum potential of all citizens, whatever that may be. This is what Dewey meant by equality. It had nothing to do with making all people the same within society. Dewey, therefore, feared not only centralized governmental power that could impinge on individual freedom, but also the dogmatic authoritarianism of those who saw capitalist free market principles as the essential mechanism that needed to undergird society. Both of these could threaten a citizen's ability to realize his or her full potential. Most progressive educators were certainly more concerned with achieving equal educational opportunity, based on Dewey's definition of equality, than with a radical transformation of society. However, when Friedrich A. Hayek wrote his book *The Road to Serfdom*, Dewey saw the theoretical underpinnings of this book as an attempt to replace his equalitarian ideals of education with laissez-faire individualism.[30]

Friedrich A. Hayek: From the Darkness a Conservative Voice

One of the most influential conservative economic and political theorists that stepped forward during this time was Austrian-born Friedrich A. Hayek. While working in London during the 1940s, Hayek wrote *The Road to Serfdom*, first published in 1944. Within this book conservatives found a compelling voice that would quickly begin to bolster the conservative cause. Hayek would eventually impact the economic and political ideas of other conservative economists such as Milton Friedman and Murray Rothbard, both of whom recognized the importance of his work.[31] During the post-WWII era, Hayek's economic and political theories would find a ready audience among conservatives critical of the New Deal and the encroachment of a supposed collectivistic socialist state.

In *The Road to Serfdom* Hayek warned about what he perceived to be the dangers of excessive economic controls that impinged on individual liberty through overreaching socialistic state planning and central government intervention.[32] Hayek's in-depth analysis was at first given little attention by many American economists who had relied on a Keynesian economic approach for bringing economic relief during the Great Depression. Hayek's economic and social theories, however, would find a cadre of conservative economists, ideologues, and corporate elites who would use his theories to promote a free market, antistatist agenda. Even Keynes, however, in a letter written to Hayek, congratulated him on a "grand book" and stated that he was "morally and philosophically in agreement . . . with virtually the whole of it; and not only in agreement with it, but in a deeply moved agreement."[33]

Significantly, however, Keynes seemed to express satisfaction because Hayek admitted that the degree of government intervention in order to solve the complex economic and social challenges of a society was a "question of knowing where to draw the line."[34] Hayek had somewhat tempered his total faith in free markets in *The Road to Serfdom* by explaining that some degree of central government planning was necessary in order to meet the needs and challenges of society. However, for both Hayek and Keynes, "planning" did not mean a radical transformation of social organization would lead to the creation of a socialist or communist state. Hayek also felt that his economic and social theories did not entail "a dispute on whether we ought to employ foresight and systematic thinking in planning our common affairs." Rather, it was "a dispute about what is the best way of so doing." This is certainly one reason why Keynes did not find Hayek's ideas completely out of order. And while Hayek was resolute against the dogmatism inherent within socialist economic theory and social order, he also opposed a "dogmatic laissez faire attitude" . . . that would leave "things just as they are."[35]

Although Hayek believed that effective competition was the best way to "guide individual effort," in order for competition to work, a "legal framework" needed to be in place that would allow his notion of free competition to take place.[36] While competition was the key principle of social organization, Hayek admitted that maintaining competition would require "certain kinds of government action." In the social arena, however, he believed that some institutions provide services "which can never be adequately provided by private enterprise." For Hayek, competition was not "incompatible with an extensive system of social services—so long as the organization of these services is not designed in such a way as to make competition ineffective over wide fields."[37] To all of this Keynes seemed to heartily agree. But where were the lines of government intervention and planning to be drawn—and on what side of the line would public schools fall?

After its publication in 1944, *The Road to Serfdom* would assume a manifesto-like quality in America after a 20-page condensed version was published in the *Reader's Digest* prior to Hayek's American lecture tour in 1945. The lecture tour was initially intended to be academic lectures for economic scholars, but it was transformed into venues suitable for audiences of several thousand and broadcasts over the radio. Hayek was embarrassed by the adulation he was experiencing as a result of the *Reader's Digest* condensation of his book as well as the appallingly simplified cartoon version of *A Road to Serfdom* that was published by General Motors and subsequently reproduced in *Look Magazine*. He was also increasingly concerned about the misuse of his ideas. A Chicago newspaper quoted Hayek as stating,

> I was at first a bit puzzled and even alarmed when I found that a book written in no party spirit and not meant to support any popular philosophy should have been so exclusively welcomed by one party and so thoroughly excoriated by the other.[38]

When speaking to the Economic Club of Detroit, Hayek emphasized that he was not advocating against all government intervention, explaining:

> I think what is needed is a clear set of principles which enables us to distinguish between the legitimate field of government activities and the illegitimate fields of government activity. You must cease to argue for and against government activity as such.[39]

Later, in a 1956 forward to his book, Hayek admitted that he "had given little thought to American readers when first writing it." He was also surprised by the fact that when it was published in the United States it was met with either "acclamation or disdain."[40] For American conservatives, however, Hayek's book became a rallying cry warning against what they perceived to be increased socialist government authoritarianism that took decision making out of the hands of the individual. Although Hayek said very little about education in his book, what he did say gives insight into the conservative disdain and fear of progressive education and the institution of public schools. He explained that it was socialists who, in order to get people to accept a "definite set of values," were the first to "create most of the instruments of indoctrination of which Nazis and Fascists have made effective use." Education was one of those instruments. According to Hayek, German education was problematic because it had "shifted a greater part of its educational system from the 'humanities' to the 'realities' between 1840 and 1940."[41] Post-WWII conservatives who adhered to the conservative ideas of Albert Nock, found Hayek's analysis compelling. During this period other conservative political, social, and economic theorists would step forward and accelerate the conservative attack on what they saw as the socialist institution of American public schools. The attack would take place within the context of Cold War rhetoric, increased federal aid to public schools, and federal government efforts to dismantle racial segregation.

THE COLD WAR: STOKING THE CONSERVATIVE ATTACK

The Cold War would provide additional fuel for the conservative attack on public schools.[42] However, America's fear of communism and the resulting Cold War rhetoric was not just a result of conservative hysteria, as both liberals and conservatives felt the need to challenge Soviet expansion. Even before the Cold War, John Dewey, who had been accused of being a full-blown Marxist by some of his critics, opposed and feared the impact of communism and the Soviet Union on democratic societies. In 1942, Dewey had already warned America of a Communist threat developing in the Soviet Union. During WWII a formal alliance was made with Great Britain and the communist Soviet Union under the leadership of Joseph Stalin. Dewey did believe the United States needed to provide aid to the Soviet Union in order to stop Hitler during the war, but he also believed that this did not mean America should ignore Stalin's repressive regime. As America's alliance with the Soviet Union deepened, Dewey reminded America that "totalitarianism and democracy will not mix." He then explained that America's "future would be much more secure than it now appears" if we were to emulate Stalin's distrust of us by not trusting him "instead of indulging in the fatuous one-sided love feast" with the Soviet Union that he felt was going on in America at the time. Dewey was troubled that the wartime alliance would result in a "lack of realism about Soviet society and politics."[43] Conservatives, however, would use the Cold War as another means to demonstrate how public schools, an institution they now believed was under the increasing control of radical socialists and communists, was undermining the education of America's children and threatening the security of the United States.

The conservative search for Communists in America's public schools had begun prior to WWII. During the late 1940s, however, public schools became embroiled in super-heated Cold War rhetoric and intensified Red-baiting. In 1949, for example, President Truman made a speech entitled, "Education Our First Line of Defense: Learning Alone Can Combat Tenets of Communism." This would be a common theme for others as well, such as James B. Conant, former Harvard president and a significant influence on educational policy, and Admiral Hyman Rickover, the father of America's nuclear naval program, both of whom felt that only 15 to 20 percent of American students had the ability to go on to college or university study.[44] The "Duck and Cover" film, now accessible on the Internet, was created in 1951 by the U.S. government and subsequently viewed by millions of American school children. It warned of the Soviet nuclear threat and attempted to ameliorate the impact of a nuclear war in the minds of children. The film, which now seems absurd and ridiculous, explained to America's children the actions they needed to take in order to avoid being severely injured in the event of a nuclear explosion.

The House on Un-American Activities Committee (HUAC) held hearings on the extent Communists had infiltrated schools, and published a pamphlet titled "100 Things You Should Know About Communism and Education."[45] HUAC had become a permanent committee in 1945 and immediately began to expand its hunt for radical institutions and individuals the committee felt threatened America. In 1946, the committee even considered investigating the Ku Klux Klan for "violence and murder," but decided to not take this course of action because, according to HUAC's chief counsel Ernest Adamson, the committee had decided that it lacked "sufficient data on which to base a probe." Adding to this rationale, committee member John E. Rankin, Democrat from Mississippi and a future "Dixiecrat," observed, "After all, the KKK is an old American institution."[46] Although the KKK would avoid the probing eyes of HUAC, the institution of American public schools would not get off so easily when the committee decided that there was plenty of data that connected progressive educators to the Soviet political and educational system.

Although a classic example of the hunt for "Reds" in public schools occurred in Pasadena, California, in 1950, it is even more than that. This is because the Pasadena incident was an example of how conservative groups added the Red Scare to their arsenal of weapons that would be used to stop, what they perceived to be, America's march to becoming a socialist state. A right-wing conservative group first began the assault on how Superintendent Willard Goslin was running the Pasadena school district. The district's problems were complex, and also influenced by issues of race, immigration, and increased taxes. Conservatives, however, would unite in Pasadena in a campaign to brand Goslin as a Communist in order to force his resignation.[47] In 1951, *Time* described the campaign as "the sort of attack that hurls irresponsible charges without denning terms, or even finding out whether the charges are true or not."[48] Eventually a State Senate Investigating Committee was charged with looking into the situation. The committee became known as the Dilworth Committee named after its chairman Republican Senator Nelson Dilworth. After probing deeply into the Pasadena situation, Dilworth's committee found no evidence of communist or subversive activity in the schools despite all attempts by committee members to uncover "commie" activity. Despite this attempt at Red-baiting, Goslin received a standing ovation after testifying before the Dilworth Committee. Although in the end there were many people who saw through this witch hunt and stood by his side, and the committee did exonerate him,

Goslin was still dismissed even after the Red-baiting trump card was eliminated.[49]

By 1949 and through the 1950s, conservative hostility and suspicion of public education was being manifested through an increasingly scathing criticism specifically directed against these schools and progressive education. Public educators, however, did respond to this criticism. For example, the NEA's Defense Commission reported to NEA members that there was an enemy attacking public schools. The Defense Commission, as Stuart Foster explains, was created in 1941 as an "early response of professional educators to anti-communist attacks on public schools."[50] And although the Defense Commission, according to Foster, was successful in both uniting and alerting teachers to the enemy attacking public schools and limiting the use of "red-scare tactics," the tactics were never eliminated. Foster further explains that the commission also experienced "limited success in diffusing the political motivation" of these attackers.[51] When it came to even somewhat altering the political motivation of the conservative faithful, however, the commission never really had any chance at all. The main reason was because of the deeply entrenched allegiance to immutable conservative principles that fortified the attackers.

SOCIALISM AND THE INTELLECTUAL THRUST AGAINST PUBLIC SCHOOLS: BELL, SMITH, AND BESTOR

Supporters of public schools seemed to underestimate the potential power of conservatism to unify diverse factions when they did identify the source of criticisms being leveled at public schools. For example, in 1952, Archibald Anderson, historian and editor of *Progressive Education*, believed that there were basically two types of public school critics. He felt that the first group was sincere in attempting to improve an institution they supported. However, he seemed to underestimate and marginalize the second group who he characterized "as a motley assortment of chronic tax conservatives, congenital reactionaries, witch hunters, super patriots, dogma peddlers, race haters, and academic conservatives."[52] Two years later, however, C. Winfield Scott and Clyde M. Hill edited a book titled *Public Education Under Criticism* that began to clarify the source of this criticism, and it was clearly coming from the conservative right. The book was "dedicated to those parents and teachers, the true friends of our public schools . . . who have created the greatest system of free education in the world." The articles included in this volume detailed the criticisms of education, including a belief that the curricular focus in public schools was academically watered down, that teacher education programs and the teachers they produced engaged in educational "quackery," and that public schools were socialist in nature, which threatened the security, freedom, and Christian values of the United States. But of all the many articles published in this book, it might be John T. Flynn who captured the fundamental conservative criticism of public schools at the time and which ultimately, for conservatives, became the root cause of all the educational evils present in these schools. In his article, "Who Owns Your Child's Mind?" first published in an October 1951 issue of *Reader's Digest,* Flynn declared,

> I do not say that our schools have been taken over by either Communists or Socialists. I do insist that there are schools where the invasion has been started, and that where this exists in a school it is apt to be found in the social-science departments (where only a few teachers can do immense harm) . . . I do not charge that even the guilty teachers are teaching communism (though a few may be Communists). I say *they teach socialism.*"[53]

By the time Flynn wrote this article, however, he was no mere blip on the conservative radar. Flynn had already had a long, influential career in journalism that also included radio broadcasts from the late 1930s to the early 1950s, focused generally on his contempt for socialism and Roosevelt's New Deal. After WWII, Flynn would join the ranks of the many conservatives who would attack, what they perceived to be, the influence of socialist progressive educators on public schools. His book titled *The Road Ahead*, however, bears mentioning not only because it sold several million copies, but also because it reflected a conservative theme that persisted well after the Cold War was over, and because the book aided in an eventual conservative coalescence. First, Flynn made it clear that even if there was no Communist Red Scare taking place, the threat of socialism would persist. Second, one of the personifications of this socialist threat was taking place in the South as a result of civil rights initiatives. This is why he dedicated one entire chapter to what he called, "The War on the South."[54] According to John Moser, however, Flynn believed that "the communist threat to America was primarily moral and intellectual; the war was to be fought in print and in the schools, not in Europe and Asia." As a result, he was opposed to increased military spending and interventionism as a reaction to the communist threat. When he submitted an article to William F. Buckley's new conservative *National Review* in which he expressed this belief, his submission was rejected. Buckley, the magazine's editor, claimed that Flynn's opposition to "militarism" was "difficult to defend in the absence of any discussion whatever of the objective threat of the Soviet Union." Buckley eventually apologized for his harsh critique. Regardless, Flynn's antimilitarism and anti-interventionism would preclude any direct role as an insider within a new conservative resurgence.[55]

A shift in American social and political thought that was also a reaction against progressivism in general was beginning to coalesce during the early years after WWII.[56] A great deal of the intellectual thrust of public school criticism during this time was provided by three authors, Bernard Iddings Bell, Mortimer Smith, and Arthur Bestor. For conservatives, the scathing claims by these three that all public schools were failing added credibility to their assault on both the institution of public schools and progressive education. These critics saw America's public schools, and the colleges of education that supplied the teachers within these schools, as institutions of narrow elitism that assumed too much responsibility in nonacademic areas, while attenuating the curriculum that needed to be taught to all students in the United States. For many conservatives in 1949, Bell's *Crisis in Education* and Smith's *And Madly Teach: A Layman Looks at Public School Education*, both published that year, became the most influential books specifically about education that added to the conservative cause since Nock's *Theory of Education in the United States.*

Bell was a close friend of Albert Nock and dedicated *Crisis in Education* to Nock's son Samuel. Both Bell and Smith were in agreement as far as the abysmal state of education. Bell, in his foreword to Smith's book, warned, "American education is so defective in theory and practice as seriously to threaten the long continuance of the way of life to further which this nation was founded."[57] Both books were based on the same two basic themes best described by Cremin: (1) the schools had failed to teach the most elementary skills, and (2) education itself had been systematically divested of its moral and intellectual content. More specifically, academic rigor was eliminated in schools, schools took over domestic functions that belonged to parents, and schools excluded religion, which for conservatives meant education had no ultimate moral purpose.[58] But while Bell did not blame the teaching profession for all the problems, Smith squarely placed the blame on the shoulders of the teacher/pedagogue. As far as intellectual power and influence is concerned, however, the works of Bell and Smith paled compared to that of Arthur Bestor when he wrote

Educational Wastelands: The Retreat from Learning in Our Public Schools, first published in 1953.

The Educational Wasteland of Public Schools

Clarence Karier insightfully points out that Bestor's educational concern "grew not so much out of Cold War fears" but rather dissatisfaction with the life-adjustment progressive reform movement and "the perceived anti-intellectual stance of American educators" who had been "attempting to meet a student's individual needs through a differentiated curriculum that appeared to be increasingly trivialized."[59] Bestor, however, believed that the problems of education were not caused by earlier pre-WWII efforts of progressive educators like John Dewey, but rather what he now called the shift that had taken place in progressive education after WWII. He renamed this shift "regressive education." This shift was problematic for two important reasons. The first had to do with the lack of academic rigor in public schools. Bestor warned, "Less adequately financed educational systems in other countries are superior in the intellectual discipline which they provide in languages, history, mathematics and science."[60] His measure of academic success, however, is interesting; he declared:

> If the schools are doing their job, we should expect educators to point to a significant and indisputable achievement in raising the intellectual level of the nation—measured perhaps by larger per capita of books and serious magazines, by definitely improved taste in movies and radio programs, by higher standards of political debate, by increased freedom of speech and of thought, by a marked decline in such evidences of mental retardation as the incessant reading of comic books by adults.[61]

This shift was particularly problematic for Bestor and other longtime critics of progressive education when the "life adjustment movement" created a curriculum track that began appearing in public schools after 1945. This track became part of a larger differentiated curriculum that was being created at the turn of the century. The life-adjustment track, which was indeed nebulous and academically watered down, dealt with the physical, mental, and emotional health of students. For students placed in this track, specific courses might focus on such things as developing proper personal hygiene, sociability, personality, and a good work ethic. On the other hand, it is important to know that there remained an academic track for those students in public schools who were identified as more academically capable. The criticism of the life-adjustment curriculum, however, was so intense and widespread that the movement collapsed in 1954. Nevertheless, the curricular legacy of the movement would provide fuel for those opposed to progressive education well after that year.

The second reason that supposedly caused public schools to fail was an extension of the first. Bestor condemned teachers and the teacher education programs that created these "pedagogues" for their "intrusion into curriculum making" that was "divorced from the basic disciplines of science and learning." Their intrusion into curriculum was then solidified as state officials, in league with schools of education, created a process of teacher certification that entailed substantial course work in pedagogy, course work that was so excessive that it became academically vacuous.[62] Bestor called these requirements "the taproot of the great educationist upas tree," a tree that yielded a latex poison used on arrows! The state-enforced overbloated pedagogical requirements for becoming teachers violated what Bestor felt was the correct approach to creating effective teachers.[63] He believed that teachers first needed to gain a degree in the liberal arts and then study courses in pedagogy that lead to certification. Bestor also recognized, however, that all professors in the liberal arts needed to take more responsibility for the education of the future teachers who were in their classes.[64]

But did this mean that every one of these professors needed to help teachers understand how their courses in math, science, history, or English were supposed to be applied in different grades? After all, teachers learn a great deal about teaching subject matter through their liberal arts courses. Or did most professors teaching these classes in colleges and universities simply see their educational roles in the same way as when they taught any other student? Certainly teachers need an academically rigorous in-depth knowledge of the subject matter they teach, and probably more so than the average citizen unless the subject is directly related to the citizen's eventual profession. The often excessive number of redundant education courses in many undergraduate and graduate teacher certification programs needed to be evaluated, something that holds true even to this day. There was, however, an essential need for the "educationist." America could not rely on professors if they only saw their educational role as "founts of knowledge" and approached the education of teachers as an aside.

Writing in 1985, Karier describes Bestor's faith in the liberal arts to somehow miraculously create teachers in this way:

> Bestor had his blind side, which was to be found in his idealism regarding higher educational institutions themselves. There was a reason why educationists so quickly came to power and influence. A significant part of that reason lies in the failure of leaders in the academic disciplines to invest their time and effort in public education problems for any sustained length of time.[65]

Someone, indeed, had to take ultimate responsibility for making a teacher, and the "educationist," probably naively, did that. In the process, however, they opened themselves up to critics who would find ways to dismiss other factors that stood in the way of a child's educational achievement when a teacher's ultimate success would be determined by "high stakes testing."

The Sputnik crisis, however, seemed to validate Bestor's criticism of public schools when the Soviet Union, on October 4, 1957, was the first to place a satellite in orbit around the Earth. Andrew Hartman describes America's reaction to this event as one of "shock and awe."[66] Blame for America's failure for being bested by the Soviets fell squarely on the shoulders of public schools. These schools and their teachers had failed to meet their responsibility to rigorously educate students in science and math, plain and simple. It made no difference that less than five months later, on January 31, 1958, America placed its own satellite in orbit. America had scored a quick touchdown, and Americans knew they were back in the game! No one, of course, posited that somehow public schools had miraculously created the scientific minds and the resources to make this happen in just five months! Nor did anyone seem to consider that American William Pickering, a Caltech graduate, had already developed the Jupiter rocket that launched America's first satellite. Nor did anyone seem to recognize that Werner von Braun, the scientist and father of the Nazi rocket program during WWII, now working for the United States after surrendering to the Americans at the end of the war, had assembled a team that was working on other American rocket programs at the time. Von Braun would later be in charge of developing America's Saturn rocket that enabled the United States to be the first country to put a man on the moon in 1969, just 11 short years after America's first satellite was launched. According to critics, it was America's public school system under the guidance of progressive educators that was the problem. And when Hyman Rickover connected Sputnik to the educational failure of progressive education, for conservatives, the corrupting influence of a socialist educational institution had once again reared its ugly head.[67]

Russell Kirk: The Founder of Modern American Conservatism

Russell Kirk has often been described as one of America's leading thinkers, the founder of modern American conservatism and a leading proponent of traditional conservatism. He was a political theorist and moralist as well as a social and educational critic. When Kirk wrote *The Conservative Mind,* first published in 1953, he hardly imagined that he had placed himself on a path to legendary status among future conservatives.[68] Between 1953 and 1994, the year he died, this giant of conservatism produced a prodigious amount of writings, most of which focused on conservative social, political, and educational thought. Upon Kirk's death, one speaker memorialized him as now being "at one with the great tradition he helped articulate and recover."[69] For decades, what Kirk articulated and recovered was a supposed eternal spiritual essence that he believed defined conservatism. Kirk argued that conservatism was not ideological but rather "a state of mind, a type of character, a way of looking at the civil social order. The attitude we call conservatism is sustained by a body of sentiments, rather than by a system of ideological dogmata."[70]

Within this body of sentiments was a suspicion of public schools and a detestation of progressive education and John Dewey. His abhorrence of Dewey's social, political, and educational ideas was summed up in *The Conservative Mind*, and it would reflect his views of public education for the decades before he passed away. Kirk's view of public schools and progressive education probably began as early as WWII when he was drafted in 1942. An individual who actually opposed America's intervention in the war, Kirk spent four years serving in what Nash calls "the **desolate wastes** [emphasis added] of Utah and later at a camp in Florida."[71] Freed from the day-to-day exigencies of the actual war front, he was able to read the works of Albert Nock and even communicated with him.[72] Interestingly, one year before the *Brown v. Board of Education* decision, Kirk lauded the ideas of the "Southern Agrarians . . . who endeavored to remind America of the values of the Old South."[73] According to Kirk, however, in much of the United States there were many other things that were wrong. One of these "wrongs" had to do with America's public schools and the influence of Dewey. Kirk was disdainful of Dewey's belief in the need to take into consideration the natural tendencies of a child in the educative process because it denied "the whole realm of spiritual values," and thus "nothing exists but physical sensation, and life has no aims but physical satisfaction."[74]

Kirk believed that one reason America had problems was because of the educational ideas of people like John Dewey. Kirk scoffed at Dewey's theory of education. In particular, he ridiculed the idea that a "child is born with a *natural* desire to do, to give out, to serve, and should be encouraged to follow his own bent, teaching being simply the opening of paths." Seeming to take his cue from Nock, Kirk claimed that Dewey "advocated a sentimental equalitarian collectivism . . . and he (Dewey) capped this structure with Marxist economics, looking forward to proletarian ascendency and a future devoted to efficient material production for the satisfaction of the masses, a planners' state." Kirk further argued that "every radicalism since 1789 (The French Revolution) found its place in John Dewey's system" and that this system appealed to, among others, "that distraught crowd of semi-educated." Supposedly, "Veneration (of the old American traditions) was dead in Dewey's universe, indiscriminate emancipation was cock of the walk."[75] And to make matters worse, Kirk believed that a socialistic federal government in collusion with progressive educators was helping make this happen.

Based on these views, it is little wonder that even after the Sputnik crisis, Kirk would oppose direct federal aid to America's public school system; a system of education he felt was so corrupt that it threatened the very fabric of American society. The importance of Kirk's ideas to the conservative cause, and the influence of these ideas on the expansion and unification of the conservative base, cannot be overlooked. Within Kirk's conservative mind, in one way or another, anti–New Deal economists, traditional conservatives, conservative academicians, Christian fundamentalists, conservative politicians, southern segregationists, and libertarians found an ally. And one important bond that would coalesce these seemingly disparate factions, in one way or another, was their suspicion of America's "socialist" public schools.

Frank Chodorov: The Disciple of Nock

Nash believes that "if Albert Jay Nock had lived on, he might have become the 'grand old man'" of postwar American libertarianism. With his death in 1945, however, the mantle passed to his principle "disciple."[76] That disciple was libertarian thinker and free market supporter Frank Chodorov. By the 1930s, Chodorov was already criticizing what he believed to be excessive government intervention and collectivism into the political and social life of American society. In 1948, Chodorov turned his critical lens on public education with the publication of "Why Schools Are Not Free" in the October issue of *analysis*, excoriating public education as a "state-owned institution" of "socialized education" that "cannot possibly be separated from political control." According to Chodorov, reforming education meant "desocializing it."[77] Six years later, Chodorov warned that the 1954 *Brown v. Board of Education* decision, in its quest for social justice, simply marked "another step in the direction of centralization of power in the federal government."[78] In an article titled "A Solution of Our Public School Problem," published in the May 19, 1954, edition of *Human Events*, Chodorov stated that the federal government had "undertaken to disregard the prevailing sentiment" of local communities and "to force these people to be 'good'" by abolishing segregation within public schools.[79]

Chodorov's solution to the public school problem was simply "competition," and he advocated for the remission of tax revenues for public schools to parents who would then be free to use those funds to send their children to the private or public schools of their choice. The remission of tax revenues for public schools, later called vouchers, would be a way to both negate governmental collectivist efforts and destroy progressive education, which for him was synonymous with socialized education. Chodorov asserted that "there are no faults in the public school that competition would not eradicate. And the improvement would come easily and automatically, entirely without resort to political methods. The mere matter of tax remission would settle all our school problems."[80] Chodorov, therefore, was actually a proponent for school vouchers at least one year before economist Milton Friedman put forth this idea. In 1953, Chodorov also forged a relationship with the young William F. Buckley when Chodorov founded the Intercollegiate Society for Individualists (ISI). Nash described the society as an "antidote to the Intercollegiate Society for Socialists." Buckley became the first president of the ISI.[81]

William F. Buckley Jr.: Public Intellectual of the Conservative Right

Upon his death in 2008 at the age of 82, the *New York Times* memorialized William F. Buckley Jr. with these words: Buckley had "marshalled polysyllabic exuberance, famously arched eyebrows, and a refined, perspicacious mind to elevate conservatism to the center of American discourse."[82] Buckley, a plenitudinous writer, was even as a young man a conservative who combined traditionalism with anti-communist zeal and an allegiance to laissez-faire economics. That being the case, he was particularly appalled about what he believed was the cultural and intellectual deterioration of American society being facilitated within institutions of higher education. In 1955, Buckley summed up his outrage against liberal thinkers within these institutions, claiming, "The largest cultural menace in America is the conformity of the intellectual cliques which, in education as well as the arts, are out to impose upon the nation their modish fads and fallacies, and have nearly succeeded in doing so."[83] Like many other conservatives at the time, Buckley believed John Dewey was the biggest perpetrator of this menace. Using Yale University as an example of the wide-ranging influence of Dewey's ideas about education and society, Buckley believed that Dewey represented the shift toward a "theistic relativism" in academia and society at large. He further believed that "the teachings of John Dewey and his predecessors have borne fruit," and now "there is surely not a department at Yale that is uncontaminated with the absolute that there are no absolutes."[84]

During the second half of the 1950s, Buckley would use *National Review*, the publication he founded, to express conservative outrage against what was perceived as increased government collectivist efforts to impact society and potentially cause total social transformation. For example, in 1956, Buckley warned that "the socialist tidal wave continues to build up a titanic power, and it is on the move."[85] Buckley was particularly concerned with what he considered to be the Eisenhower administration's liberal efforts to somehow carve out a "middle ground between right and wrong" or, in other words, between liberal and conservative political, social, and economic ideas. Tensions within the Republican Party, however, were already mounting since Eisenhower's advisors in 1954 had warned the president that more conservative factions were vying for party dominance. His advisors described them as "Neanderthal Men . . . laying the ground work for a reassertion of party control."[86] For Buckley, federal aid to education, supported by the Eisenhower administration, was obviously one manifestation of this socialist incursion into America's way of life. Buckley considered this kind of federal action as a further "institutionalization of socialist measures and paraphernalia" that would further erode American society and individual freedom.[87]

During the 1950s, Buckley's allegiance to antistatism and anticollectivist government intervention provided him with a rationale that even overcame the tension that existed between issues of social justice and racist totalitarian power within individual southern states. This was the same rationale that enabled segregationists to continue their Jim Crow society under the banner of state's rights, anticollectivism, antisocialism, and anticommunism. Buckley, in his devotion to what he considered immutable conservative principles, extended his anticollectivist arguments to endorse the continuation of a southern segregated society because of "the median cultural superiority of White over Negro."[88] According to Buckley, southern segregationists were entitled to maintain their social hierarchy, in spite of being a numerical minority in much of the South, because they were "the advanced race." Using his typical lavish literary style, Buckley rationalized:

> National Review believes that the South's premises are correct. If the majority wills what is socially atavistic, then to thwart the majority may be, though undemocratic, enlightened. It is more important for any community, anywhere in the world, to affirm and live by civilized standards, than to bow to the demands of the numerical majority. Sometimes it becomes impossible to assert the will of a minority, in which case it must give way, and the society will regress; sometimes the numerical minority cannot prevail except by violence: then it must determine whether the prevalence of its will is worth the terrible price of violence.
>
> The axiom on which many of the arguments supporting the original version of the Civil Rights bill (1866) were based on Universal Suffrage. Everyone in America is entitled to vote, period. No right is prior to that, no obligation subordinate to it; from this premise all else proceeds.
>
> That, of course, is demagogy. . . . The great majority of the Negroes of the South who do not vote do not care to vote, and would not know for what to vote if they could. . . . The problem in the South is not how to get the vote for the Negro, but how to equip the Negro . . . to cast an enlightened and responsible vote.[89]

Buckley believed that the fundamental and immutable principle of maintaining ancestral tradition in opposition to what conservatives felt was "collectivist" federal authority, even if this meant maintaining a segregated society in the South, trumped the use of federal authority to dismantle that society. Using this authority, even in the name of social justice, was viewed as a violation of this immutable principle, a sine qua non upon which true conservative political, social, and economic life needed to be based. Although Buckley would change his position during the late 1960s as he came to see the fallacy in his thinking regarding southern desegregation, he had taken part in bringing southern segregationists into the conservative fold.

SEGREGATIONISTS, CONSERVATIVES, AND THE SOCIALIST THREAT

During the early post-WWII years, while social, political, and economic conservative thought and action was beginning to solidify in America, in the South, white citizens in dominant positions of power channeled a great deal of their energy into preserving a segregated society. However, the uniqueness of the South's social order and the economic realities of a southern economy, still overwhelmingly agrarian in nature, were at odds with certain essential tenets of conservative economic principles. Nevertheless, southern segregationists would find allies among conservative intellectuals through a selective allegiance to the tenets of conservative economic and social theory. This process would then allow the unification of southern conservative segregationists with a consortium of free market antistatist conservatives who had found the Eisenhower administration too progressive.

The preservation of the southern way of life had been a consistent theme in southern culture since Reconstruction, whether through the writings of William Faulkner, Tennessee Williams, Margaret Mitchell, and William Alexander Percy, to name just a few, or through the cultural perpetuation of an idyllic southern ethos handed down word of mouth from generation to generation. During the 1950s, Buckley's *National Review* participated in the perpetuation of this ethos. Anthony Harrigan, writing for *National Review* in 1958, extolled the virtues of the South, stating that visitors are amazed and enchanted as they "enjoy and admire Southern houses, highways, flowers, smiles and victuals."[90] Harrigan further lauded the "essential conservatism" of the South, proclaiming,

> The South has a sort of built-in power brake, which is a most effective piece of historical equipment. It has an essential conservatism, which has kept it from skidding into some very unhappy patterns, enthusiasms and crazes. Looking back at their land and its traditions, Southerners have come to realize that the mind of the South took its shape in an age of realism in men and affairs, back in the eighteenth century. The original shapers of the Southern tradition believed that progress resulted not from equality of condition, but from fruitful inequalities.[91]

Despite judicial, legislative, and media pressure, southerners were generally united in a determined effort to sustain the social manifestation of this way of thinking in order to preserve the segregated society it helped create. One result of this effort was the formation of militant southern resistance groups. Among the southern resistance groups that arose in the South during the 1950s was the Citizens' Council that began in Mississippi as a response to the *Brown v. Board of Education* decision in 1954. The founder of the Citizens' Council, Robert Patterson, a manager of a 1,583 acre plantation in Leflore County, Mississippi, feared that desegregating public schools would lead to mongrelization, communism, and the destruction of the southern way of life. He vowed, "I for one, would gladly lay down my life to prevent mongrelization."[92] In July 1954, Patterson, along with 14 business owners, civic leaders, and elite citizens founded the Citizens' Council. Recruiting members from civic organizations such as the Rotary Club, Kiwanis, and the Civitans, the Citizens' Council grew to include an estimated eighty-five thousand members in Mississippi and sixty thousand in Alabama by mid-1956. Citizens' Council organizations eventually became operational in all southern states and several nonsouthern states like California, Illinois, and Ohio.[93]

The widespread growth of the Citizens' Council was further facilitated through the publication of the organization's tabloid newspaper, *The Citizens' Council*. In 1955, William J. Simmons, the newspaper's editor, estimated that the newspaper had a monthly circulation of forty thousand, much of which was outside of Mississippi.[94] By that year, certain fundamental tenets of conservatism were firmly in place in the hearts and minds of southern segregationists. And while "racism remained in the nucleus of its thought," as Neil McMillen makes clear, "the Councils' ideological circumference had expanded to encompass the political and economic attitudes characteristic of conservatism." So while the ultimate goal of the Citizens' Council was always to maintain a segregated society, the Council rationalized that this goal was based on larger conservative tenets. As McMillen goes on to explain, for southern segregationists and conservatives in general, "the apparently ceaseless expansion of a centralized and bureaucratic government, the philosophy of a welfare state and the social gospel, the erosion of state's rights, confiscatory income taxes and the increasingly collectivized pattern of American life were all manifestations of a total all-out assault against American conservatism."[95] Citizens' Council members, therefore, railed against what they perceived to be "the tyrannical actions of the Supreme Court," particularly as these actions related to the *Brown* decision and its social ramifications.[96] The Citizens' Council warned, "The present trend brings joy to Communists and their fellow travelers who want to see all power centered in the federal government because they can more easily influence one government in Washington than the 48 governments in 48 states."[97]

For Delta planters who supported the activities of the Citizens' Council in order to maintain a segregated society, conservative anti-statism, which they endorsed on social issues, conflicted with the necessity of maintaining their economic way of life. As James Cobb explains, the Delta planters were willing to take the economic and political assistance of Washington to maintain their planter lifestyle while vigorously denouncing the "regulatory and social welfare activities of the federal government." This generally reflected a fear by the Mississippi Delta's white leadership that by accepting essential economic assistance, it would also mean being required to accept the federal government's demand to desegregate society.[98]

In 1954, Judge Tom P. Brady of Mississippi delivered a speech entitled *Black Monday* that was subsequently published as a book. This book would become a manifesto for the Citizens' Council and white resistance groups in general. Brady's diatribe would be an amalgam of historical and anthropological chicanery, the science of eugenics, and conservative political, social, and economic theory. Most telling is the fact that he dedicated his book "to those Americans who firmly believe socialism and communism are legal 'messes of porridge' for which our sacred birthright shall not be sold."[99] In this manifesto, Brady asserted that the decision of the Supreme Court of the United States in the *Brown* case was "socialistic . . . usurping the sacred privilege and right of the respective states of this union to educate their youth. This usurpation constitutes the greatest travesty of the American Constitution and jurisprudence in the history of this nation."[100]

While advocating for the abolition of public schools in the event the federal government actually enforced the *Brown* ruling, Brady offered an alternative course of action to circumvent forced school desegregation. Quoting from conservative economist Frank Chodorov, Brady suggested an economic solution for public schools:

> Whatever is wrong with the public school system, including the voodooism of the New Education [Progressive Education], is due to the compulsory attendance laws and the compulsory taxes which support it. The public school is a socialized or politically monopolized institution, and suffers from weakness inherent in all monopolies. The only thing that prevents the public school from decaying completely is the fact that it is not a complete monopoly. Local control of the school gives the taxpayer and parent some say in its management, even to the point of occasionally throwing out "progressive faddism." If the plans of the Educationists succeed, if the public school is centrally managed

by an entrenched bureaucracy, then the present faults of the school will seem insignificant; it will be a political department, not a place of learning. Nothing will do more to better education in America than the breaking of the public school trust. And if it is broken, nothing else need be done to eradicate its faults.

This is not a proposal to abolish public schools. It is a proposal to put them into competition with free enterprise schools, so they can prove their worth. And this can be done by the remission to parents of the taxes they are compelled to pay to support politically-controlled schools, in an amount comparable to what they pay for private schooling.[101]

THE CONSERVATIVE COALESCENCE BEARS FRUIT

By the early 1960s, amid an evolving conservative coalescence, many public school teachers seemed unaware of the conservative view of their schools, while the "educationists" within teacher education programs and liberal educational policy makers either marginalized conservative ideas or completely ignored them. If educators were aware that there was movement to the right in American social and political thought, as Cremin suggests, "too many educators thought they would be progressives in education and conservative in everything else." Then, in a rather prophetic manner, Cremin stated, "The combination, of course, is not entirely impossible, though it may well be intellectually untenable."[102] If the late 1940s and early 1950s were the dark days of conservatism, then the 1960s would be the pinnacle of liberal power and influence in America. When President Johnson, with a Democratic-controlled Congress, was able to pass the 1964 Civil Rights Act, this did not sit well with southern segregationists or the newly developing more conservative libertarian wing of the Republican Party. That wing began coming to power with the Republican nomination of Barry Goldwater for president in 1964.[103] And when President Johnson was able to pass his Great Society initiatives, a set of programs that addressed numerous social problems and issues in America including poverty and education, the more conservative wing of the Republican Party saw this as another example of an invasive socialist welfare state. As a result of this initiative, the 1965 Elementary and Secondary Education Act (ESEA) was passed as an important part of Johnson's "War on Poverty."

During the 1960s, a number of U.S. Supreme Court rulings on prayer in schools inflamed the Christian Right. For example, in *Engle v. Vitale* (1962) the court determined it was unconstitutional for state officials to compose an official school prayer and endorse its use in schools even if it is voluntary and nondenominational. In 1963, in *Abington Township School District v. Schemp*, it ruled that school-sponsored Bible reading in public schools was unconstitutional, although studying religions and their writings including the Bible without proselytizing as a way to understand human development was allowed and even encouraged. Five years later in *Epperson v. Arkansas* (1968) the Supreme Court invalidated an Arkansas statute that prohibited the teaching of human evolution in the public schools. In the decades ahead, other U.S. Supreme Court decisions that addressed school prayer and the teaching of evolution in public schools would simply further conservative Christian discontent and help drive these individuals into the increasingly conservative Republican fold and help in the creation of groups such as Jerry Falwell's Moral Majority.[104]

Conservative criticism of public schools would continue during the 1960s and 1970s. Published in 1968, James D. Koerner's book *Who Controls American Education?* is an example.[105] Koerner, a former executive secretary with the conservative Council for Basic Education (CBE), in conjunction with the CBE, continued the decades-long conservative criticism of public education. Interestingly, Koerner chose to begin his book by quoting Albert Jay Nock: "The First condition of progress is a lively and peremptory dissatisfaction."[106] But Koerner now believed that the layman needed to be concerned with more than "particular deficiencies in the curriculum or the standards in their schools." They now needed to worry about the way in which education was "governed in the United States."[107] Some of the things he believed needed to be evaluated were the misguided power of the federal government in education policy, the corrupting influence of teacher organizations such as the NEA and AFT, and the increasing power of accrediting agencies like the National Council for Accreditation of Teacher Education (NCATE) working in conjunction with teacher education programs. Koerner stated:

> I am convinced that the greatest problems in teacher education and certification are created and sustained by a system of control that lacks checks and balances and that has plainly demonstrated an incapacity to reform itself. What I am saying is that the big decisions about how teachers and administrators are trained and licensed are now reposed in too far a degree in the hands of professional educators, who, after all, represent only one segment of the educational community, not to say the public interest.[108]

Koerner and the CBE, however, also recognized that much of America's educational challenges rested in its "inner cities," and as we have already seen, was something NCEE members who wrote *A Nation at Risk* also believed but would not overtly state. Significantly, Koerner mentioned that new proposals were being put forward to better meet these inner-city challenges because of the failure of public schools to do so. One of the proposals in 1968 was for the "creation of a national network of new, independent privately owned schools for the children of the Nation's inner cities."[109]

In 1971, libertarian economist and political theorist Murray Rothbard continued the conservatives' drumbeat of their attack on public schools when he wrote *Education: Free and Compulsory.* On the front cover of his book Rothbard defiantly proclaimed: "We Are Ready—How About You? SCHOOLS AT WAR!" According to Rothbard, the public school system and compulsory education in America, just like in Europe, was a central "state usurpation of parental control [of] their children; an imposition of uniformity and equality to repress individual growth; and the development of techniques to hinder the growth and reasoning power and independent thought of children." Compounding the problem was progressive education and "the state of current teaching in the public schools."[110]

Seeming to take a page from Nock's *Theory of Education in the United States*, Rothbard did not hesitate to put himself up as an expert in pedagogy and child development when he declared, "It is clear that one of the major problems comes from the dullest" group of students. "The progressive educationists saw that the dullest could not be taught difficult subjects, or, indeed, simple subjects." Rothbard then rationalized, "Instead of drawing the logical conclusion of abandoning compulsory education for the uneducable, they decided to bring education down to the lowest level so that the dullest could absorb—in fact, to move forward the elimination of subjects or grading altogether." According to Rothbard, a centralized state system of compulsory education "forced into schools children who have little aptitude for instruction at all. It so happens that among the variety of human ability there is a large number who are not receptive to instruction. To force these children to be exposed to schooling, as the State does almost everywhere, is a criminal offense to their natures."[111] Again, as if taking his cue from Nock, Rothbard confidently stated,

> It is evident that the common enthusiasm for equality is, in the fundamental sense, antihuman. It tends to repress the flowering of individual personality and diversity, and civilization itself; it is a drive toward savage uniformity. Since abilities and interests are naturally diverse, a drive toward making people equal in all or most respects is necessarily a leveling downward. . . . Because each person is a unique individual, it is clear

> that the best type of formal instruction is that type which is suited to his own individuality. Each child has his different intelligence, aptitudes, and interests.[112]

Of course, within Rothbard's educational theory there were those "ineducables" who were left out because they had no aptitude for learning. In the decades ahead, educational reformers like those who wrote *A Nation at Risk* or accrediting agencies like NCATE felt they needed to remind teachers that "all children can learn." It seems, however, this reminder would have been better directed toward a conservative like Rothbard, and those who might have endorsed his educational ideas, than to the thousands of public school teachers educating America's children. The issue, of course, was and still is not that all children can learn, but whether all children can learn the same things and at the same high academic level of achievement as measured on high-stakes tests. As an important aside, no formal written statement by any progressive educator exists that declares there is a group of "ineducable" students who could not learn. On the other hand, there were some conservative educational theorists who clearly stated that this was the case. Rothbard, however, did not stop with his take on child development and progressive education. He was also dismissive of the professional skills required to teach effectively when he simplistically endorsed his idea of what later would be called "home schooling," while also ignoring social and economic realities:

> Almost all parents are qualified to teach their children, particularly in the elementary subjects. Those who are not so qualified in the subjects can hire individual tutors for their children. Tutors may also be hired where parents do not have the time to devote to the formal instruction of their child.[113]

According to Rothbard, and so many others as we have seen, academic learning in public schools was abysmal and public schools were failing in general. On the other hand, it also seems that when the creators of *ANAR* claimed the ubiquity of public school failure, while ignoring differences in intelligence, aptitudes, and interests among students, or alluding to successful schools as educational aberrations, they engaged in a bit of educational chicanery. Significantly, however, through a convoluted interpolation and screening of economic, political, social, and educational facts and ideas, an educational zeitgeist or spirit took form that would be infused into the American psyche regarding public schools. Through this process an ad hominem catch phrase was created that would be used by all public school critics as a rallying cry for future systemic education reform initiatives—"Public schools are failing!"

By the 1970s, a new powerful conservative movement continued to coalesce in order to make its move in American politics. In the past, conservatism was often its own worst enemy because of its factional nature, in addition to lacking a larger populist base that was needed in order to gain real and overwhelming political power. By 1980, the time was right. Political libertarians united with traditional conservatives, while southerners were shifting their allegiance to the Republican Party in response to such things as federal intervention regarding Civil Rights initiatives like desegregation and school busing. Federal court rulings, particularly about prayer in schools and the teaching of evolution, were helping drive fundamentalist Christians into the more conservative Republican camp. Economic conservatives amid rising inflation, increased oil prices, and a downward spiraling stock market warned of an evermore increasingly socialistic authoritarian federal government that was causing these economic problems and America's supposed inability to compete in the global arena. More and more, government institutions would be used as examples of this encroaching socialist menace that was at the root of America's crisis. In turn, these institutions would help unite the conservative cause. By 1980, millions of Americans were convinced, as President Reagan would claim, "in this time of crisis, government is not the solution to our problem; government is the problem." Antigovernment sentiment, however, would need specific social and political adhesives to create a bond between conservative factions in order to unify conservative thought and action. For conservatives, certain government institutions had already become those adhesives. An important one of these was the institution of public schools, and no individual reflected the conservative distrust and disdain for this institution than did libertarian economist Milton Friedman.

Chapter 3

Friedmanomics, School Vouchers, and Choice

Ronald Reagan ran for president on a platform of small government and fiscal responsibility. His economic policies reflected a sharp ideological change from the Keynesian policies embraced by previous presidents, most notably the New Deal policies of President Franklin D. Roosevelt, to a new vision of free market, supply-side, trickle-down economics. This vision and the economic policies associated with Reagan would be given the moniker *Reaganomics,* a name that has endured over the years. In the words of Rich Thomas of *Newsweek*, however, "Before there was Reaganomics, there was Milton Friedman," whose economic theories formed the foundation of Reagan's economic policies. The Nobel laureate economist, Milton Friedman, developed an almost legendary status among Reagan supporters and became known as the "guru" of the Reagan administration.[1]

Friedman's economic theories, or *Friedmanomics*, have endured as America's free market economic doctrine since the Reagan presidency. Most important, however, *Friedmanomics* has dramatically altered the education landscape in America by promoting the notion of the free market as the wellspring of education reform. According to Friedman, the problem with the American public school system rests with the government's complicity in creating schools, disdainfully calling them "government schools," that were socialist institutions. For example, in 1980 he argued that the public school system in the United States is "an island of socialism in a free market society."[2] For more than 60 years, Friedman promoted a free market approach to education reform, asserting that a voucher system was the panacea for all that was wrong with American schools. As a result, Friedman's ideas about education reform have been used to circumvent federal policies, such as the separation of church and state and the desegregation of public schools, and his ideas about competition and school choice have become a permanent fixture in education policy decisions and proposed legislation at the state and national level since the 1980s.

THE FUNDAMENTALS OF *FRIEDMANOMICS*

From 1946 to 1966, Milton Friedman was a professor of economics at the University of Chicago, and it was during this time he did what he considered to be his most important economic work. In 1963, he published *A Monetary History of the United States, 1867–1960* with economist Anna Jacobson Schwartz, a book that is considered a classic in economic theory.[3] In this book, Friedman and Schwartz challenged the commonly held beliefs that the Great Depression was caused by excess speculative buying that culminated in the crash of the stock market on October 29, 1929, and that government intervention in the form of monetary controls eased the devastation of the Depression. The authors relabeled the Great Depression, instead calling it the Great Contraction of 1929–33, and asserted that the economic crisis that occurred was the fault of the Federal Reserve System, whose management of monetary policy in the United States was so inept that what would have been a moderate economic contraction became a major catastrophe. Roosevelt's New Deal policies have generally been credited with easing the economic crisis during the Great Depression and saving capitalism. According to Friedman and Schwartz, however, Roosevelt's policies were the wrong cure for the wrong disease and actually prolonged the Depression and made it worse.[4] They claimed that without interference by the federal government, an unfettered free market would have corrected itself and the Depression would have been shorter and less devastating. Friedman and Schwartz's reframing of governmental responsibility with regard to economic and social policies once again reflected the sharp contrast that existed between the more liberal, progressive economic theories of John Maynard Keynes and the conservative, free market economic theories of Friedrich Hayek.

Friedman's ideas about the Great Depression align with his earlier conclusions about economic systems in general. In the late 1940s, he conducted research for the National Bureau of Economic Research to investigate fluctuations in the market as a result of monetary and banking phenomena, a concept economists often refer to as the "business cycle." Friedman concluded that there was no such thing as a predictable, recurring business cycle. Rather, he believed that "there is a system that has certain response mechanisms and that system is subject over time to external forces."[5] Economic fluctuations, according to Friedman, are natural "reactions to a series of random shocks."[6] The stock market crash of 1929, therefore, was a shock to the economy and government interference during the Great Depression was "a testament to how much harm can be done by mistakes on the part of a few men when they wield vast power over the monetary system."[7] Of course, no one will ever know if this is true or what would have ultimately happened to the American economy after the stock market crash without Roosevelt's New Deal policies, and, therefore, Friedman's theories about what might have been are purely hypothetical and theoretical. Nonetheless, Friedman's theoretical analysis, albeit hypothetical and challenged by other economists, was widely embraced by like-minded conservatives who saw most government intervention as a problem.[8]

According to the tenets of *Friedmanomics*, any form of government interference in the marketplace is wrongheaded. Federal policies that control the supply of money in the market are problematic insomuch as they limit the power of the market to right itself during times of economic crisis. Following this logic, according to Friedman, government should employ a laissez-faire approach when it comes to affairs of business and taxation. By reducing the level of regulation and taxes especially for the wealthy, businesses are able to thrive as wealthy individuals reinvest in the market and strengthen it. This was the basic notion behind the trickle-down theory espoused by the Reagan administration. According to the fundamentals of *Friedmanomics*, making sure the wealthy are allowed to make as much money as possible will, theoretically, benefit everyone. The wealth of those at the top of the economic food chain will trickle down to the rest of the members of a society through the creation of jobs made possible from a greater amount of their money being in the market. Higher employment among the middle and working classes will enable them to purchase new cars, homes, and televisions, the result being even more money circulating through the economy. This increase in demand by the working and middle classes for manufactured goods will create additional jobs as business owners invest their capital to expand or build factories to meet the demand. And the more people buy, the greater the profit for the wealthy and the cycle will continue.[9]

Therefore, according to *Friedmanomics*, government interference in the form of business regulations or taxation policies that require the wealthy to pay more taxes than less affluent Americans is detrimental to the health of the economy. According to Friedman,

> The scope of government must be limited. Its major function must be to protect our freedom both from the enemies outside our gates and from our fellow-citizens: to preserve law and order, to enforce private contracts, to foster competitive markets.[10]

Friedman asserted that taxes should never be raised in an effort to increase government revenues in order to balance the federal budget. According to the tenets of *Friedmanomics*, federal policy makers and Congress should oppose any tax increase, always demand cuts in government spending, and "accept large deficits as the lesser of evils."[11] To *Friedmanomic* loyalists, cutting taxes is a way to "starve the beast" and force the government to cut government spending, and, even if cutting taxes results in a high budget deficit, this is considered an acceptable alternative.[12] As Friedman's biographer, Lanny Ebenstein, pointed out, however, Friedman incorrectly prognosticated that the economy would suffer when George H. W. Bush raised taxes in 1990 in an effort to curb the budget deficit. What followed Bush's tax increases, and the Clinton administration's further increases in taxes, was a decade of sustained economic growth.[13] In spite of this blow to an essential tenet of *Friedmanomics*, free market devotees have continued to fight any and every effort to increase taxes, particularly for more wealthy Americans, as a way to balance the federal budget.

In 1980, the "great communicator," presidential candidate Ronald Reagan, explained the fundamentals of *Friedmanomics* to the American public. In clear, simple words he explained the common sense of shrinking the government, cutting taxes for the wealthy, and embracing a free market approach to the economy. It all seemed to make sense and offered hope to America. The country placed its faith in the grandfatherly wisdom of Ronald Reagan, elected him president, and entered an era of free market economic policies.

Friedmanomics and Public Schools

Milton Friedman wrote extensively about public education, beginning in 1955 with the publication of *The Role of Government in Education*.[14] The overarching theme of this essay and all of Friedman's subsequent publications about education is that the American government operates a monopoly over its public schools and that the entire educational system is socialistic. In 2003, he continued this theme, writing, "The elementary and secondary school system is the single most socialist industry in the U.S."[15] For five decades, Friedman steadfastly persevered, with missionary zeal, proclaiming that he had the solution for all that was wrong with the American education system. Government should get out of the way. Schools should be treated according to the principles of a free market society. Parents and their children are "consumers" of a product—schooling—and, in a free market education system, they would have an array of choices in what type of schooling they wish to purchase. According to Friedman, teachers and school administrators, as part of the education establishment, owe their allegiance to union officials who seek to maintain greater centralization and bureaucratization within a government school monopoly and, therefore, have a vested interest in limiting the power of parents. Public schools, according to Friedman, should always be referred to as "government schools" because he thought the term *public schools* is misleading.[16] The grand solution Friedman proposed in 1955 for breaking up the monopoly of government schools was a voucher system. According to his plan, parents would receive a voucher with which to purchase education for their children at the private or public school of their choice:

> Government, preferably local governmental units, would give each child, through his parents, a specified sum to be used solely in paying for his general education; the parents would be free to spend the sum at a school of their own choice, provided it met certain minimum standards laid down by the appropriate governmental unit. Such schools would be conducted under a variety of auspices: by private enterprises operated for profit, non profit institutions established by private endowment, religious bodies, and some even by governmental units.[17]

For Friedman, a voucher system was the silver bullet that had the power to transform an educational system that he believed was in complete disarray. Friedman has been referred to as the "Father of School Vouchers," although Frank Chodorov preceded Friedman in proposing the concept of school tax vouchers in his 1954 article, A Solution of Our Public School Problem."[18] However, Friedman can be credited with promoting the idea on a national scale using his political influence to facilitate its acceptance in the decades after proposing his idea in 1955. Because Friedman believed his voucher idea was a masterful application of free market principles in order to reform schools, he was always prepared to defend this idea against any and all challenges. Over the years, Friedman would promote his voucher idea in a way that seemed elegantly simple and, like *Friedmanomic* theories in general, seemed to make sense. Wouldn't it make sense, as Friedman claimed, to simply let parents have a voucher for the amount of money a state spends annually to educate a child and let the parent use it to pay for a private school? To Friedman, any complexities associated with his proposition could be easily explained away with simple arguments and metaphors from the free market.

Voucher critics have argued that the universal use of a school voucher system could lead to unequal educational opportunities for children as some parents could take their voucher funds and supplement them with their own private funds to send their kids to more elite private schools. Friedman, however, did not see this as a problem as he seemed to casually explain that "life is not fair" and some children do, in fact, "have a greater advantage over others simply because they happen to have wealthy parents."[19] And very importantly, for Friedman, the goal of society should never be to ensure equal outcomes for all citizens. In fact, he claimed that it is understood by Americans that some parents will only be able to afford to provide their children with a basic education, paid for by a government tax voucher, and other parents will be able to pay for a more expensive private school, supplemented with a government tax voucher. For Friedman, that is simply how the world works within a free market economy. In fact, he felt schools are much like restaurants. For example, he explained that while some restaurants (in 1979) sell very expensive hamburgers, like "the 21 Club charging $12.25" for its "Hamburger 21," this did not mean "that McDonald's could not sell a hamburger profitably for 45 cents and a Big Mac for $1.05."[20] Certainly, however, if one was even able to afford to go to "the 21 Club" and eat their signature hamburger, one would probably taste the difference between that and a McDonald's burger! One thing is sure, however, comparing burgers to schools was even more illogical than comparing apples to oranges!

Voucher critics have argued, too, that some parents would use vouchers to send their children to religious schools and that this violates the separation of church and state doctrine. But according to Friedman, this was not a problem. By issuing the voucher to parents and not schools, there would be no Constitutional violation since, technically, no government funds would be transmitted directly from the government to private religious schools. Friedman, in fact, thought parents should be able to use tax vouchers to purchase education at religious schools because, after all, "public schools teach religion, too - not a formal, theistic religion, but a set of values and beliefs that constitute a religion in all but name."[21]

Voucher critics have also argued that providing tax dollars to send children to private schools would take money away from public schools, thereby weakening the public school system that for many is fundamental for helping to realize American democratic ideals. By using a voucher system, public schools faced with shrinking enrollments and thus shrinking budgets would lose resources to adequately educate their students and, ultimately, face closure. According to Friedman, however, government schools could use a good dose of competition to make them improve. As private schools enter the market, Friedman argued, "the quality of all schooling would rise so much that even the worst, while it might be *relatively* lower on the scale, would be better in *absolute* quality."[22] Besides, Friedman asserted, if public schools are "doing such a splendid job," why should they fear competition from private schools? And if public schools are not doing so splendidly, why should anyone object to their destruction?

The economic imperative for Friedman was competition and the ability of a free market of schools to provide parents with a variety of choices. The free market approach to education would ensure a variety of alternatives. Parents could organize their own nonprofit schools and use vouchers to pay for the expenses. Friedman believed "vegetarians" could even have their own schools, as could the "Boy Scouts and the YMCA." "Mom and Pop" schools could open in neighborhoods.[23] For Friedman, the educational possibilities were endless! What would determine each school's ability to remain in the free market of education would be their ability to compete and attract parents and children to use their school tax vouchers to attend the school. Schools unable to compete would be forced out of the market, in much the same way that a restaurant is forced to close if it fails to attract enough patrons.

But what about "hucksters" who, interested only in profit, opened a private school with little regard for educational quality? In 1971, voucher proponents Judith Areen and Christopher Jencks acknowledged that in a free market educational system hucksterism could exist. For these two, however, critics who "envisage the entry of large numbers of profit-oriented firms in the educational marketplace" did not have a valid argument. After all, they explained, there already existed some private schools that were nothing more than diploma mills, but the quality of their services was not necessarily any lower than public schools. The authors predicted that private schools run by hucksters would be the exception in a voucher program within a free market educational system.[24]

Southern Segregationists

When voucher critics cited the use of Friedman's voucher concept by southern states to maintain racially segregated schools, Friedman's initial reaction was to consider this a possible flaw in the system since it would exacerbate class distinctions. He would not be deterred, however, in his belief that his free market solution could overcome any challenge, since his ultimate goal was to remove the government from education. In fact, this is what the southern states were doing. Friedman actually opposed any federal enforcement of desegregation, considering it to be a violation of individual rights, and on this point he agreed with southern segregationists. For him, a voucher system, as a model of free market economic theory applied to education, however, could solve any problem, even the racial apartheid that existed in racist southern societies. In the world of *Friedmanomics*, competition was the key. According to Friedman,

> Under the system, there can develop exclusively white schools, exclusively colored schools, and mixed schools. Parents can choose which to send their children to. The appropriate activity for those who oppose segregation and racial prejudice is to try to persuade others to their view, if and as they succeed, the mixed schools will grow at the expense of the nonmixed, and a gradual transition will take place.[25]

Friedman believed that a voucher system would eliminate racial tensions. For him, much of the racial conflict that existed over the issue of desegregation was based on a "well-founded fear about the physical well-being of children and the quality of their schooling" and not because of any sort of deep-seated racism.[26] According to Friedman, the government, by enforcing desegregation of public schools, was the problem, not the racist beliefs that required federal intervention. Allowing parents and their children to *choose* which school to attend using government tax dollars would solve any problem. The historical record, however, seems to indicate the opposite. Racist attitudes were the problem and the federal government had to intervene in order to protect children who were using their right to *choose* in order to attend a desegregated school. When the Little Rock Nine *chose* to attend Central High School in Arkansas, the response from the white community was violent. And when Arkansas Governor Orval Faubus refused to intervene in order to protect a child's right to choose, President Eisenhower had to place the Arkansas National Guard under federal control and send one thousand Army paratroopers from the

101st Airborne Division to restore order. When little Ruby Bridges chose to attend William Frantz Elementary School in New Orleans in 1960, she was met with a crowd of angry whites shouting racial epithets and some even making death threats against the frightened little girl. President Eisenhower had to send Federal Marshals to escort the little girl to and from school each day to keep her safe from harm. For both the Little Rock Nine and Ruby Bridges, in order to attend the schools of their *choice*, intervention from the federal government was used to ensure their safety from white racists. This was clearly the proper role of the government in a free society—protecting the rights of these children and their families to *choose* the schools they wished to attend.[27]

Friedman would idealistically write, "We should all of us, insofar as we possibly can, try by behavior and speech to foster the growth of attitudes and opinions that would lead mixed schools to become the rule and segregated schools the rare exception."[28] Through persuasive speech and behavior, racial tensions would be erased and desegregated schools would triumph over the few segregated schools that would remain. Perhaps Friedman's disregard for the events that unfolded in the years following the *Brown v. Board of Education* decision was naive, or perhaps he simply had an uncanny faith in the human spirit and that racists would somehow be miraculously transformed and see the error of their ways. Or, perhaps, his allegiance to his free market theories blinded him to the reality of racist societies. The fact remains that while the nation was watching news accounts of: the murder of Emmett Till; Freedom Riders being beaten for attempting to challenge Jim Crow laws in the South; Bull Connor ordering the use of attack dogs and fire hoses on adults and children participating in peaceful demonstrations in Alabama; the murder of idealistic young Freedom Summer workers in Mississippi for attempting to register black Americans to vote; and little girls dying among the rubble of a church bombing by members of the Ku Klux Klan, Friedman wrote, "The appropriate solution is to eliminate government operation of the schools and permit parents to choose the kind of school they want their children to attend."[29]

He ignored the reality that only two years after *Brown v. Board*, almost one hundred fifty thousand white residents of Mississippi and Alabama had joined "Citizens' Councils" for the sole purpose of ensuring that black children would never attend white schools in their states by using whatever legal or social means necessary.[30] Friedman also ignored the rising resistance among southern state governments that led to a bevy of laws and regulations with a range of goals, from prohibiting interracial marriage, repealing compulsory school attendance laws, and thwarting attempts by organizations such as the National Association for the Advancement of Colored People (NAACP) to file "agitation suits" to enforce federal laws. For Friedman, these realities were less consequential than the need to remove the federal government's role in education and let the free market reign.

While Friedman's optimistic suggestion that racists could be transformed through positive role models did not readily bear fruit, his voucher idea was seized upon by segregationists. Senator Robert Byrd of Virginia is credited with pioneering the strategy of "Massive Resistance" in his state in 1956. It became legal in Virginia to close public schools and provide state-supported tuition grants, or vouchers, for white students to attend all-white private schools. Virginia, then, became the first state to actually adopt Friedman's voucher idea, at least for white children. Public schools in Norfolk, Charlottesville, and Warren Counties were officially closed in 1958 and early 1959 rather than send their thirteen thousand white students to desegregated schools. In Prince Edward County, public schools were closed and private "segregation academies" were opened for white students, funded by a combination of public tax funds and private organizations. Many black children went without any formal education for four years until the Supreme Court's ruling in *Griffin v. County School Board* in 1964.[31] Mississippi would also adopt Friedman's ideas for a voucher system to maintain segregated schools and white segregation academies opened across the state, funded in part by tax dollars through a variety of schemes, a practice that continued for two decades after the *Brown v. Board* decision. In 1974, for example, one Mississippi newspaper reported that in one such scheme more than a quarter million tax dollars had been used to send the white children of Parchman State Penitentiary employees to segregated private schools since 1969.[32]

Southern schools would also employ the use of "freedom of choice plans" to maintain an illusion of compliance with the Civil Rights Act of 1964. Under these choice plans, all children, white or black, could, after submitting the proper forms, attend any school of their choice. It was implicitly understood, however, that under choice plans, no white parents would choose to send their children to black schools and most black parents would not dare send their children to white schools. Nonetheless, officials within the Department of Health, Education, and Welfare (HEW) accepted the premise that choice plans were an effective means for desegregating public schools. Lloyd Henderson, who was in charge of enforcing compliance with federal civil rights laws in Mississippi in 1965 would later say that he "wondered how federal officials could have expected southern black families to dare to send their children to all white schools after more than a century of racism and violence."[33] In one rural school district in Mississippi, only one black family exercised their right to *choose* a white school for their children to attend. Four nights after delivering their freedom of choice forms to the white high school, gunshots blasted onto the roof and through the windows of their home, with bullets hitting the wall behind the bed where two children were sleeping. Fortunately, no one was physically injured and the family did not back down. However, what followed for the children were years of taunting, name calling, and isolation. Only about 2 percent of Mississippi's black children utilized choice plans to attend white schools and their parents overwhelmingly faced retaliation by the white community in the form of canceled credit, loss of jobs, eviction from homes, and, sometimes, violence. In many schools, the children who broke the color barrier were isolated from white students on segregated buses, in segregated cafeterias, and in completely segregated classrooms.[34]

In 1969, as Joseph Crispino explains, the federal courts determined that voucher programs in Mississippi would have to end because they "established a system of private segregated schools as 'an alternative for white students' seeking to avoid desegregated public schools."[35] At its annual convention in 1970, the NEA voiced strong opposition to voucher systems, contending that school vouchers would lead to "racial and economic divisions while contributing to the social isolation of children."[36] The NEA called for federal and state legislators to prohibit voucher plans, expressing concern that these plans would weaken, or even destroy, the public school system. Friedman, however, remained undeterred from his conviction that vouchers were the panacea that would right all that was wrong with education in America. It was inconsequential that his ideas were espoused by segregationists, and he easily dismissed this as a deterrent. Similarly, he would ignore all other complexities that would render a voucher system problematic. He would continue to try to influence education reform over the decades. By using his influence as a Nobel Prize–winning economist, Friedman would have access to politicians, presidents, and policy makers as an advisor in matters of economic and social policy.

Friedman's Presidential Politics

After the publication of *A Monetary History of the United States*, Friedman used his emerging status as the leading conservative economist in the country to fulfill his interest in public policy. He had become very popular among conservatives. He was a prolific writer, publishing over three hundred editorials for *Newsweek*, in addition to articles that appeared in *The New York Times, The Washington Post*, and other national publications. Friedman authored or coauthored several books, produced a series of documentaries entitled "Free to Choose" for Public Broadcasting, and endowed the Friedman Foundation for Educational Choice. Already a popular figure among leading conservatives in the country, Friedman's influence was magnified after being awarded the Nobel Prize for Economics in 1976, and he used that influence to promote his economic and social ideas in both national and international arenas.[37]

Friedman's first foray into presidential politics occurred during Republican Barry Goldwater's 1964 campaign for president, serving as Goldwater's chief economic advisor. Although Goldwater's conservative ideas were considered extreme by many moderate Republicans at the time, Friedman agreed with him politically, particularly with regard to limiting the role of the federal government. Goldwater opposed the 1964 Civil Rights Act because he believed it was an intrusion of the federal government into the affairs of states. This opposition, along with his pro-state's rights stance, brought Goldwater overwhelming support among southern states that were immersed in widespread resistance to *Brown v. Board* and school desegregation. In spite of the fact that white southerners were overwhelmingly Democrats in 1964, having reaped the benefits of Roosevelt's New Deal policies, they cast their presidential ballot for the candidate they felt represented their own interests regarding desegregation, hoping to stop the federal government from enforcing the *Brown v. Board* decision. Goldwater lost his presidential bid in a landslide to Democratic incumbent President Lyndon Johnson. However, he won in his home state of Arizona and five states in the Deep South—Alabama, Georgia, Louisiana, Mississippi, and South Carolina. Future conservative Republican candidates would learn from Goldwater's campaign, however, and this would change national politics in the coming decades.

Friedman would again lend his support to a presidential candidate in 1968, serving as an economic advisor to Republican candidate Richard Nixon. Nixon's successful campaign was not primarily based on his conservative economic policies. Rather, a great deal of the success of his presidential campaign has been attributed to the employment of the "Southern Strategy," a strategy developed after Goldwater's overwhelming support by states in the Deep South.[38] Using the Southern Strategy, Nixon tapped into the anger of segregationists, bitter over federal enforcement of civil rights laws and *Brown v. Board*, by promising to roll back federal intervention in the desegregation of public schools, and, in particular, the use of busing policies.

Following Nixon's election as president, Friedman would continue to advise Nixon on economic and domestic policy. While Nixon had great respect for Friedman, he was not a stalwart devotee of free market economics. He did, however, listen to Friedman on issues of social policy, and his ideas about school vouchers as a mechanism for school reform would find a toehold at the federal level under the Nixon administration.

According to Gary Orfield and Susan E. Eaton of the Harvard Project on School Desegregation, in keeping with campaign promises he made as part of his Southern Strategy, a key part of Nixon's education policy initiative included his administration's attempts to dismantle a number of the federal desegregation enforcement policies through judicial and administrative measures.[39] In 1969, however, the Nixon administration added credibility to Friedman's voucher concept by funding the Educational Voucher Project through the U.S. Office of Economic Opportunity (OEO), under the directorship of Christopher Jencks, former executive director of the Center for Education Policy Research at Harvard University. The project was intended to be an experiment to test the effectiveness of a school voucher system to better meet the needs of low-income students attending schools in urban areas. The OEO invited major school districts from around the country to participate in the study by becoming a site for an experimental voucher system. While five school districts originally received preliminary study grants, only one of these districts, Alum Rock, California, agreed to continue its participation in the experiment.[40] The implementation of a voucher system at Alum Rock proved much more complicated than anticipated and the experiment was short lived. Friedman later blamed the failure of the Alum Rock voucher experiment on the "educational establishment."[41]

The failure of the Alum Rock experiment to establish the validity of a voucher system as a viable education reform alternative was coupled with another failed attempt by the Nixon administration to impose a voucher system on a national level. In 1971, he established a Presidential Commission on School Finance to offer recommendations for fiscal challenges faced by America's public schools. One of the recommendations that resulted from this commission was the proposal of a "Parochiaid" program, a system for providing public money for students attending parochial schools. That same year, however, the Supreme Court ruled in the *Lemon v. Kurtzman* decision that providing tax dollars to private religious schools was unconstitutional, violating the separation of church and state doctrine. As a result, the Parochiaid initiative was not pursued.[42]

In many ways, Nixon's educational agenda foreshadowed future events in the education arena. In 1970, Nixon's proposal to Congress for the formation of the National Institute of Education (NIE) began with this statement, "American Education is in urgent need of reform."[43] The primary responsibility of the NIE would be the facilitation of educational research. However, Nixon also proposed a new concept in education—accountability—and, in order to make education more accountable, the NIE would work toward the development of new measurements of educational output as a means of assessing the effectiveness of local schools. Interestingly, according to President Nixon, the creation of a national accountability system would help forestall the imposition of a national curriculum; he explained:

> For years the fear of "national standards" has been one of the bugaboos of education. There has never been any serious effort to impose national standards on educational programs, and if we act wisely in this generation we can be reasonably confident that no such effort will arise in future generations. The problem is that in opposing some mythical threat of "national standards" what we have too often been doing is avoiding accountability for our own local performance. We have, as a nation, too long avoided thinking of the productivity of schools.[44]

Nixon's approach to the implementation of a system of testing, as a measure of accountability, however, was decidedly different from the accountability systems that would evolve in the coming decades. First, Nixon acknowledged that:

> we will want to be alert to the fact that in our present educational system we will often find our most devoted, most talented, hardest working teachers in those very schools where the general level of achievement is lowest. They are often there because their commitment to their profession sends them where the demands upon their profession are the greatest.[45]

Any comparison of schools, therefore, according to Nixon, should be between schools and districts with similar economic and geographical features. Nixon asserted that, while teachers and administrators should be held accountable for their performance, "success should be measured not by some fixed national norm, but rather by the results achieved in relation to the actual situation of the particular school and the particular set of pupils."[46] Finally, Nixon suggested that any new system for measuring educational achievement "should pay as much heed to what are called the 'immeasurables' of schooling . . . such as responsibility, wit and humanity as it does to verbal and mathematical achievement."[47] The NIE was congressionally approved in 1972 under the leadership of the Education Division of HEW and, upon the creation of the federal Department of Education in 1980, was renamed the Office of Educational Research and Improvement (OERI).

Friedman and Reagan

By far, Friedman would find his greatest presidential ally in President Reagan. They first met in 1967 when Reagan was serving as governor of California and Friedman was a visiting professor at the University of California at Los Angeles. Friedman would later say of his first meeting with Reagan that he was "delighted to find that he was not only a warm, attractive human being, but his views on educational issues were very much in line with my own."[48] Friedman served as economic advisor to Reagan during his presidential campaign. Following the Southern Strategy playbook, Reagan's Republican campaign staff strategically launched his campaign at a county fair in Mississippi, in the county made infamous by the murders of three civil rights workers in 1964 by the Ku Klux Klan, invoking what historian Joseph Crispino describes as, "a mantra that had sustained a generation of southern segregationists." Reagan told the crowd of supporters, "I believe in states' rights," and he promised to "restore to states and local governments the power that properly belongs to them."[49] Southern voters were, in 1980, still incensed over the role of the federal government in education and throughout his campaign Reagan promised to work for passage of legislation that would provide tuition tax credits and vouchers, permit voluntary school prayer, and abolish the federal DOE. Reagan won the election with a landslide victory.

Early in his first term, it was clear that Reagan's attempts to abolish the DOE were futile. Likewise, he would not be able to impact the issue of prayer in schools, an issue that had been repeatedly adjudicated by the Supreme Court. The one area that Reagan could have some impact, however, was in providing a forum to promote Friedman's ideas about school vouchers on a national level. The American public, however, didn't readily accept the voucher concept and Reagan was unable to pass legislation through Congress to implement a voucher system. According to David Berliner and Bruce Biddle, Reagan's failed attempts to fund school vouchers through federal legislation in 1982, 1983, and 1984 were due to the perception of the proposals as "elitist."[50] This lack of acceptance may have been fueled by the use of school tax vouchers by white segregationists to maintain educational apartheid in the South. However, a larger controversy about school vouchers was based on their use to fund private religious schools.

In 1980, the Internal Revenue Service launched an investigation into private religious schools in Mississippi that claimed tax-exempt status. IRS regulations required that private religious schools had to demonstrate that they were not guilty of discrimination. The IRS investigations were not only egregious to conservative Christians across the South, but also to right-wing Christian institutions of higher learning, such as Bob Jones University that prohibited interracial dating and marriage. When Bob Jones was denied tax-exemption status by the IRS, the Reagan administration came to the rescue and reversed the IRS ban on tax exemptions to racially discriminatory schools, a move that the *New York Times* called "tax-exempt hate."[51]

When Reagan's legislative attempts to implement voucher plans failed, he shifted his discussions of vouchers in two ways that ultimately made the concept more palatable to the American public. First, he changed the language associated with the concept from that of "school tax vouchers" for private schools to the more benign language of "school choice." Although they meant the same thing, according to Alex Molnar, "President Reagan successfully separated educational choice from its racist and sectarian roots."[52] The second shift was to propose vouchers as a way to provide a higher quality education for low-income students, primarily in inner-city schools. According to Kevin Dougherty and Lizabeth Sostre,

> Conservatives decided to repackage school choice in a form that its opponents might find more palatable or at least harder to oppose. In the first installment of this new campaign, the Reagan administration introduced a bill to provide vouchers to low-income youth to purchase remedial education at whatever school, public or private, they would like.[53]

This second shift did facilitate wider acceptance of the voucher movement, in particular by groups concerned with the declining quality of inner-city schools serving large populations of low-income minority students. In 1973, Friedman wrote, "I have long been puzzled that black leaders have not been the most vigorous proponents of the voucher plan."[54] According to Friedman, black leaders, who frequently sent their own children to private schools, were guilty of not helping their own people by making private schools an option for them through vouchers. Vouchers could, according to Friedman, "free the black man on the street from domination by his leaders." Nearly two decades later, the black community would look toward Friedman's ideas as a solution for the deplorable state of many of the inner-city schools in America. For black citizens, the public school system had long been a civil safeguard in a democratic society. However, it was clear by the 1980s that the state of many public schools serving largely minority student populations, particularly in urban areas, were in need of reform. Due to shrinking tax bases to support public education, poverty, and isolation, these schools were deplorably inadequate. For example, Jonathan Kozol described the inner-city schools of East St. Louis as, "a monument to apartheid in America."[55] The shift in language from school vouchers to school choice as a way to improve the educational lives of low-income students during the Reagan administration would prove to be a very successful strategy, enabling some otherwise reticent supporters on the right and left to envision choice as a reform initiative rather than an attempt to dismantle public schools.

George H. W. Bush, School Choice, and Vouchers

Following the election of George H. W. Bush as Reagan's successor to the White House, Friedman's newly packaged school choice concept would find greater traction. While federal policies regarding school choice and vouchers were not in place, states and local school districts had the ability to adopt school choice plans. Minnesota was the first state to enact a public choice "open enrollment" law in 1988. The second state to follow Minnesota in enacting a statewide choice program was Arkansas under Governor Bill Clinton.[56] Other states followed over the next decade, implementing various programs that would enable students to attend schools other than those assigned to them by their local school district. Conservatives would continue to advocate for private school vouchers, but, for Friedman, the fact that the idea of school choice was gaining respect at federal, state, and local levels gave him hope.

President H. W. Bush referred to himself as the "education president," and he promised to promote education reform once in the White House. He openly supported the voucher movement as part of his education reform policies, and, as a matter of fact, vouchers and school choice was a higher priority for his administration than educational standards.[57] When black activists, working in conjunction with the Wisconsin state legislature and the Bradley Foundation, successfully led the effort to implement the Milwaukee Parental Choice Program (MPCP), Bush lauded their use of a system to provide vouchers for low-income students to enroll in private schools. The 1990 program, however, faced legal challenges from groups such as the NAACP, the People for the United Way, teachers' unions, and the American Civil Liberties Union. Nevertheless, voucher advocates in Milwaukee were victorious in maintaining their program, and, in 1998, the MPCP was extended to include not only nonsectarian private schools, but religious schools as well.

In 1990, John E. Chubb and Terry M. Moe published *Politics, Markets, and America's Schools*, a book that refueled discussion about vouchers at the national level. In their book, the authors reasserted Friedman's claim that government funded schools were incapable of reforming themselves, boldly proclaiming that "reformers would do well to entertain the notion that choice *is* a panacea," having "the capacity *all by itself* to bring about the kind of transformation that, for years, reformers have been seeking to engineer in myriad other ways."[58]

While supporting the idea of vouchers and choice as the most powerful tool for reforming education, Bush proceeded to promote his educational agenda on other fronts as well. The proposed reforms outlined in *America 2000* were a result of his 1989 summit of state governors in Charlottesville, Virginia, a meeting devoted to education. Taking the spotlight at the summit was Governor Bill Clinton of Arkansas who had attended a similar summit of state governors in 1983 when Terrel Bell had been invited by Vice President Bush to discuss *ANAR*. This time Governor Clinton would take a more prominent role and is credited with doing much of the work in writing *America 2000*. President Bush later explained the goals of *America 2000*. By the year 2000:

1. All children in America will start school ready to learn.
2. The high school graduation rate will increase to at least 90 percent.
3. American students will leave grades four, eight, and twelve having demonstrated competency in challenging subject matter including English, mathematics, science, history, and geography; and every school in America will ensure that all students learn to use their minds well, so they may be prepared for responsible citizenship, further learning, and productive employment in our modern economy.

4. U.S. students will be first in the world in science and mathematics achievement.
5. Every adult American will be literate and possess the knowledge and skills necessary to compete in a global economy and exercise the rights and responsibilities of citizenship.
6. Every school in America will be free of drugs and violence and will offer a safe, disciplined environment conducive to learning.[59]

Responsibility for reaching these goals would not, according to Bush, rest in the hands of the federal government, but would be the responsibility of state and local governments. *America 2000* would increase accountability through student testing as well as perpetuate the notion that schools carry the responsibility for producing students who can compete internationally within a global economy and bolster the American economy through productive employment. As a one-term president, Bush was not able to see *America 2000* passed by Congress. *America 2000* would, however, be successfully implemented with slight revisions and renamed *Goals 2000* by Bush's successor, President Bill Clinton.

Unlike President Nixon, George H. W. Bush promoted the idea of a set of national educational standards. Lamar Alexander, Bush's secretary of the DOE, directed his department to facilitate the creation of national standards in history, English language arts, science, civics, economics, the arts, foreign languages, geography, and physical education. These efforts were facilitated through grants to professional groups of teachers and scholars, and, because of legal mandates that prohibited the federal government from imposing a curriculum on states and school districts, the DOE stressed that adoption of these standards by states would be strictly voluntary. The creation of these standards was stalled, however, because of a rancorous debate that ensued about the proposed history standards. In newspaper editorials and talk radio shows, the standards were blasted as "the epitome of left-wing political correctness."[60] The debate pitted the right against the left, with some conservatives claiming that the standards were attempting to downplay the role of great white men in American history, in favor of the role of women and minorities. In short, the attempt by the DOE under George H. W. Bush to create a set of national standards created a big stink.

In his final education reform attempt, George H. W. Bush proposed a "G.I. Bill for Children" in 1992. This initiative would provide a $1,000 voucher for children in families with incomes below the national average to attend a private school. Although Congress did not act on Bush's proposal, the idea did stimulate national attention for the idea of school vouchers.[61] In spite of not being able to implement his education reform initiatives on the federal level, President Bush was effective in keeping Friedman's voucher idea alive. Cleveland, Ohio, implemented a voucher plan similar to Milwaukee's MPCP program. The Ohio legislature approved the plan in 1995, providing vouchers in the form of scholarships by lottery, with preference for low-income families to attend secular or religious schools. Again, the voucher program was challenged in the courts. However, in 2002 the Supreme Court ended the legal disputes, ruling that the voucher program in Cleveland was constitutional and did not violate the separation of church and state clause because it allowed individuals to choose between secular and religious schools.

Both Milwaukee and Cleveland voucher plans targeted low-income students in inner-city schools, and this bolstered their appeal to minorities who saw this as a way to finally see improvements in schools that were failing for a variety of reasons. Voucher proponents were enthusiastically hopeful that the Cleveland and Milwaukee plans would ignite a flurry of other such programs across the country. However, this would not be the case. Any time a voucher program was placed on the state ballot during a general election, citizens rejected the idea as a statewide reform initiative.[62] A true voucher system would not be implemented again until 2003 when the Republican-led Congress established the "Opportunity Scholarship Program" for the schools in Washington DC, providing vouchers for two thousand students to attend private schools, many of which were Catholic schools.[63]

The voucher concept was not completely dead to be sure. While American citizens, when given the opportunity to vote on the issue of vouchers, have rejected the idea, state governments controlled by conservative legislatures have continued to implement various vouchers plans. In 1999, Florida implemented a statewide voucher system that would enable any student enrolled in a "low-performing school" to transfer to a private school, secular or religious, or another higher achieving school. By 2006, the Florida voucher program would be found by the state Supreme Court to be unconstitutional and much of its original program was dismantled. What remained, however, was the McKay Scholarship program that provided vouchers for students with disabilities to attend private schools. In 2011, the *Miami New Times* published a scathing critique of this program, revealing widespread abuse, fraud, and substandard schools.[64] Nevertheless, Florida continues its efforts to implement a statewide voucher program, in spite of a lack of general support by Florida citizens. In 2012, Florida voters summarily rejected an effort to amend the state constitution to permit vouchers.[65]

In 2012, Louisiana Governor Bobby Jindal and the Republican-controlled state legislature implemented the most far-reaching of any voucher program. Any student in a school carrying a rating of average or below by the state could transfer to any other educational institution. This included not only private schools of any kind, but also any for-profit company in the business of education—whether an actual school or an online virtual school. By May 2013, the state's highest court ruled that the funding of vouchers from public school funds was unconstitutional. Undeterred, however, Louisiana continues to implement choice programs in other ways.[66]

Evaluating the Effectiveness of Voucher Programs

As a result of the 1990 implementation of the Milwaukee voucher program, there has been a substantial research base established over the years to test the validity of Friedman's claims that the voucher concept is the panacea for education reform. Since the beginning of the Milwaukee voucher program over 25 years ago, a great deal of research has been generated, with a number of the studies being sponsored by pro–free market conservative foundations, such as the Walton Family Foundation, the Friedman Foundation for Educational Choice, and the Bradley Foundation, that unabashedly promote vouchers and school choice. It's not surprising, therefore, that research funded by these groups would highlight any and all of the positive impacts of voucher programs. But while some studies seemed to point to the Milwaukee program as a success, a closer examination of the research generated from the MPCP program reveals quite a different picture. Friedman and other voucher proponents have maintained their belief that a voucher program would not only help the students who enroll in private schools, it would also lead to improvements in the public schools as well.

In 2009, almost 20 years after implementing its voucher program, the Milwaukee public schools participated in the NAEP testing program for the first time. The results were dismal. Milwaukee performed among the lowest cities in the nation on the reading and math assessments. Black students, who were intended to benefit the most from the voucher program, scored among the lowest performing students in the nation in both fourth and eighth grade in English and math. When Milwaukee schools participated in NAEP testing again in 2011, the results were no better. Most important, however, low achievement was not limited to the public schools. The promise of private schools to improve the educational achievement of the low-income, primarily black students in Milwaukee has never been realized. Students enrolled in private voucher schools, and the charter schools that have emerged as the new choice option in recent years, did no better than those who remained in the public schools.[67]

The voucher program in Cleveland revealed similar results. Students attending public schools in Cleveland have typically performed better on state tests than students attending voucher schools. On national tests, Cleveland students, like those in Milwaukee, were among the lowest performing in the nation. In spite of the failure of the voucher program to improve academic achievement for any of their students, regardless of race, ethnicity, or socioeconomic status, the state of Ohio expanded its voucher program statewide to include any student in a low-performing school or any student with a disability. As a result, by 2011, over $100 million tax dollars were being diverted away from public schools to private voucher schools.[68] In Washington DC, the voucher program fared no better. A congressionally mandated evaluation of their "Opportunity Scholarship Program" concluded that there was no evidence that the program had any affect at all on student achievement. Students enrolled in private voucher schools performed no better than their counterparts in public schools.[69]

Voucher advocates have claimed that, even if test scores do not reveal consistent improvement among students, researchers have found that those who attend private schools receiving vouchers are more likely to graduate from high school and attend college. However, this finding has been challenged. It is impossible to say that students who attended private schools through a voucher program would not have graduated and attended college had they remained in a public school. Arguably this is because students who participate in voucher programs tend to be more motivated and this may explain their desire and ability to graduate from high school and go on to college. One can debate whether or not the continued enrollment of these more highly motivated students in public schools would have helped raise the accountability ratings of the public schools, or if they had continued in these schools their motivation would have gone away.[70]

In spite of the lack of any empirical evidence that a voucher system is the panacea for low student achievement, conservative advocates for vouchers continue to promote this failed idea. For them, according to Diane Ravitch, the lack of evidence in improvements in student achievement doesn't matter. It is a matter of principle. The true benefit of a voucher program is that it will "end government control, supervision, and regulation in schooling."[71] In the years following the Reagan and George H. W. Bush administrations, the voucher/choice idea has continued to evolve, with charter schools becoming the most recent tool for implementing school choice and the free market ideal in education. By 2005, the charter school movement would be fully in place across the country, embraced by both the political left and right.

Opportunism and Vouchers

Friedman continued to promote his vision for education reform until his death in 2006 at the age of 94. The Friedman Foundation for Educational Choice remains a strong voice in advocating for school vouchers and choice. Along with other conservative think tanks, Friedman's foundation has seized upon any and every opportunity to promote their vision for remaking public education through free market ideas. In 2005, when New Orleans was hit by Hurricane Katrina and the city was devastated on an epic scale, Friedman would see this as an opportunity to promote his free market theories. In the *Wall Street Journal*, on December 5, 2005, Friedman wrote:

> Most New Orleans schools are in ruins, as are the homes of the children who have attended them. The children are now scattered all over the country. This is a tragedy. It is also an opportunity to reform the educational system. . . . The New Orleans schools were failing for the same reason that schools are failing in other large cities, because the schools are owned and operated by the government.[72]

Hurricane Katrina, according to Friedman, presented the perfect opportunity to completely reinvent the school system in New Orleans by implementing a voucher system using tax dollars to send all children, once they returned to the city, to privately operated schools. In 2007, Naomi Klein, prompted in part by the events of Hurricane Katrina, provided an extensive evaluation of Friedman's economic policies and their impact on not only New Orleans, but in other international arenas. According to Klein, Friedman, in the months following the hurricane, saw this crisis as an opportunity, citing his earlier essay on contemporary capitalism in which Friedman stated,

> Only a crisis - actual or perceived - produces real change. When that crisis occurs, the actions that are taken depend on the ideas that are lying around. That, I believe, is our basic function: to develop alternatives to existing policies, to keep them alive and available until the politically impossible becomes the possible.[73]

As Klein explained, Friedman was convinced that, when a crisis has struck, "it was crucial to act swiftly, to impose rapid and irreversible change before the crisis-racked society slopped back into the 'tyranny of the status quo.'"[74] Hurricane Katrina was the crisis, and if handled properly, could dismantle the existing public school system in New Orleans and replace it with a privatized voucher system.

Even before Friedman published his thoughts about Hurricane Katrina in December, 2005, conservative think tanks were already mobilized in efforts to take advantage of the opportunity. On September 13, 2005, a little more than two weeks after the hurricane's impact was felt in New Orleans, the Heritage Foundation convened a meeting with conservative leaders and Republican lawmakers to develop a list of pro–free market ideas for responding to the Katrina crisis. Among the 32 policies proposed at this meeting was one that called for providing parents with vouchers to send their children to charter schools.[75] All of the proposed measures were endorsed by President George W. Bush and thousands of teachers were fired in order to facilitate the complete reinvention of the educational system in New Orleans. Privately operated charter schools quickly replaced almost all of the public schools in the city. Before Hurricane Katrina, there were 123 public schools and 7 charter schools. After the storm, however, 4 public schools remained and 31 charter schools were in operation. And that was just the beginning. By 2013, New Orleans led the nation in the percentage of its students who attended charter schools, with 79 percent of their students attending these schools.[76]

The encroachment of free market theory into the educational arena has been largely unchallenged by federal policy makers. While there have always been skeptics of this approach to education reform, their voices have been silenced, lost in the cacophony of criticism of teachers and schools since *ANAR* claimed that basically "all public schools are failing." Ironically, history has demonstrated that Friedman's economic theories have not been proven to be correct. His ideas were, in fact, theoretical, awaiting empirical evidence to prove their worth. And when his voucher idea did not yield valid empirical evidence to prove its worth, it mattered very little to voucher proponents, whose primary goal was to remove the government from schooling and allow the free market to guide the progress of American education. Nor has it mattered to voucher advocates that the American public has never wholeheartedly embraced vouchers as an effective school reform option. Any time a voucher system has been placed on a state ballot, citizens rejected the idea. Even voucher advocate Terry M. Moe has admitted that the American public overwhelmingly supports its public schools, seeking to reform the system rather than dismantling it in favor of a privatized system.[77]

In a survey sponsored by the Friedman Foundation for Educational Choice, published in January 2014, Americans again rejected vouchers as the best option for reforming America's schools. As a matter of fact, vouchers were not even second or third on the list of seven educational reform options. Survey respondents cited smaller class sizes as the most promising reform option, followed by increased technology and stronger accountability. Try as they might, after six decades voucher advocates have simply not been able to convince American citizens that a tax voucher system is the panacea for education reform.[78] In the words of Diane Ravitch, "How embarrassing for the Friedman Foundation."[79]

Over the years, Friedman's voucher concept has evolved and been relabeled, with the terms vouchers and choice becoming interchangeable. And the evolution continues, with the most recent iteration of vouchers being relabeled as charter schools. As will be discussed in the coming chapters, the educational landscape would over the years increasingly reflect the free market ideas of Friedman, with the idea of competition being embedded in every discussion about education, while America has been left with an educational system continuously enmeshed in a tangled web of educational reform initiatives. While conservatives have, in many ways, successfully created a free market for education, ironically, they have, in spite of their repeated assertions that government is the problem, helped create both a gigantic federal Department of Education system and a Draconian accountability system.

Chapter 4

Corporate Superstars and an Inconvenient Truth

Under the Reagan administration, deregulated free markets were removing the shackles from corporate tycoons on a crusade to save the free world from what, they believed, was the tyranny of big government and high taxes. In 1987, the U.S. Congress, under President Reagan, passed the Malcolm Baldrige National Quality Improvement Act as a way to recognize preeminent public or private organizations that exemplified excellence and quality.[1] Education would soon be caught up in the headiness of corporate "heroism" and corporate superstars would be looked upon as the big minds with the big ideas about how to systemically reform public education in the United States. The path to the Common Core State Standards would, in large part, be carved by these corporate superstars.

In November 1989, Xerox was presented the Baldrige Award, largely based on the efforts of its CEO, David T. Kearns, in turning around the corporation since assuming leadership in 1977. Kearns' career in big business began with IBM before he became the CEO of a troubled Xerox corporation as it was languishing and losing its battle for profits to Japanese companies that, quite simply, were making better copy machines. For the next decade Kearns worked tirelessly reinventing Xerox, making it a corporation worthy of the Baldrige Award. Kearns was presented the award at a White House ceremony by President George H. W. Bush who commented on the Xerox CEO's "can-do, no-excuse attitude" and "aggressive impatience with the status quo."[2] Within two and half years, Bush would call on corporate superstar David Kearns to apply his can-do, no-excuse attitude and aggressive impatience with the status quo to education policy, appointing him deputy secretary of the U.S. DOE in 1991.

According to Kearns, the principles of Total Quality Management (TQM) were the keys to his success as CEO of Xerox. These same principles, Kearns asserted, if applied to public schools, would yield the same results. In much the same way he reinvented Xerox, Kearns vigorously promoted the reinvention of America's public education system using a business model to promote quality, customer satisfaction, and system-wide restructuring. TQM quickly became a buzzword among educational leaders in the United States. For example, the November 1992 issue of *Improving School Quality* featured an article by John Jay Bonstingl about the impact of TQM on public schools entitled "The Quality Revolution in Education."[3] Other such articles were soon to follow.

The concept of TQM originated with W. Edwards Deming and a team of researchers working in Japan in the decade following WWII. Deming's mission was to assist Japanese business leaders to "reverse their well-established reputation for shoddy, cheap goods by designing quality into their work systems."[4] Still recovering from the devastation of the war and desperately trying to recover economically, Japan eagerly adopted Deming's suggestions. Japan was so successful in reinventing its manufacturing sector that by the 1970s, Japan had overtaken the United States as a preferred source for many manufactured goods like automobiles and copy machines.

Although Deming's ideas had been largely ignored by U.S. manufacturers in the decades following WWII, his principles would be resurrected in a 1980 television documentary entitled, "If Japan Can, Why Can't We?"[5] Education leaders jumped onboard the TQM bandwagon, confident that if schools were run according to the principles of successful businesses, the result would be successful schools with high quality "output" that would translate into high test scores. In 1992, Bonstingl described the Four Pillars of Total Quality as:

1. The organization must focus, first and foremost, on its suppliers and customers;
2. Everyone in the organization must be dedicated to continuous improvement, personally and collectively;
3. The organization must be viewed as a system, and the work people do within the system must be seen as ongoing processes; and
4. The success of TQM is the responsibility of top management.[6]

The implementation of TQM required a complete reinvention of the very notion of public schools. Students were no longer merely learners, but they were the school's "primary customers" as well as "workers" whose product is their own continuous improvement and growth measured by test scores within a TQM model. Within this model, teachers don't simply teach but rather "deliver educational services" to children.[7]

In order for TQM principles to be successful in American schools, however, required the underlying belief that: (1) American schools were in peril, much like manufacturers in Japan after WWII, and in need of complete restructuring; and (2) schools were nothing more than businesses. The concept of TQM, however, begins to break down when thinking of public schools as mere businesses. In one sense students were considered consumers, in that they "consumed" the education provided at a particular school. But according to TQM principles, these students were also considered workers, in that they were engaged in the production of learning, test scores, and the creation of *themselves* as learned individuals. So to make this comparison more bizarre, these same students were also the product of the company, i.e., schools! This process was very different than when a worker produces a car for Ford or a hamburger for McDonald's. At least one thing that most Americans can agree upon is that children are not hamburgers—nor are they cars!

The education of any child is just too complex to simply reduce this process in terms of a simplistic TQM business approach. The effectiveness of the tidal wave of TQM models that swept the education landscape throughout the 1980s and 1990s continues to be widely debated. Nevertheless, what has remained is the concept that schools are nothing more than businesses in which a product results in the form of student learning that can only be validly measured through standardized testing, which, in essence, ultimately becomes a school's measurable profit.

A new model for reforming public schools would be created by another corporate superstar. In 1989, Lou Gerstner, then CEO of RJR Nabisco facilitated the creation of the company's Next Century Schools (NCS) program. This program provided $30 million in grants over three years for education leaders who were willing to radically restructure individual public schools that would serve as models of market reform in education. Governor Bill Clinton served on the original NCS Advisory Board along with President George H. W. Bush's secretary of education, Lamar Alexander, and soon to be appointed deputy secretary of education, corporate superstar David Kearns.[8]

According to Leanna Landsmann and Mary Harbaugh, the NCS project represented a shift in education reform from one of restructuring to revolt, quoting President George H. W. Bush as declaring, "There will be no renaissance without revolution." Gerstner was quoted as stating that Nabisco's money should go toward "arming the insurgents" and "guerrilla educators." Gerstner's NCS conferences would be called "China Breakers"—a metaphor for what one might do with an inferior set of dinnerware.[9]

As the NCS's three-year program began to wind down, the New American Schools Development Corporation (NASDC) was formed to further infuse corporate dollars into education reform initiatives. This time, however, the federal government would provide some of the money, thanks to President George H. W. Bush. Gerstner would play an important role in the NASDC. Larry Cuban, explaining the influence of the NASDC and its corporate dollars on federal education policy, quotes James Jones, chairman of the American Stock Exchange. Jones rationalized, "Privately financed federal initiatives to transform schools would 'take the shackles off' and would 'think big to make education something that improves the productivity, the competiveness, the quality of all students going through the system.'"[10]

Gerstner would go on to become one of the enduring corporate superstars in the 1990s and well into the twenty-first century. In much the same way that Kearns is credited with saving Xerox, Gerstner is credited with saving IBM, when he left RJR Nabisco to assume leadership of the floundering technology giant in 1993.[11] Certainly, IBM and Xerox needed saving and there was plenty of empirical evidence that these businesses were failing due to the inferior products they were manufacturing. Rescuing these failing businesses through systemic change, however, did not mean that Kearns and Gerstner were charged with completely restructuring the United States' business system writ large, nor were these two individuals claiming that *all* businesses were failing. They were engaged in restructuring one business by improving the business practices and the quality of the manufactured goods produced by that business.

Far from being satisfied with being corporate giants, however, Gerstner and Kearns extended their corporate lives to engage in a messianic-like mission of saving what they saw as a failed public school system. And far from saving one school or one school district, they envisioned their role in a more grandiose way—saving an entire American school system on a national basis. Of course, these efforts were predicated on the assumption that all schools were failing and in need of rescue as if all schools were producing inferior products, or as if the entire public school system in America was merely a business and comparable in any way to a major corporation such as IBM or Xerox.

The Fallacy of Public Schools as a Business

In 2013, IBM employed 434,246 employees worldwide. To be sure, that's a lot of people to manage. However, that's really "small potatoes" when compared with the number of people "employed" by public schools in the United States. If, indeed, as the TQM model proposes, students are considered workers, customers, and products of public schools, then the 50.1 million students enrolled in public schools in 2013 would be counted as employees of this vast education system in addition to being customers and products. Then add to that the 3.3 million full-time teachers employed within American schools. In addition, according to the Department of Education and the Bureau of Labor Statistics, public schools also employ 231,500 principals, superintendents, and other school administrators.[12] Therefore, if the public school system in the United States is to be treated like a business, then any proposal for reforming public schools in the same way that a large corporation is restructured must take into consideration the need to manage over 53.5 million employees (not counting other staff positions such as secretaries, maintenance workers, bus drivers, or substitute and part-time teachers)—all with diverse backgrounds, needs, strengths, and weaknesses and serving very diverse communities in inner-cities, in addition to rural and suburban areas in all 50 states within America. And of course, all of these schools, people, and locales have profound social and economic infrastructure needs that must also be met in order to become successful.

Free marketers would no doubt assert that the essential strength of America's business system rests with a competitive market that forces businesses to improve or perish. Likewise, they assert that competition is exactly what the public school system needs in order to force schools to either improve or perish. What free market school reformers ignore is that the "system" of public schools has always felt the sting of competition. School districts have always competed for tax dollars—dollars that were often increasingly scarce in urban areas that experienced "white flight" and shrinking tax bases. As a result, students attending urban schools, situated within deteriorating urban neighborhoods and communities where high unemployment and crime are a consistent reality, have always felt the sting of reductions in funding for the programs and buildings that would make their schools competitive with more affluent suburban communities, in which schools benefit from expanding tax bases, better neighborhoods, and higher parental incomes. The same is true of students in rural areas across the United States.

Schools are not businesses. If they were, then few corporate CEOs would even consider opening a school in many of the destitute communities in which public schools exist. After all, corporations are often very selective when it comes to where they locate their business offices and factories. They certainly don't expect their employees to walk through drug-infested, gang-ridden, and squalor-filled neighborhoods to go to work. Businesses, and in particular corporations, look to the local and state governments, who court the CEOs, to invest in infrastructure that would make a community worthy of the business's presence. For example, deals are made to ensure adequate roads, good sources of water and power, and tax incentives. Businesses want to ensure that the employees they relocate to an area have good schools for their families and nice neighborhoods. In other words, CEOs of corporations envision the community as a source for ensuring the profitability of their business.

If schools were businesses like those based on a corporate model, then citizens would be empowered to do the same thing, demanding, for example, that city officials clean up the neighborhoods before requiring students to navigate the drug-infested, gang-ridden streets between their homes and the school. Parents could demand that state and city governments repair decaying school buildings before the first day of school. And parents could demand programs that would enrich their children's educational lives, such as music and the arts, before they subject their children to an endless stream of mandated standardized tests.

Nevertheless, schools are not businesses. Public schools serve children, their families, and their communities. They serve a different system—not the system of public schools as governed by Washington or the state departments of education, but the system of the community in which they are located. At the very least, systemic reform, therefore, must simultaneously include reforming the community. Until that occurs, public schools within economically disadvantaged and socially troubled communities cannot be held accountable to the same standard as their more affluent and socially stable counterparts in suburban areas. By demanding this, public school supporters are asking no more than what corporations require before their factories or corporate headquarters are built in a particular community.

The Elementary and Secondary Education Act (ESEA), as an essential component of President Johnson's War on Poverty, acknowledged that schools exist within community systems. Therefore, reforming education and improving educational outcomes could only be effective within a comprehensive approach to providing equity for all children, families, and communities. According to Alain Jehlen, writing for *NEA Today*, public schools made substantial gains in closing the achievement gap in the years directly following the implementation of War on Poverty programs. Perhaps, as noted by Jehlen, the defunding or underfunding of War on Poverty programs over the decades since 1970 can be cited as a reason for the stagnation in student achievement for students living in impoverished communities.[13]

As an important aside, as we will see, charter school operators employ some of the same tactics as business CEOs when opening new schools. It's common practice, for example, for new businesses to request—and receive—certain tax breaks from state and local governments in order to ensure their profitability. Charter schools, too, would be given all kinds of concessions. While public schools serve all students, regardless of ability, disability, or any social, emotional, or physical factor that might impact education achievement, charter schools are permitted to operate with policies that enable them to select students who will increase their profitability (in terms of higher test scores). Students with special needs are often counseled away from charter schools and students and parents who violate their contracts are conveniently eliminated before high-stakes tests are administered.[14] And, in the case of New York City, private charter schools are provided rent-free space within public school buildings and operate concomitantly as both public and private entities, using tax dollars to provide profits for the business owners while receiving rent-free space in public buildings.

In 1994, Gerstner published his book *Reinventing Education: Entrepreneurship in America's Public Schools* with coauthors Roger D. Semerad, former senior vice president of RJR Nabisco, Denis Philip Doyle, senior fellow of the Hudson Institute, and William B. Johnston, executive vice president of the global public relations company Burson-Marsteller and senior fellow of the Hudson Institute. The authors described themselves as "venture capitalists,"[15] willing to provide financing for bold ideas for educational entrepreneurs who have the ability to radically restructure the American school system which was, according to the authors, in "deep trouble."[16] In the book's foreword, Gerstner explained that his involvement in education reform was not "just philanthropic" but was "fueled by intense anger" and frustration over "the slowness and indifference our country brings to the crisis in public education reform."[17] He further explained: "The Chinese character *crisis* is made up of two characters, one for *danger*, and the other for *opportunity*. Our schools are in trouble, yet we know enough to act." Gerstner and his coauthors provided the blueprint for success for public education by invoking the language of TQM and business reform. Interestingly, they employed some of the same language as other free market reformers, such as Milton Friedman, while promoting school choice as a reform initiative, when they proclaimed, "Public elementary and secondary schools are a protected monopoly, owned and operated by government and enjoying captive clienteles."[18]

AN INCONVENIENT TRUTH: THE SANDIA REPORT

In the decade following *A Nation at Risk*, its findings went largely unchallenged, and, therefore, education reform efforts were predicated on the highly suspect findings of that report and fueled by its alarmist tone. Corporate superstars and government officials routinely referred to *ANAR* in their public pronouncements of a failing public school system and the need for systemic reform. What if, however, a government report surfaced that called into question the validity of the findings in *ANAR*? It was one thing for liberal university professors to challenge the notion that schools were failing and publish articles that only university intelligentsia would read in academic journals. It was another thing entirely for the U.S. government to issue a report that challenged the findings issued by the DOE in 1983.

In 1990, Admiral James Watkins, the Department of Energy secretary, instructed Sandia National Laboratories to undertake a study of American education, although he did not foresee the firestorm this study would create.[19] Watkins was a protégé of Admiral Hyman Rickover who was a staunch critic of America's public schools; and although Watkins was not the rabid education critic of Rickover's caliber, he readily accepted the opportunity to join in the assault on America's public schools. Watkins proclaimed, "We have to pick up our society by its bootstraps and find a new mechanism to obtain science and math literacy"[20] Sandia National Laboratories seemed like the perfect entity to undertake an investigation into public schools with its long history as a highly respected research center.[21]

Daniel Tanner, writing in 1993, explained that "the basis for undertaking the study was to provide Sandia a foundation for planning its activities in education."[22] The key to assessing the importance of Sandia's evaluation of education is the fact that it was begun with no previous premises about education that needed to be proved. In other words, the researchers began their investigation with no preconceived notion that schools were failing. Sandia researchers presented their report, originally titled "Perspectives on Education in America" in spring 1991. The report would later simply be known as the Sandia Report.[23]

Sandia researchers knew that their report would not be well received by education policy makers. An early version of the report stated, "Unfortunately, much of the current [education] reform agenda, though well intentioned, is misguided."[24] They further went on to assert, "Based on a 'crisis' mentality, many proposed reforms do not properly focus on actual problems."[25] However, the researchers were also concerned that their report would be, at best, suppressed by the DOE, and, at worst, their federal research funds would be cut as a result of the report's findings. Their concerns seem to have been well founded.

In an attempt to circumvent critics and ensure the accuracy of their report, Sandia researchers began circulating annotated drafts to educators and researchers in late 1990, amid rumors that the administration intended to "kill the report."[26] When the Sandia researchers first presented their report to the DOE in the spring of 1991, they were met with angry reactions, particularly from former CEO of Xerox and then deputy education secretary David T. Kearns. According to Gerald Bracey, Kearns told the researchers, "You bury this or I'll bury you."[27] Julie A. Miller, writing for *Education Week*, reported in October 1991 that Washington sources told her that the researchers "were told it [the report] would never see the light of day, that they had better be quiet." Her source further commented, "I fear for their careers."[28]

After presenting the Sandia Report to the DOE in spring 1991, the findings of the report became the subject of a congressional hearing. The findings of the briefings, however, were not immediately released to the American public. Tanner explains, "The briefings had prompted strong demands [from DOE officials] that the report not be issued in its present form [summer 1991] and that it be subjected to review by officials of the National Science Foundation (NSF) and the DOE's National Center for Education Statistics (NCES)."[29] According to Tanner, this was an "unprecedented agreement" that "effectively held the report from being officially released" to the media and American citizens. While one of the goals of the extended evaluation was supposedly to judge the validity of the report's findings about education in America, this extended process "helped neutralize its potential impact."[30] Most telling is that in July 1991, the NCES, after evaluating the report, commented that the report was rather unique in that it presented "a balanced view" of American education.[31] In fact, Emmerson Eliot, a member of the NCES, was rather complimentary when he stated,

> I applaud the attempt represented here to present a balanced view of education since that is frequently not the approach analysts take. (This report presents both positive and negative aspects of the condition of education in the nation, and there are certainly trends that support both perspectives.) This is an important aspect of the report, and balance should be sought throughout the revision process. In addition, the report covers a great deal of ground in attempting to address a full range of issues in education. This provides a comprehensive and intriguing compilation of information. Still the report needs much work before it is published or is widely disseminated.[32]

What is of key importance is that while Eliot also went on to explain that the "much work" he was talking about had to do with supposed flaws in the report, the flaws still did not invalidate the report's findings and conclusions. Throughout the extensive revision process, according to Tanner, "the Sandia Report remained virtually intact in every major respect."[33] One of the Sandia researchers asserted that the DOE and NSF reviewers could not invalidate the data because most of it was actually "compiled by these very same agencies."[34] As a matter of fact, on the final draft of the report, in April 1992, one frustrated reviewer of the report simply wrote "Nuts" without further commenting upon or challenging its findings. The final version of the Sandia Report included a statement that the peer reviews by the DOE and NSF would be included in an appendix. The Sandia researchers were confident that the appendix would further strengthen the credibility of their report.[35] And it was these findings and conclusions that were causing consternation among DOE officials and other critics of American public schools who had jumped on board the education reform bandwagon of *A Nation at Risk* and *America 2000*, the frame of this wagon resting on wheels that spun the tale that America's public schools were failing except for a very few—plain and simple.

The Bush administration never cleared the Sandia Report for publication. To date, the report has only been published in the *Journal of Educational Research* in its May–June 1993 edition, which devoted the entire issue to the report.[36] Although the researchers did not lose their jobs, they were reassigned and the Sandia Laboratories discontinued their proposed research and development program for education. This led Tanner to cynically state, "Obviously, nuclear weapons research is far safer than the maelstrom of politics that swirls around our public schools."[37] But even more troubling, according to Bracey, the researchers were "forbidden to leave the state of New Mexico to talk about the report."[38] And while former Bush administrators to this day have continued to deny that the Sandia Report was suppressed, according to Bracey, Lee Bray, the Sandia vice president who oversaw the research, after his retirement admitted, "Yes, it was definitely suppressed."[39]

So what did the Sandia Report conclude that caused such angst among education policy makers, prompting them to go to such extraordinary lengths to suppress its findings? For policy makers at the DOE, the Sandia Report, if released to the public, had the potential to derail efforts to systemically reform public education by demonstrating the America's public schools were not failing.

Sandia researchers' findings regarding SAT scores mirrored similar findings by the College Board in the mid-1970s. While there had been a decline in SAT scores since the 1960s, this decline arose from the fact that more students in the bottom half of the class were taking the SAT. With more people aspiring to achieve a college education, the national SAT average was lowered as more students in the third and fourth quartiles of their high school classes took the test.[40] It was the case that minorities continued to significantly lag behind their white counterparts on the SAT. However, they concluded that "this disparity may be better correlated with home setting or family variables than with race or ethnicity," particularly for disadvantaged urban and rural students.[41] SAT scores for "traditional" test takers, according to the Sandia Report, had "actually improved over 30 points since 1975." The researchers, therefore, concluded that "the issue of student performance on SAT is far too complex to be discussed in terms of decline or improvement in average scores."[42]

When examining student performance on NAEP, Sandia researchers found that in the years leading up to 1990, there had not been "recent declines in performance on skills tests," further stating, "if anything, today's students are performing better than previous students."[43] As was the case with SAT scores, the researchers found that there continued to be a discrepancy between the NAEP scores for minority students and those for their white counterparts. However, they noted that this was a result of the education system's focus on "increased access and improved basic skills."[44] Sandia researchers further stated, "Our investigation of the NAEP data revealed that performance has been steady or improving in nearly all subject areas tested, and that the greatest gains have been made in basic skills. Furthermore, these gains have not been at the expense of advanced skills."[45]

According to the Sandia researchers, education reformers' claims about high dropout rates were misleading. While "dropout rates were not carefully calculated in many school districts" prior to the mid-1980s, census data revealed "an impressive increase in graduation rate from 1870 to the mid-1960s," and, "after 1965, the graduation rate from traditional schools has remained steady at about 75%." Furthermore, if GED completion was included, the high school completion rate was over 85 percent.[46] For black students, the decrease in dropout rate was particularly impressive in the 20 years leading up to their research, dropping from 28 percent to 15 percent. Dropout rates for Hispanic students, on the other hand, had not changed. Sandia researchers found, however, that Hispanic dropout rates were heavily influenced by immigration, with roughly 50 percent of the Hispanics reported as dropouts being first-generation immigrants who had in reality never enrolled in school in the United States. Sandia researchers asserted, "We believe that it is misleading to count adult immigrants as dropouts from the U.S. education system if they never attended a U.S. school."[47] And far from being an issue that required total systemic reform of the American education system, problems with dropouts were concentrated in inner cities where students, "regardless of race, tend to dropout at a higher rate than students in other community types."[48]

Sandia researchers further questioned the assertions of education reformers that the United States was not producing enough students capable of earning bachelor's degrees in the sciences (today generally referred to as STEM areas). The researchers found that between 1960 and 1980, the percentage of U.S. students earning degrees in the sciences was relatively stable at nearly 4 percent. And, interestingly, they found that engineering PhDs were "at or near an all-time high" and physical science PhDs were "within a few percent of an all-time high."[49] Furthermore, the Sandia researchers called into question claims by business leaders that the lack of skilled workers was a major problem. They noted that, in reality, only 15 percent of business leaders surveyed had difficulty filling skilled positions. After more closely examining claims of skilled-worker shortages, researchers concluded that "these positions existed in the chronically underpaid occupations such as nurses, skilled secretaries and clerks, and in craft apprentice trades." These shortages were, according to the researchers, attributable to "the fact that many people formerly filling these high-skilled, non-college jobs are now attending college and obtaining higher paying positions."[50] Additionally, Sandia researchers found that business leaders surveyed were "generally satisfied with the skills levels of their employees" and any complaints they had with workers tended to be related to work ethic and social skills. The researchers concluded that any dissatisfaction with workers did not "point to the K-12 education system as the root cause."[51]

Two other points raised in the Sandia Report bear mentioning as well. First, they found that "the average teacher in Japan earns almost 50% more than his/her American counterpart, relative to incomes in their respective nations" and that, "in constant dollars, beginning salaries [for teachers] in 1990 are the same as those of the 1970s."[52] Second, in response to public school critics complaining about increases in expenditures for education since the early 1980s, the Sandia researchers found that, while there had been an increase in total per-pupil spending, "much of the increase in expenditures . . . had been for special education." Roughly 25–30 percent of the expenditures were "directed to 10% of all students." Spending on "regular" education had remained steady.[53]

Clearly, findings such as these, especially coming from this highly respected politically neutral group of scientific researchers at the Sandia National Laboratories, was something that needed to be tucked away in some inconspicuous place where the American public, and, in particular, the American media, would probably not consider looking. And what better place than a respected professional journal about education—the *Journal of Educational Research*! With the Sandia Report suppressed, the crusade could continue for the systemic reform of public schools.

Systemic Reform and Local School Boards

Clearly the findings of the Sandia Report were an inconvenient truth that had the power to derail systemic education reform initiatives grounded in the belief that public schools were failing. However, with the Sandia Report sufficiently buried, critics of public schools could continue their campaign to radically reform America's public schools. Once critics of public schools had established that these schools were in crisis and therefore failing in total, the next step was to call for "systemic reform," which ended up being code for a total radical transformation of America's system of public education.

For these critics, it was to their advantage to never acknowledge that there are "many" public schools in America that were, indeed, performing well, as the Blue Ribbon Schools panel acknowledged even before *ANAR* was published.[54] To acknowledge this, at the very least, would have been an inconvenient truth for proponents of a radical course of systemic education reform. Instead, one essential strategy for achieving systemic reform was to divert attention away from acknowledging that some schools were performing quite well by labeling these schools as an aberration. Nevertheless, the drive for total systemic reform in education would be the natural outcome of creating a crisis mentality among Americans when it came to their public schools. When it was established that achieving total systemic reform must be the primary goal of education reform, a Pandora's Box of corporate-driven free market educational initiatives and solutions became a real threat to the local control of public schools that have personified American democracy.

Locally controlled public schools have served American students quite well. As a matter of fact, far from being aberrations, there are many public schools in locally controlled school districts across the country that are sources of pride to their communities and states. It is widely acknowledged that inner-city schools have suffered for many years, laboring to ameliorate the negative impacts of poverty, crime, shrinking tax bases, unemployment, and social factors beyond the ability of schools and teachers to solve. Nonetheless, there are abundant examples of successful schools and school districts in the United States. Therefore, citizens in every state across America need to begin asking themselves why some public schools always seemed to be doing well, while others always seemed to be facing challenges that stand in the way of education success. Is their success or failure simply a matter of good versus bad teachers and administrators, or good versus bad school boards—or does the degree of success or failure among these schools also have to do with other factors that are beyond the control of teachers, school board members, and individual citizens?

For the critics of public schools, however, addressing questions such as these would have undoubtedly revealed a number of inconvenient truths that could have potentially distracted from the narrative that all public schools are in crisis and the only solution to this crisis is to systemically reform the entire public education system. This narrative, indeed, became the driving force behind public school reform, the result being, as Kathy Emery explains, to "transfer educational policy making from local school boards to the state government for the purposes of subordinating educational policy to the corporate agenda."[55]

In the United States, local school boards have played an essential role in maintaining the proper relationship among diverse stakeholders concerned about public school education. Archie Carroll and Ann Buchholtz, in their book *Business and Society: Ethics and Stakeholder*

Management, explain the relationship between organizations such as school boards and the communities they serve.[56] Whether one is on the libertarian right or progressive left, it is essential to consider how the wishes of the individual citizen decision maker, as well as special interest groups such as the business community, become manifested in the United States.

According to Carroll and Buchholtz, "A society's pluralistic nature makes for business and society relationships that are more dynamic and novel than those in some other societies."[57] The authors explain that "pluralism refers to a diffusion of power among society's groups and organizations,"[58] and "a pluralistic society is one in which there is a wide decentralization and diversity of power. . . . Power is dispersed among many groups and people. Power is not in the hands of any single institution such as business, government, labor, or the military or a small number of groups."[59] According to the authors, one of the strengths of a pluralistic society is that it "prevents power from being concentrated in the hands of a few. It also maximizes freedom of expression and action. Pluralism provides for a built-in set of checks and balances so that no single group dominates."[60]

Carroll and Buchholtz go on to point out that one weakness in a pluralistic society to keep in mind is that it can create "an environment in which diverse institutions pursue their own self-interests with the result being that there is no ***unified direction*** [emphasis added] to bring together individual pursuits."[61] When it comes to America's public schools, this is where the means to manifest public decision making within a democracy enters the picture. This has to do with the role, power, and responsibility of local school boards that act as both arbiter and decision maker as individual boards go about considering the ideas of certain groups regarding education, and the degree of impact these individuals and groups and their ideas need to have in the education of the children for which the board is responsible. It is the local school board that creates a unified direction when it comes to public schools. After this process takes place, the local school board is responsible for deciding a proper educational course of action.

For school boards, there is always a tension over which organizations or interest groups best serve the educational needs of children in preparation for their eventual multiple roles in society, both as workers and citizens. The local school board is therefore engaged in a dynamic process that constantly must assess and then reassess the ideas of multiple stakeholders in the education process, and then be flexible enough to adapt a school's curriculum and environment to the social, economic, and political context in which the board's local schools exist. The major challenge and responsibility for any school board is deciding how to (1) create a positive learning environment that maintains high academic standards, which includes hiring quality teachers to help facilitate this process; (2) effectively deal with larger socioeconomic realities that impact students and their families; (3) democratically address the multicultural nature of American society; (4) create good citizens in a democratic republic; (5) meet the needs of the business sector; and (6) meet the needs of the individual parent, teacher, administrator, and, most important—the individual needs of every student. To accomplish all of this, school boards must be allowed to engage in a symbiotic, cooperative relationship with diverse education stakeholders by considering stakeholder needs and ideas while maintaining board autonomy.

Although certainly not a perfect system, in theory America's public schools rely on local school boards to reflect the wishes of a democratic pluralistic society. If the community does not like board decisions then solutions at minimum can be achieved through future elections or appointments. However, in more extreme cases of a school board's malfeasance, different individuals or groups can take legal action against a school board for violating laws that govern their action. Legally, no school board has complete dictatorial power, which is why, as Ruth Kolb and Robert Strauss pointed out, it is also essential to have strict laws in place that help "assure that our schools are served by local leaders who are, as much as possible, free from the distracting influence of self-interest."[62] Local public school boards are governed by laws while serving at the behest of the individual citizen, and membership within these boards becomes a democratic defense that prevents power from being concentrated in the hands of a few. This means, for example, that the business sector, federal and state governments, religious and multicultural groups, and yes—teachers' unions—can all represent centers of concentrated power.

THE BUSINESS ROUNDTABLE IN A DEMOCRATIC PLURALISTIC SOCIETY

Since at least the 1980s, the business sector has been well represented in discussions of education reform in the United States. And since that time, a driving force behind the move for total systemic reform of public schools has been the Business Roundtable (BRT). As Kathy Emery and Susan Ohanian explain, the BRT is "an association of chief executive officers who examine public issues that affect the economy and develop positions which seek to reflect sound economic and social princples."[63] The BRT was established in 1972 through the merger of three existing organizations: the March Group, the Construction Users Anti-inflation Roundtable, and the Labor Law Study Committee. Notably, according to the BRT website, "These groups founded Business Roundtable on the belief that in a pluralistic society, the business sector should play an active and effective role in the formation of public policy."[64]

This statement is important. In one sense, the BRT is meeting its responsibility within a pluralistic society by having America's business sector play an active and effective role in the formation of—in this case—education policy. The BRT, in fact, has not only a right but also a responsibility to do that. This is, however, the same active and effective role other special interest groups like those mentioned above have a right and responsibility to play within America's democratic pluralistic society. And while the educational goals of these diverse special interest groups should overlap, the marginalization of one group over the other, or even worse, the eventual dominance of one group over all the rest cannot be allowed if a democratic pluralistic society is to exist. But most problematically, using the rationale that one has a right and responsibility to play an active and effective role in the formation of education policy, and then going about working to eliminate local school boards in order to achieve total domination, is an act of authoritarian subterfuge that cannot be allowed.

No individual or group should have complete autonomy when it comes to public school education. However, as we will see, in the case of the BRT, education reform initiatives on the path to the Common Core State Standards (CCSS) will end up being a quest for power and dominance over the wishes of citizens manifested through local school boards and other public school stakeholders such as teachers and parents. For a special interest group such as the BRT, through the guise of "systemic school reform," the ultimate goal of this approach will be the usurpation of local control of public schools. In this way systemic reform eliminates any real power to influence school reform by other stakeholders, unless these stakeholders are in lock step with the education agenda of the BRT and its ideological allies. In fact, local public school boards on America's path to the CCSS became viewed as an impediment to the educational agenda of the BRT and its allies. Local school boards have been marginalized in the era of systemic education reform. As Joseph Beckham and Barbara Klaymeier Wills point out,

> Local school boards have been characterized as the largest losers in the reform efforts of the 1980s and 1990s. State legislatures have generated educational policies and regulations directed to academic standards, professional certification and preparation, and curriculum development. Bypassing local school boards in the haste to reform public education, additional legislation has emphasized choice as well as quality, and encouraged the development of charter schools with limited regulatory ties to the local school system, school-based management, vouchers, tax credits, and home-schooling options.[65]

By 2008, corporate and political leaders, critical of not only America's public schools but also the local school boards that were given the democratic responsibility of representing the public, would become so emboldened that they would no longer even beat around the bush about their feelings. For example, in 2008, Matt Miller, a senior fellow at the Center for American Progress, an organization that labels itself as a center of "progressive ideas for a strong, just, and free America," would write an article in the *Atlantic* in which he proposed what he called "a modest proposal to fix the schools." And what was this modest proposal all about? As the title of his article made clear, "First, Kill All the School Boards!"[66] That same year, Lou Gerstner, in a *Wall Street Journal* editorial, suggested this same course of action.[67]

Clearly, by 2008, America was continuing on its path to the CCSS and along the way democratic decision making was being taken out of the hands of the American citizen. Six years later on March 2, 2014, Diane Ravitch, in an empirically informed and impassioned speech about the assault on America's public schools, would proclaim, "I am absolutely furious that the Democratic Party has merged with the Republican Party around a bipartisan agenda that actually is a Republican agenda."[68] But how did this happen? How did the conservative right and the liberal left finally converge in an all-out unified assault on the democratic institution of America's public schools?

One organization would be essential in this convergence. The corporate financed American Legislative Exchange Council (ALEC) was formed in 1973. ALEC describes itself as:

> a nonpartisan membership association for conservative state lawmakers who shared a common belief in limited government, free markets, federalism, and individual liberty. Their vision and initiative resulted in the creation of a voluntary membership association for people who believed that government closest to the people was fundamentally more effective, more just, and a better guarantor of freedom than the distant, bloated federal government in Washington, D.C.[69]

During the Reagan administration, ALEC's role within the policy arena was greatly expanded, as conservative legislators and ALEC staff members worked closely with the Reagan administration to promote a conservative political agenda. When Reagan formed a national Task Force on Federalism, ALEC followed suit by establishing task forces of their own in several areas including education. The publication of *ANAR* bolstered the organization's resolve to engage in and influence federal education policy and provided an opportunity for ALEC to promote their free market reform agenda for education. ALEC published a two-part report in response to *ANAR* in which the organization "laid the blame for the nation's educational decline squarely where it belonged - on centralization, declining values, and an increasingly liberal social agenda that had pervaded schools since the 1960s." As a result, ALEC "offered such 'radical' ideas as a voucher system, merit pay for teachers and higher academic and behavioral standards for students as possible solutions to the problems."[70]

In the first two decades of its existence, ALEC primarily served as a "clearinghouse of ideas" submitted by its members. However, at the end of the Reagan administration the organization's task forces shifted their role within the government policy arena, serving as "think tanks and model bill movers." Over the next three decades ALEC actively solicited input and financial support from the private sector. According to the organization, this shift enabled them to seize upon their "long-time philosophy that the private sector should be an ally rather than an adversary in developing sound public policy."[71] This shift also positioned ALEC as a major player in the systemic education reform arena.

With the power of corporate dollars behind them, ALEC has wielded a mighty hand in public policy. One of their most influential roles as conservative policy agents has been to craft model legislation for state legislatures. To date, according to their website, "ALEC's Task Forces have considered, written and approved hundreds of model bills on a wide range of issues, model legislation that will frame the debate today and far into the future. Each year, close to one thousand bills, based at least in part on ALEC Model Legislation, are introduced in the states. Of these, an average of 20 percent become law."[72]

The full impact of the convergence between the political left and right would begin to take place under the guidance of President Bill Clinton. During the Clinton era, the influence of corporate elites with massive amounts of money would profoundly impact education reform at the state and federal levels with the overt cooperation of individual state governors. Even ALEC's conservative small government, states-rights agenda would bend under the pressure of corporate dollars to facilitate a free market of education initiatives. The organization's assertion that "government closest to the people was fundamentally more effective" would give way to government policies that yield the most profit for corporate power and distance citizens from public school policy.

CHAPTER 5

PUBLIC SCHOOLS AND A THIRD WAY OF GOVERNING

"I love Bill Clinton. Maybe not his politics, but I love Bill Clinton. My husband, Bill Clinton and I have become friends. And Bill visits us every summer. We don't agree politically, but we don't talk politics. Bill's father wasn't around, and I think he thinks of George a little bit like the father he didn't have."[1] In February 2014, Brent Budowsky explained that "many Americans warmly smiled" when the former first lady made this genuinely sincere statement. Budowsky went on to state, "the respect and affection between" these two presidents "is genuine and very American," claiming that "it hearkens back to an Americanism dating back to the early republic of Jefferson and Adams, which voters would greatly value today, when political opponents collaborated with mutual respect to advance national interests."[2]

One of the national interests that would unite Presidents Bush and Clinton and help create a good relationship between the two was education and the need to systemically reform America's public schools. George H. W. Bush wanted to be the education president, but only one term in office would not make that wish come true. An heir to his educational legacy, however, was close at hand and it would not come from Bush's own Republican Party. Twenty-two years after Bill Clinton unseated Bush for president of the United States, we now know that the two former competitors have been close friends for quite some time. And although Barbara Bush makes it clear that the two former presidents may differ politically, when it comes to education policy, Bush could well have thought that he was replaced in the White House by his son. As we have already seen, Clinton, when still a governor, was closely aligned with Bush and his ideas regarding education reform, which led to *America 2000*. As we will see, the Clinton administration would make some changes to *America 2000* and create *Goals 2000*. This legislation would set the tone for education policy decisions during Clinton's years in office, leading up to No Child Left Behind.

The journey along the path to the Common Core State Standards (CCSS) is not straightforward. There was certainly no secret conspiracy on the part of one group of ideologues to dominate public school policy decision making at the expense of another group's interests. To view the path in this way would ignore the complex roles of a number of competing groups, each with its own overt agenda, ideas, and interests. According to Diane Ravitch, "Bill Clinton and the New Democrats championed a 'third way' between the orthodox policies of the left and the right."[3] The book *Reinventing Government: How the Entrepreneurial Spirit Is Transforming the Public Sector from Schoolhouse to Statehouse, City Hall to the Pentagon* by David Osborne and Ted Gaebler, published in 1993, would provide a blueprint for reinventing government through the adoption of TQM principles, privatization, outsourcing, and downsizing.[4] Newly elected President Bill Clinton would be swept up in the TQM movement, and within months after his inauguration, his administration would implement far-reaching strategies for reinventing the government through market reforms. As a result, business entrepreneurs interested in systemic education reform made it possible for competing agendas, in one way or another, to find common ground within the Clinton administration's third way of governing. And very importantly, business entrepreneurs brought plenty of money in their apolitical effort to ensure that their ideas about education reform would gain traction.

A precedent for this approach had already been established when Bush's *America 2000* initiative was stalled in Congress, and the business community consolidated their efforts to push forward their agenda for systemic education reform. Leading the charge was the Business Roundtable (BRT). Following the 1989 meeting of the National Governors Association, the BRT used their considerable resources to promote the *America 2000* plan for reforming education by launching a massive public relations campaign to promote their education agenda. For example, a national series of advertisements warned the American public that the economy was in danger because of the nation's public education system. School reform was needed, according to the ads, because America did not have a good labor force, the result being that "people here and abroad want Japanese cars, Korean TVs, Scandinavian furniture and Italian shoes."[5]

With the election of Clinton as president, the BRT found a ready ally in their efforts to promote systemic education reform. Most important, Clinton's choice for secretary of the DOE, former governor of South Carolina Richard Riley, was very appealing to the BRT because he had a strong record of working closely with the business community. According to Jesse H. Rhodes, one DOE official recalled that the Clinton administration openly courted the business community, pitching, "our agenda is your agenda."[6]

THE REAUTHORIZATION OF THE ELEMENTARY AND SECONDARY EDUCATION ACT AND GOALS 2000

One of Clinton's early tasks during his first term in office was the reauthorization of the Elementary and Secondary Education Act (ESEA), which by law must be reauthorized every five years by Congress. According to Rhodes, in order to facilitate the reauthorization process, the Clinton administration relied heavily "on unelected political entrepreneurs for what became the 'Clinton education agenda.'"[7] Preparations for the reauthorization of the ESEA had actually begun in late 1990 with the formation of a Commission on Chapter 1, named after a key component of the ESEA. This component had to do with the education of low-income children. Commission members represented a wide array of groups: the Pew Forum on K-12 Education Reform; the Council of Chief State School Officers' Resource Center on Educational Equity; the Citizens' Commission on Civil Rights; the Center for Law and Education; the Children's Defense Fund; the Southwest Center for Academic Excellence; the National Center on Education and the Economy; Stanford University; the NEA; the AFT; and the Council of Chief State School Officers. The Commission's primary goal was to develop a plan to "use or change Chapter 1 to provide a challenging educational program of deep content to educationally disadvantaged students."[8]

Although group representation within the commission appeared to have been allied with more liberal-leaning constituencies, what is important to note about their work is that they looked to the business community to develop their plan. For example, the commission invited William Kolberg of the National Alliance of Business to join their group and, according to Rhodes, they explicitly relied "on the Business Roundtable's publication *Essential Components of a Successful Education System* to help structure their views."[9]

The Chapter 1 Commission's report, "Making Schools Work for Children in Poverty," was published in 1992 just before Clinton became president. In many ways, the commission's recommendations foreshadowed the basic tenets of the No Child Left Behind policies that would become the law of the land in 2002. For example, according the commission, federal ESEA funds should be tied to certain requisite state policies, such as:

1. High standards for all students.
2. Performance benchmarks that measure student progress against standards.
3. Assessments that gauge student progress toward meeting standards.
4. Annual report cards tracking schools' yearly progress in achievement of all students as well as the achievement of disadvantaged groups.
5. Criteria for establishing adequate yearly progress.
6. Mandatory accountability systems for rewarding or punishing districts and schools based on student achievement.[10]

The commission also recommended a provision for schools serving high populations of disadvantaged students that would discontinue "pull-out" programs for struggling learners, expand teacher professional development programs, and target ESEA funds for schools within districts serving low-income, disadvantaged communities. Most important, the commission recommended the implementation of "opportunity to learn" standards to address financial inequalities between districts and schools in order to provide all children with greater opportunities to achieve at high levels.[11]

The commission's findings were well received by both the education community and Congress. Soon after the report was published, President Clinton entered office. With several members of Congress willing to sponsor a bill for restructuring ESEA based on the commission's report, newly appointed secretary of education, Richard Riley, solicited commission member Marshall S. Smith, the dean of the school of education at Stanford University, to draft the administration's ESEA reauthorization report.[12] The Clinton administration's final proposal was announced in September 1993 and generally reflected the Chapter 1 Commission's recommendations.[13] This proposal for reauthorization and modification of the ESEA would now be called the Improving America's Schools Act (IASA). It is important to understand that any points of divergence between the commission's recommendations and the final draft of the IASA primarily had to do with the politics of ensuring the bill's passage in Congress. For example, acquiescing to the liberal education community's concerns about the negative and discriminatory impact of testing and stringent accountability measures on children, teachers, and schools, the Clinton administration's final proposal did not contain as much specificity regarding testing, accountability, and reporting as the commission thought was needed. The concerns of conservatives were appeased when the "opportunity to learn" standards were removed based on the rationale that the inclusion of this provision would necessitate tax increases at the state and local levels. Most important, any provision for withholding federal funds to schools and districts for noncompliance was deemed by the Clinton administration as politically inexpedient and, therefore, was not included in the reauthorization of ESEA/IASA. The DOE would have to rely on states to implement ESEA policies through exhortation and political pressure.[14]

The ESEA/IASA, signed into law in October 1994, also became the essential legislation needed for federal approval and support of public school choice plans and the creation of charter schools. According to this legislative initiative, charter schools held the promise of providing new models for public schools and could serve as "a mechanism for testing a variety of educational approaches." The act clearly stated that charter schools could be "exempted from restrictive rules and regulations if the leadership of such schools commits to attaining specific and ambitious educational results for educationally disadvantaged students consistent with challenging state content standards and challenging State student performance standards for all students." The ESEA/IASA was significant because it enabled state legislatures to rationalize that charter schools "can embody the necessary mixture of enhanced choice, exemption from restrictive regulations, and a focus on learning gains," and, therefore, the federal government should provide "financial assistance for the design and initial implementation of charter schools."[15]

In order to ensure that ESEA/IASA reauthorization would result in systemic education reform, the cornerstone of his education policy agenda, Clinton had to use a two-pronged legislative approach. The first legislative step in achieving systemic reform was accomplished in March 1994 through the passage of *Goals 2000: The Educate America Act.* This act provided grants to states to develop standards and assessments for the purpose of implementing standards-based reforms within individual school districts. However, these grants did not target disadvantaged students. Instead, the grants were designed to broadly address system-wide reforms. Clinton was strategic by first ensuring *Goals 2000* was passed in March 1994, which made funds available for the implementation of standards and assessments. In this way, with the passage of *Goals 2000*, the reauthorization of ESEA/IASA seven months later would have more impact.

According to the *Goals 2000: The Educate America Act*, the Clinton administration declared that by the year 2000 the following would take place:

1. Children will start school ready to learn.
2. At least 90 percent of all students will complete high school.
3. All students will leave grades 4, 8, and 12 having demonstrated competency over challenging subject matter including English, mathematics, science, foreign languages, civics and government, economics, arts, history, and geography. All schools will ensure that students are prepared for responsible citizenship and productive employment.
4. The nation's teaching force will have access to professional development to enable them to improve their professional skills so that they are able to prepare American students for the next century.
5. U.S. students will be the first in the world in mathematics and science.
6. Every adult American will be literate, with the knowledge and skills to compete in a global economy and exercise their rights and responsibilities of citizenship.
7. Every school in the United States will be free of drugs, violence, and the unauthorized presence of firearms and alcohol.
8. Every school will promote partnerships to increase parental involvement.[16]

Although these were idealistically and politically grand goals, they were, in fact, impossible to reach in six years. They did, however, reflect the nature of Clinton's third way of governing and policy making. Within *Goals 2000* there was a little something for everyone. For example, among liberals the provision for increased attention and funding for early childhood programs found favor. For conservatives, parental involvement acknowledged the rights of parents in making decisions about their child's education. For the business community, there was an acknowledgment of the role of schools in developing a strong workforce. And there was enough language about citizenship to provide an aura of democracy that undergirded America's public school system. Of course, it's hard to imagine that anyone who supported *Goals 2000* actually believed that every adult would be literate by the year 2000 or that fewer than 10 percent of the nation's high school students would drop out of school.

As it turned out, the goals were in reality mere window dressing for the ESEA/IASA, providing the impetus for the primary intent of the act—the implementation of widespread systemic education reform. According to Michael M. Heise, writing for the Fordham Law Review in 1994, *Goals 2000* reflected a "dramatic expansion of the federal government's role in education."[17] The act included a provision for "Voluntary National Content Standards." According to Heise, this signaled Congress' attempt "to structure a uniform national curriculum, developed and approved by bipartisan groups consisting of members of Congress and state legislatures, professional educators, academics, representatives of business, industry, labor, universities, low-income and minority groups, and other civic leaders."[18] The key to creating national standards was the creation of a National Education Standards and Improvement Council (NESIC) that would approve the various education standards created voluntarily within states. Assessments, therefore, would need to be developed in order for fourth, eighth, and twelfth grade students to demonstrate their competence in all the subject areas, and an accountability system would need to be in place in order to demonstrate each state's efforts in meeting *Goals 2000* through a comparison with other states.

With the implementation of *Goals 2000* in March 1994, and IASA in October 1994, the United States entered a new era of education accountability. Prior to the IASA, states were permitted to assess underprivileged students based on a set of less-rigorous standards. As a result of IASA, states were required to assess all students based on the same set of standards. While this seems, on the surface, to be a reasonable policy, it does foreshadow another key concept that would become a part of the No Child Left Behind policies of the future. No longer would poverty, status as an English language learner, disability, or any other factor be considered in student achievement or accountability rankings. America's public school policy makers, as a result of IASA, would now begin adopting a "no excuses" mentality.[19] Unfortunately, throughout the years that would follow the 1994 ESEA reauthorization as IASA, more and more children would be ensnared and victimized by testing policies that required them to take high-stakes tests in spite of any disabling condition or other factor than might impede their success—such as being speakers of a new language (having just immigrated to the United States) or living with the detrimental impacts of intergenerational persistent poverty.

The one-two punch provided by the passage of both *Goals 2000* and the IASA left many conservatives concerned with the expansion of the federal government's role in education. Both parties, however, thought national standards were problematic. Although both Republicans and Democrats thought voluntary state standards were acceptable, they generally believed that federal standards were an intrusion on state's rights. For example, in January 1995, the U.S. Senate voted almost unanimously (99–1) to censure the U.S. History Standards that had been developed under the George H. W. Bush administration.[20] Republicans, in order to weaken attempts to strengthen federal control over public schools, successfully passed several amendments to *Goals 2000* in 1996. One of these amendments eliminated the *Goals 2000* provision for a national council to evaluate state standards. As a result, the NESIC was never appointed. Another amendment permitted states to use *Goals 2000* federal funds to purchase technology for schools rather than to fund the development of standards and assessments. This amendment also enabled schools to receive *Goals 2000* funds without having to submit detailed plans for how they intended to use the money. The Republicans had already successfully released states from any obligation to develop strategies or standards to ensure "opportunity to learn."[21] As a result, states were no longer required to provide additional infrastructure or resources that would equalize education programs in order for all students to achieve. Conservatives were confident, therefore, that they had successfully made sure that the role of the federal government would be limited.

In an additional nod to the primacy of business leaders in establishing the agenda for systemic education reform, shortly after the passage of *Goals 2000*, President Clinton signed into law the School-to-Work Opportunities Act in May 1994. The president, in announcing this legislation, noted its close alignment with *Goals 2000* and its importance. The purpose of the School-to-Work Opportunities Act was to provide federal "venture capital to stimulate State and local creativity in establishing statewide School-to-Work Opportunities systems."[22]

The National Education Summit: Willie Sutton Goes Where the Power Is

Lou Gerstner was an honored guest at the 1995 National Governors Association meeting where he ironically explained his presence by stating, "I'm here because of Willie Sutton. Willie robbed banks, the story goes, because he realized that's where the money is. I'm here because this is where the power is—the power to reform—no, to revolutionize—the U.S. public school system."[23] His speech was direct and to-the-point, beginning with the infamous quote from *A Nation at Risk*: "If an unfriendly foreign power had imposed our schools upon us, we would have regarded it as an act of war."[24] Gerstner excoriated the governors and the American public for the lack of progress made in education reform in the years since the publication of *ANAR*, reminding the governors of their meeting in 1989 when they formulated education goals that eventually would become the *Goals 2000: Educate America Act* in 1994. Gerstner railed,

> Six years have passed since those wonderful goals were set. More important, 1616 days remain until the year 2000 arrives. I wonder how many people in our country are committed to achieving those goals. I wonder how many people think we have a chance of achieving them. I often think how many people even know they exist. . . .
>
> The bottom line is that if our kids are failing in the classroom, it's not just their fault. It's our fault. And that, my friends, underscores a very frightening reality. Setting goals for U.S. education is one thing. Reaching them is another. The only way it will happen, the only way that we have even a ghost of a chance of getting there, is if we push through a fundamental, bone-jarring, full-fledged, 100 percent revolution that discards the old and replaces it with a totally new performance-driven system.[25]

Gerstner challenged the governors, who he referred to as the "CEOs of the organizations that fund and oversee the country's public schools," to "add an 'R' to our traditional reading, 'riting, and 'rithmetic—An 'R' for revolution."[26] He then invited them to join him at the IBM headquarters in Palisades, New York, for a meeting to plan the revolution. Gerstner told the governors, "We'll pull it all together but we'll need your help. And you'll have to be there. You'll have to invest a day—not a few hours. Because, as I said before, real change requires the participation of the CEO."[27]

The Palisades' National Education Summit

For Gerstner and governors such as Wisconsin's Tommy Thompson, who was on the Palisades summit's planning committee, this would become their version of education reform from the "ground up." Thompson explained that if state governors were involved, then education "standards will be set by communities and states, not by the federal government." Thompson then made a statement that now seems prophetic when he declared, "This will spark a **race to the top** [emphasis added] as each community—and eventually each state tries to outperform others."[28]

The nation's "CEO" governors took Gerstner up on his invitation to attend the National Education Summit held March 26–27, 1996, in Palisades, but they did not come alone. At Gerstner's urging, each CEO governor brought a CEO of a major corporation. It was an impressive array of the big minds and big ideas that would shape the education revolution. The corporate superstars who worked alongside Gerstner to organize the summit included the CEOs of AT&T, BellSouth, Eastman Kodak, Proctor and Gamble, and the Boeing Company. The Republican CEO governors serving on the summit planning committee included Tommy Thompson of Wisconsin, Terry E. Branstad of Iowa, and John Engler of Michigan. Democrat CEO governors included Bob Miller of Nevada, Roy Romer of Colorado, and James B. Hunt Jr. of North Carolina.[29] The assemblage of the moneyed and powerful was so impressive, according to Denis P. Doyle, who attended the meeting as a representative of the Heritage Foundation and also coauthored Gerstner's book *Reinventing Education*, that "there were more security people in attendance than participants."[30]

The CEO's education summit was a rather private affair. While President Clinton was invited to speak on the second day, DOE Secretary Richard Riley was only an invited guest, with no place on the program. Other than the CEOs, the invitation list only included 35 "resource people," who Doyle described as "the usual suspects . . . a motley crew of special-interest pleaders, state education leaders, foundation executives, think tank intellectuals, and policy analysts." Among the "motley" crew were Al Shanker of the AFT and Keith Geiger of the NEA, and, they, like the members of the other "special interest crowd," were "among the silent throng at the back of the hall."[31] Joyce A. Elliott of Arkansas was the only teacher in this group of resource people. Clearly, the education summit was not intended for professional educators or for any representatives of local school boards. Nevertheless, the National Education Summit resulted with a policy statement in which the CEOs, gubernatorial and corporate, committed to do the following:

1. Within one year, businesses participating in the Summit will require job applicants to demonstrate academic achievement through transcripts, diplomas and portfolios.
2. Within one year, an external, independent, non-governmental group will be in place to provide public leadership, a national clearinghouse, national and international benchmarking, technical

assistance, and support for public reporting on the annual progress made by each state and by businesses.

3. Within two years, the Governors will establish internationally competitive academic standards and assessments to measure academic achievement and accountability systems within their individual states.
4. Businesses participating in the Summit will place high priority on the quality of a state's academic standards and student achievement when determining business location decisions.[32]

The bipartisan spirit of the summit was impressive. On the second day, President Clinton delivered a speech that Doyle described as "calculated to please."[33] Doyle explained, "Not surprisingly . . . it was a speech 95 percent of which any Republican could have delivered with complete conviction." Chester Finn, who attended the summit as a representative of the conservative Hudson Institute, noted that "it was a speech which Ronald Reagan could have given."[34]

Indeed, much of Clinton's speech aligned very well with what education critics believed about public schools, beginning with a reference the president made to *ANAR* as the beginning point for education reform. Clinton lauded the corporate superstars for organizing the summit, stating that the "business leaders know well, perhaps better than any other single group in America, what the consequences of our failing to get the most out of our students and achieve real educational excellence will be for the Nation." In his speech, the president even gave a shout out to Bill Gates, a rising corporate superstar who would later join the ranks of CEOs with the big minds and big ideas about education reform, by referring to Gates' book, *The Road from Here*.[35]

Clinton stated, in his usual politically dexterous manner, that "many of our schools are doing a very good job, but some of them don't." And as far as teachers were concerned, Clinton stated, "We know that many of our teachers are great, but some don't measure up." The president, however, also pointed out some "interesting challenges" that he thought were "somewhat unique to our country in this global environment." According to the president, an interesting challenge that was somewhat unique to America was the fact that "we have a more diverse group of students in terms of income and race and ethnicity and background and, indeed, living conditions than almost any other great country in the world." In addition, Clinton averred, "We know that our schools are burdened by social problems not of their making, which make the jobs of principals and teachers more difficult." Nevertheless, Clinton felt that these numerous social problems and challenges could be overcome by schools.[36]

Clinton went on to claim, for example, that "our country has an attitude problem about education" because "too many people in the United States think that the primary determinant of success in learning is either IQ or family circumstances instead of effort." The key to educational success is "the right kind of educational opportunities, the right kind of expectations." Therefore, what America needed was "a revolution of rising expectations." Clinton argued that IQ is inconsequential in the learning process, stating that if you stack up "all the Americans together in order by IQ, you couldn't stick a straw between one person and the next." According to the president, effort outweighs intelligence, as he asserted, "A lot of people, even in education, need to be reminded of that from time to time." Unless these simple facts are acknowledged, efforts "to have accountability through tests and other assessments will not be as successful as they ought to be." Clinton also told the audience that the reauthorization of ESEA by his administration acknowledged the need to hold all children to the same high standards. Significantly, while at first acknowledging the immense social problems public schools needed to deal with, the president also reminded the audience that poverty was no longer a consideration in educational achievement. If you believe "these kids can learn," then you "have to give them a chance to demonstrate it." According to the president, high standards and greater accountability would give poor children that chance—and excuses for education failure like poverty or living in dangerous neighborhoods would no longer be considered valid.[37]

Both liberals and conservatives claimed victories as a result of the Palisades Summit. Clinton acknowledged the educational challenges associated with teaching children living in poverty and realities of an educational system that serves America's vastly diverse population. Liberals wholeheartedly embraced this acknowledgment. However, Clinton also gave a nod to public school critics by asserting that the larger social and economic challenges associated with poverty and diversity could be overcome merely through a set of rigorous standards, assessments, and accountability measures within public schools. High expectations and effort was the key to academic achievement. Altering a child's life of destitution and social trauma were not seen as a precursor to educational achievement, nor was it even seen as an essential educational partner when actually measuring the success or failure of a public school since ultimate accountability did not go beyond the walls of the school. Public schools, in fact, had once again become the scapegoat for the larger social and economic ills that plagued America, something David Hursh would again point out in 2014 when America's path to the CCSS was completed.[38]

The educational problem was simple. It rested with unaccountable poorly trained teachers with low standards who had equally low expectations for poor children. According to this line of thinking, it seems that middle- and upper-class children experienced educational success because of properly trained teachers with high expectations. And because minority children were far more likely to be poor than their white counterparts, by extension, it seems that when most teachers took a job teaching poor minority children those teachers were automatically poorly trained as well as having low expectations for the children they taught. It is no wonder, then, that George W. Bush's mantra of "ending the soft bigotry of low expectations" was widely embraced since it helped rationalize No Child Left Behind policies.

Conservatives were also glad to hear Clinton call for "more options for parents . . . in terms of the public school choice legislation and . . . charter schools." Interestingly, conservatives viewed the "real function" of the summit as a way to "solemnize the fact that the federal role in education is virtually at an end."[39] As Doyle explained, there was unanimous agreement on the part of the corporate and gubernatorial CEOs that because of "the idea that standards are a state and local issue," . . . "the federal role will soon be *de minimis*," and CEOS and governors "are reconciled to that new reality."[40] However, neither the liberals nor the conservatives left with a clear picture of the reality that would play out on the educational horizon in the years following the summit in Palisades. The liberal education community would learn that the true intention of the Clinton administration was the imposition of a rigid accountability system driven by high-stakes testing, while the conservative education community would learn that the underlying motive of the summit's organizer-in-chief was far different from diminishing the federal role in education. In fact, in 2008, Gerstner, writing for the *Wall Street Journal* would reveal his actual educational agenda, calling for:

1. The abolishment of all local school districts except for 70—one for each of the 50 states and one for each of the major cities;
2. The establishment of a set of national standards for a core curriculum;
3. The establishment of national standards for teacher certification and the requirement for regular re-evaluations of teacher skills; and
4. The extension of the school day and the school year for all K-12 students.[41]

Of course, what would be the point of hosting a National Education Summit if technology wasn't featured? After all, this was the period when the big "dot-com bubble" was just starting to inflate. According to Doyle, on the second morning "small groups of governors, CEOs, and resource people were moved at a forced march through more than a dozen technology exhibits" with ten-minute "carefully scripted" presentations. These exhibits were successful, as Doyle goes on to explain, "not least because of the striking example of enlightened despotism" that acquainted the summit attendees with the majority of the technology displays running on Apple software.[42] However, when Doyle observed that "there was concern in some conservative circles that the summit was no more than a new generation of 'robber barons' working their will on a malleable and hapless populace," perhaps this display of "enlightened despotism" only helped further confirm what some conservatives believed about the summit in general.[43]

One of the most significant things to emerge from the National Education Summit at Palisades in 1996 was the creation of Achieve, an organization "dedicated to supporting standards-based education efforts across the states." The organization describes itself as "the only education reform organization led by a Board of Directors of governors and business leaders." Serving at the behest of corporate and gubernatorial CEOs, Achieve would later, as we will see, assume a major role in the creation of the Common Core State Standards.[44]

ESEA: A Reauthorization Redux

With Goals 2000 in place and IASA reauthorized in 1994 to reflect the systemic reforms Clinton sought, when ESEA was set for reauthorization again in 1999, the Clinton administration was poised to propose further policies to strengthen systemic education reform initiatives. The political climate in Washington DC was quite different in 1999 than it was in 1994, however. Clinton had recently emerged from impeachment hearings, and, while his own party had supported him throughout the process, many Democrats were upset because he supported a Republican bill that cut spending for entitlement programs.[45] As a result, the Clinton administration knew that the reauthorization of ESEA with further changes would be difficult, particularly when those changes called for budget increases in order to promote systemic reform.

A key component of the 1999 ESEA reauthorization proposal included a provision that the federal government would have the right to revoke a state's ESEA funding if it failed to meet federal requirements. In particular, states would be required to improve public schools that were failing. Schools that did not improve in spite of measures such as making staff changes, would be shut down and replaced by charter schools. Other policy changes proposed by the Clinton administration included the publication of school report cards that would contain information regarding student achievement on standardized tests, teacher qualifications, class size, school safety, and attendance and graduation rates. Clinton also called for the end of social promotion. In his 1999 State of the Union Address, Clinton declared, "First, all schools must end social promotion;" hyperbolically stating, "Now, no child should graduate from high school with a diploma he or she can't read. We do our children no favors when we allow them to pass from grade to grade without mastering the material. But we can't just hold students back because the system fails them."[46]

The congressional political wrangling over the reauthorization of ESEA throughout 1999 and 2000 during two sessions of Congress was intense and divisive.[47] As both Rhodes and Vinovskis point out, during this time a number of proposals were put forth in order to get agreement regarding ESEA reauthorization. However, in particular the Public Education Reinvestment, Reinvention, and Responsibility Act, often referred to as the "Three R's," bears mentioning. Proposed by Senators Joseph Lieberman (D-CT) and Evan Bayh (D-IN), the "Three R's" sought a middle ground that was intended to make ESEA reauthorization appealing to both sides of the aisle. The "Three R's" allowed states to have flexibility when deciding how to meet federal education regulations in exchange for increased school accountability for academic achievement, which would result in a close monitoring of a school's adequate yearly progress (AYP). While this act was also defeated in Congress, it foreshadowed a major outcome of NCLB legislation.[48] In spite of congressional efforts such as the "Three R's," to get some consensus in order to reauthorize ESEA, on May 9, 2000, the Senate abandoned efforts and, for the first time since President Johnson first enacted the bill in 1965, Congress failed to reauthorize ESEA.[49] Instead of reauthorizing ESEA, Congress bought another year to consider ESEA reauthorization and funded DOE initiatives through HR 4577, an act making appropriations for the DOE and other agencies for the fiscal year ending September 30, 2001.[50]

Reauthorization of ESEA, therefore, would be the responsibility of the next president. So when the can was kicked down the road, and George W. Bush became the president of the United States in a highly contentious campaign in 2001, his administration would continue Clinton's efforts for systemic education reform. Bush's reauthorization of ESEA as No Child Left Behind would contain many of the same provisions proposed by the Clinton administration. While these provisions were subject to bipartisan debates and ultimately rejected during Clinton's last two years in the White House, the wind shifted in 2001 when, within a short period of time, there appeared broad bipartisan support for these same provisions.

THE CLINTON LEGACY

During the decades since the 1980s, there has been a proliferation of advocacy groups devoted to education reform. The lists and acronyms are dizzying in breadth and too many to mention. Each has its own policy agenda and backers; some are aligned with liberals, others are aligned with conservatives. To complicate the education arena further are the third way corporate sponsors of many of these groups, promoting free market approaches to systemic education reform. One of the troubling legacies of the Clinton era of education reform has been the fissures caused among civil rights advocates around the issue of education reform created by the Clinton administration's third way. Julian Vasquez Heilig asserts that corporate reformers have co-opted minority groups into their campaign to reform education through free market approaches. Choice has become the primary reform initiative for a number of civil rights groups as a way to ensure educational equity for poor minority students in urban schools. And charter schools are seen as the saving grace for children otherwise trapped in poor performing inner-city schools. To question charter schools and choice, therefore, becomes perilous.[51]

The ensuing divide among civil rights groups has also become increasingly contentious. On one side are the groups that Rhodes describes as the "civil rights entrepreneurs" who have found common ground with "business entrepreneurs" seeking free market approaches to education reform. These groups are strong advocates for school vouchers, school choice policies, and charter schools.[52] On the other side is the NAACP and groups that support their policies and initiatives. As the group that almost single-handedly toppled the giant of legally sponsored federal educational apartheid laws with the *Brown v. Board* decision of 1954, the NAACP perseveres in advocating for educational equality and equity for all students. They stand steadfastly against market-driven reforms, contending that the end result for these initiatives will be an increase in segregation and educational disparities among students. In 2010 the NAACP ratified its Resolution on Charter Schools, affirming their advocacy for public school education and rejecting an emphasis on charter schools as the "vanguard approach for the education of children."[53] In spite of the NAACP's denouncement of charter schools, market-reform advocates promoted their initiatives as civil rights issues. For example, as Valerie Strauss points out, in 2010 Arne Duncan announced at a screening of the documentary "Waiting for Superman," a film advocating for charter schools, that the "film signaled a 'Rosa Parks moment' that would initiate a new movement for school choice."[54]

Denisha Jones warns that the co-option of the language of the civil rights movement in the pursuit to privatize education through vouchers and charter schools will harm all children, "but especially children of color and low-income children." Jones goes on to explain, "Corporate education reform is not an ally in our fight for educational justice. We must not be fooled by those who seek to use the legacy of our struggle to turn a profit at the expense of our children's education. A strong democratic republic needs high quality public schools that offer a free and appropriate public education for all."[55]

The enduring legacy of the Clinton administration on systemic education school reform is profound. The third way of governance produced a bipartisan spirit between Republicans and Democrats in adopting systemic education reform, and the business community would be on hand to facilitate the process, creating schools that would reflect their interests. Mike Lofgren, who spent 28 years working in Congress and, therefore, has deep insights into the inner workings of government and policy makers, describes what happens when corporate Wall Street CEOs become key players in government policy making. While Lofgren focuses much of his discussions about the impact of this phenomenon on other governmental agencies such as the Department of Defense, the Department of Homeland Security, and the Central Intelligence Agency, his discussion of what he refers to as the "Deep State" is applicable to what has happened in the education arena since President Clinton relinquished responsibility for education reform to the Business Roundtable and other corporate reformers.[56]

According to Lofgren, corporate reformers "are careful to pretend that they have no ideology. Their preferred pose is that of the politically neutral technocrat offering well considered advice based on profound expertise." Lofgren asserts, "That is nonsense. They are deeply dyed in the hue of the official ideology of the governing class, an ideology that is neither specifically Democratic nor

Republican." . . . "Whether their personal views are aligned with a more conservative Republican agenda or a more liberal Democratic agenda is inconsequential." According to Lofgren, "They almost invariably believe in the 'Washington Consensus': financialization, outsourcing, privatization, deregulation and the commodifying of labor."[57] The Deep State occurs when the corporate world is able to impose their agenda on governmental policy makers in ways that bypass democratic processes and legislative and judicial efforts.[58]

Money talks, its commanding voice echoing in the education arena, increasingly reverberating along the path to the Common Core State Standards. For corporate reformers, the impetus for reforming America's public schools has always been an economic issue. Corporate superstars, such as David Kearns, Lou Gerstner, and members of the BRT, continually berated the public school system for not adequately preparing a workforce that would make American industries competitive. And when the Sandia Report demonstrated the fallacy of their assertions about education in America, the report was buried by the DOE that employed David Kearns. Interestingly, when Kearns described his stellar turnaround of Xerox in his book, *Prophets in the Dark: How Xerox Reinvented Itself and Beat Back the Japanese*, he never cited the Japanese education system as being the source for the success of Japanese industries. Instead, he discussed the business environment itself in Japan and TQM principles.[59]

It is important to understand that corporate reformers are always able to deftly side step around partisan issues and therefore emerge victorious regardless of which party is in the White House, which party dominates Congress, or which party holds the position of state governor. These reformers understand the third way, and far from adopting a bipartisan spirit as a noble effort, they understand that their power to dominate policy issues rests with their endurance over the years in spite of political affiliations in Washington. They also understand that when it comes to systemic reform of America's public schools, there is a lot of money to be had.

In October 1996, Chester Finn, former administrator within the DOE under Ronald Reagan, pointed out how much money could be made by investors in the education industry. Speaking before the Georgia Public Policy Foundation, Finn explained that smart investors could possibly "make a dime" in a booming $300 million education industry.[60] An article in the *New York Times* reported that by 1996, for-profit companies had captured $30 billion of the total $340 billion spent in the United States on education for everything from for-profit school management to textbooks, software and new technology, commercial programs, and private consulting services.[61] The investment firm Lehman Brothers sponsored the first Education Industry Investment Conference in New York in February 1996.

According to Douglas Dewey, "conferees were regaled with new opportunities in a $600 billion industry, including preschool, K-12, postsecondary, and training and development." For Dewey, writing for the conservative libertarian publication *The Freeman*, corporate entrepreneurship in the education field held the promise of finally eliminating government from education completely, "as public confidence in government schooling continues its inexorable collapse, and the whiff of billions begins stirring in the air, the savvy investor will focus his attention on the greatest emerging market in decades and treat government schools as just another competitor to blow out of the water."[62]

As the steady drumbeat for privatization continues decade after decade, it wouldn't matter if a Democrat or a Republican sat in the White House. It wouldn't matter if the favored policy of the day is school vouchers, school choice, or charter schools. The end result would be the same. There is a price on the head of every child in America. Whether this price comes in the form of tax-supported tuition for private school vouchers, public charter schools, or privately operated charter schools; or it comes from schools as consumers of expensive technology; or it comes from expensive education assessments paid for by government dollars, it matters not. And in the bargain, corporate reformers are lauded for their messianic devotion to America's school children—as if they, and they alone, are committed to improving the nation's schools. By the dawn of the twenty-first century, America was well on its way along the path to the Common Core State Standards. But before these standards could be created, a newly reauthorized and modified ESEA needed to be reckoned with. The whisper of No Child Left Behind could now be heard in the halls of Congress.

Chapter 6

NCLB and the Texas Tall Tale

Armed with the "Texas Miracle" and Rod Paige at his side, George W. Bush began his presidency ready to tackle the reauthorization of ESEA and demonstrate to the country that the education reform policies that had worked so miraculously in his home state could work equally well for the rest of America. For George W. Bush, education was "the great civil rights issue of our time."[1] Bush was able to garner enough bipartisan support for his education reform ideas to implement the most far-reaching federal education policies since the creation of the DOE 20 years earlier. According to Jonathan Parker, Bush's positioning of education reform as a civil rights issue began during his presidential campaign as a way to "create a wedge to attract support from Democrats" and garner support from civil rights groups who welcomed his attacks on those who were guilty of the "bigotry of low expectations."[2]

Even the name of the proposed legislation Bush introduced to Congress just days after his inauguration rang true to civil rights advocates. In fact, the term "Leave No Child Behind" is the trademark of the advocacy group the Children's Defense Fund, an organization founded by civil rights champion Marian Wright Edelman in 1973.[3] Marian Wright Edelman's credentials as a civil rights champion are unassailable. As an unmarried first-year law student in 1961, Marian Wright joined Medgar Evers and other civil rights workers in Mississippi, assisting black citizens attempting to register to vote. She returned to Mississippi in 1963, providing citizens with legal counsel when they were attacked and arrested by segregationist authorities. Wright's friend and colleague Medgar Evers was assassinated by white supremacist Byron De La Beckwith in front of his home that summer.[4] Wright went on to serve as staff attorney for the NAACP Legal Defense Fund in 1964, providing legal assistance for Mississippi Freedom Summer workers. When Senator Robert F. Kennedy visited Mississippi in spring 1967 to investigate implementation of policies associated with President Johnson's War on Poverty initiatives, it was Marian Wright who escorted Kennedy and his colleagues to homes in the poverty-ridden communities within the Mississippi Delta. Kennedy was shocked and deeply moved by what he saw, and it was this experience that led him to focus his efforts on the elimination of poverty.[5] Peter Edelman, legislative assistant to Senator Kennedy, accompanied him on his trip to Mississippi, where he met his future wife, Marian Wright Edelman.[6]

In 1968, Marian Wright Edelman moved to Washington DC to serve as counsel for Dr. Martin Luther King Jr.'s Poor People's March on Washington.[7] In April 1968, King was assassinated in Memphis, Tennessee, while preparing to march with sanitation workers in support of their labor concerns. The assassination of Robert Kennedy soon followed in June 1968. In the span of just a few years, Edelman witnessed the tragic murders of Medgar Evers, Martin Luther King Jr., and Robert Kennedy. By the time Edelman founded the Children's Defense Fund in 1973, she had earned the right to serve as an advocate for the rights of children and lead a campaign to improve the lives of children living with the devastating impacts of poverty.

Peter and Marian Wright Edelman would remain committed to social justice throughout their lives and careers, even when it caused schisms among some of their friends. For example, the couple have had a long and close relationship with Bill and Hillary Clinton. Hillary Clinton had served as chair of the Children's Defense Fund from 1986–92, and Peter Edelman was appointed to work for the Clinton administration.[8] However, when President Clinton enacted his widesweeping welfare reform initiative in 1996, Peter Edelman publicly resigned in protest.[9] He went on to write a scathing article entitled "The Worst Thing Bill Clinton Has Done."[10] In this article, Edelman quotes Senator Edward Kennedy who described the welfare reform bill as "legislative child abuse." Edelman warned that welfare reforms, as a result of the legislation signed into law by President Clinton, would lead to a dramatic increase in the numbers of children living in poverty. The most hard hit would be minorities and the youngest children. Although the Edelmans and Clintons were able to repair their friendship, the Edelmans have remained stalwart advocates for the poor in the United States and have refused to be silenced.[11] The Edelman's assertions about the negative consequences of Clinton's welfare reform policies would be validated over the years since 1996 by other organizations. By 2010, according to the Children's Defense Fund, 45.5 percent of all black children and 37.6 percent of all Hispanic children under the age of five were living in poverty.[12] According to the National Policy Center (NPC), the impact of Clinton's welfare reform policies has been profound for families. One measure used by the NPC to analyze the increase in poverty since 1996 is the number of families receiving assistance from the Supplemental Nutrition Assistance Program (SNAP). In 1996, 25.5 million individuals received assistance through SNAP. By 2011, that number had increased to 45.2 million.[13]

Therefore, when George W. Bush co-opted the Children's Defense Fund's trademarked mission statement, Leave No Child Behind, for his education reform policy, it was recognized by some civil rights advocates to be a disingenuous attempt to patronize minority groups.[14] Using this trademarked statement, however, would prove to be very effective during Bush's first term in office as he was garnering support for No Child Left Behind as the reauthorized ESEA. According to Rhodes, Bush "courted" Senator Edward Kennedy, the "liberal lion" of the Senate to cosponsor the NCLB bill. Rhodes explains, "Kennedy was the 'bridge' between civil rights entrepreneurs and educational liberals in the Senate who viewed Kennedy as their leader."[15] The passage of NCLB was an example of masterful deal making and politicking. Bush was assisted by Kennedy, who was, according to Rhodes, "widely recognized as a skillful legislative tactician and 'dealmaker.'" Although Democrats remained concerned about mandatory testing and federal accountability measures, they were assuaged by groups like the Leadership Conference on Civil Rights (LCCR) that represented broader civil rights coalitions, as well as civil rights entrepreneurs like the Education Trust (ET) and the National Council of La Raza (NCLR). These groups served as a "moral authority" and seemed to speak on behalf of the disadvantaged. David Shreve of the National Conference of State Legislatures, according to Rhodes, explained that civil rights groups like the ET and NCLR might have also "persuaded some Democrats" into believing that "standards-based reforms—especially tests that disaggregated performance reports by race, ethnicity, and poverty level—would reveal enduring inequities in state and local education finance regimes, providing parents and students with leverage to sue in court for additional resources."[16]

Throughout negotiations for NCLB, Republicans became increasingly uncomfortable with the amount of support Democrats were giving the bill. Conservative Republican Jim DeMint of South

Carolina dubbed the bill "leave no Democrat behind" because much of NCLB reflected the proposed ESEA provisions advocated by the Clinton administration a year earlier. Nonetheless, Republicans found themselves boxed into a corner. While Republicans were concerned about the increased role of the federal government in education and unhappy that any attempts to include a federal voucher program were eliminated from the NCLB bill, their support for standards, testing, and accountability reform was bolstered by the business community. According to Rhodes, "a vigorous lobbying campaign" was launched by corporate interests such as the Business Coalition for Excellence in Education and the Business Roundtable to execute "a comprehensive legislative blitz on behalf of NCLB" in 2001. Corporate leaders met regularly with White House officials and testified before congressional committees. Op-eds written by Business Coalition members appeared in national publications such as *The New York Times, The Washington Post*, and *USA Today* supporting NCLB, and legislators were bombarded with visits and letters by corporate lobbyists urging support for the legislation.[17] But perhaps most important, following Bush's fragile presidential victory, Republicans were hesitant to thwart the Republican president's monumental legislative education reform efforts. In short, Bush needed an early legislative victory in his first term in office.

In early September 2001, Bush was poised to finally bring together Democrats and Republicans to settle any lingering disagreements and pass NCLB into law. The congressional committee charged with reconciling the House and Senate versions of the bill was scheduled to meet on September 13. Bush, hoping to facilitate their efforts, scheduled several public appearances across the country to promote NCLB.[18] On September 11, the president found himself reading a book to a group of second graders at Emma T. Booker Elementary School in Sarasota, Florida. He was interrupted, however, and informed that a group of terrorists had launched an attack on New York City and Washington DC. Although the United States became embroiled in the aftermath of the 9/11 attacks, Congress continued to function, albeit with great difficulty, and when Capitol Hill was faced with its own anthrax crisis, there was speculation that the passage of NCLB would not occur in 2001.[19] By November, however, Republicans and Democrats were determined to continue the negotiations on the reauthorization of ESEA and pass the NCLB Act before adjourning the 2001 congressional session. A final version of the act was completed by mid-December and passed by both the House and Senate with nearly 90 percent bipartisan support. President Bush ceremonially signed the NCLB Act in Hamilton, Ohio, the home district of Republican Representative John Boehner.[20]

The 2001 No Child Left Behind Act drastically, and perhaps permanently, altered education in the United States. Standardized testing became "high-stakes" testing. States were required to attain academic proficiency for all students within 12 years. Testing data would be used to evaluate schools based on the adequate yearly progress (AYP) of all subgroups of students in achieving the goal of academic progress within 12 years. In other words, even if a school raised the test scores for many or most students, if the school was unable to raise test scores for any subgroup of students (for example, English language learners, students with learning disabilities, or students living in poverty), the school could face sanctions. The sanctions associated with failure to demonstrate AYP would increase in severity for every year a school did not adequately improve test scores for all subgroups of students.

Schools that failed to demonstrate AYP for two consecutive years would be provided technical assistance from the school district and be required to provide students with "public school choice" to attend a different school with better test scores within the district. Schools that failed to demonstrate AYP for three years would be required to offer supplemental education services, including private tutoring services at businesses like Sylvan Learning Centers. These services would be paid for through a voucher-like program to enable parents to choose the supplemental education services for their children. Schools that failed to demonstrate AYP for four consecutive years were sanctioned through the imposition of corrective actions in the form of replacement of school staff (administrators and/or teachers), replacement of curriculum, a decrease of the authority of school administration, the appointment of outside experts to advise the school, an extension of the school day or year, and/or a restructuring of the internal organization of the school.[21]

Ultimately, if a school failed to improve in spite of corrective actions, the school would face the ultimate sanction of being closed or converted to a charter school. However, as the 12-year deadline approached for having all students attaining academic proficiency, it was clear that NCLB was a failure. In 2011, for example, Arne Duncan, secretary of education for the Obama administration, would report to Congress that "82 percent of America's schools could fail to meet education goals set by *No Child Left Behind* this year." He would go on to explain that "four out of five schools in America may not meet their goals under NCLB by next year. The consequences under the current law are very clear: states and districts all across

America may have to intervene in more and more schools each year, implementing the exact same interventions regardless of the schools' individual needs." According to Duncan, the nation's schools were poised to enter the "crisis" phase and thousands of schools would be forced to "fire and replace legions of teachers," and close schools or replace them with charter schools.[22]

Critics, however, were not surprised at the failure of NCLB to effectively reform education. The "no excuses" mentality that undergirded the law's mandates were illogical, ignoring the complexities of education in general and assuming that test scores were the ultimate arbiter of a student's success. Early on, critics noted that the framework for NCLB was based on the supposed success of these policies in Texas—policies that resulted in the Texas Miracle. Unfortunately, however, for America's public schools and the children they serve, the Texas Miracle turned out to be just another Texas tall tale.

The Miracle That Never Was

As a presidential candidate, George W. Bush consistently touted the success of Rod Paige, then superintendent of the Houston Independent School District, in substantially raising student achievement and drastically decreasing the number of high school dropouts. Paige's stellar turnaround of Houston's public schools was heralded as the Texas Miracle and Paige is credited with helping to formulate the blueprint for NCLB. It was soon discovered, however, that the Texas Miracle was a sham. The United States had been sold a bill of goods and the Texas tall tale began to quickly unravel soon after NCLB became the law of the land. In fact, students had been used as pawns in Texas to game the accountability system and ensure that schools had high test scores and low dropout rates.

An assistant principal at Sharpstown High School in Houston, Robert Kimball, blew the whistle on this practice in 2003 when he learned that his school had reported a zero dropout rate for 2001–2002. "I was shocked," said Kimball, "I had been at the high school for three years, and I had seen many, many students, several hundred a year, go out the door. And I knew that they were quitting. They told me they were quitting."[23] Most of the students enrolled in Sharpstown were poor immigrants, and school district officials simply coded the disappearance of the 463 of seventeen hundred students who left the school in the 2001–2002 school year as having either transferred to another school or returned to their native country. Districts also often reported that a student had left school to earn a GED, an equivalency diploma, and the school therefore didn't have to count the student as a dropout. According to Kimball, teachers knew that the school district "was cooking the books" and it wasn't just occurring in his school but across the district. The Houston school district officially proclaimed that only 1.5 percent of their high school students dropped out. In reality, however, the dropout rate for the district was much higher, possibly well over 25 percent.[24]

Texas also widely used a "push out" strategy to prop up their high school retention rates. Low-achieving students were consistently coerced into quitting school through heavy-handed policies selectively enforced. Attendance policies, for example, were more strictly enforced for low-achieving students. In addition, students who weren't expected to score well on standardized tests were subjected to policies that enabled schools to retain students in nontested grades repeatedly in spite of passing most of their classes. According to Julian Vasquez Heilig and Linda Darling-Hammond, "push out" strategies were commonplace in Texas and schools routinely waited until after October, when state appropriations based on student enrollment data were completed, to begin to weed out problematic students. Zero tolerance behavioral policies were enforced, leading to suspensions and expulsions. Students were counseled to leave school and enroll in GED programs. In general, the school environment was inhospitable for low-achieving students and the students most often pushed out were overwhelmingly poor students of color.[25]

Texas' education reform was, therefore, far from miraculous. Over the years it would become increasingly clear that the kind of systemic reform in which high-stakes testing is the central focus would in turn produce systems in which cheating is allowed to take place and even covertly or overtly encouraged, particularly when sanctions are attached to a school's failure to produce high test scores. For example, by 2013, cities like Atlanta and Washington DC, under the leadership of Superintendent Beverly Hall and Chancellor Michelle Rhee, would be rocked by cheating scandals.[26]

How did Secretary of Education Rod Paige react when this educational miracle was proven to be a fabrication? He steadfastly defended the Texas test data, while conceding that there may have been a problem with dropouts. He was clearly angry, however, with his critics, and when the NEA publicly criticized NCLB in 2004, Paige called the NEA a "terrorist organization."[27] Paige would later recant the statement but continued to assert that the NEA employed "obstructionist scare tactics" by challenging NCLB policies.[28] It was, therefore, certainly no surprise when Paige resigned his position as secretary of education at the end of Bush's first term or that he would write a book entitled *The War Against Hope: How Teachers' Unions Hurt Children, Hinder Teachers, and Endanger Public Education* a few years later.[29] What may surprise some, however, is that upon leaving his post in Washington, Paige founded a consulting company, the Chartwell Education Group—an organization working to "advance the systemic improvement of education domestically and globally."[30] Apparently Paige's ideas that lead to the Texas Miracle were now going global. It is also noteworthy that in 2005, Paige was appointed to the Board of Trustees of the education think tank, the Fordham Foundation, one of the groups that would lead the charge to the Common Core State Standards.[31]

Reading First: Leaving No Profit Behind

Another scandal would rock the NCLB world of George W. Bush and Rod Paige during Bush's first term. A cornerstone of the NCLB law was Reading First (RF). The basic tenet of RF, scientifically based reading research (SBRR) methodology, sparked a national debate about the theoretical underpinnings of this legislative mandate. With NCLB and RF, the federal government was now directly involved in curriculum. However, this was not a surprise to many academicians, who had been sounding a clarion call for over a decade, warning educators to be vigilant in protecting their autonomy in the area of reading instruction.[32] In effect, NCLB made phonics instruction, in particular the direct instruction of a specific kind of phonics instruction, the law of the land. Whether one is a proponent of phonics instruction, a whole language approach to teaching reading, a literature-based reading curriculum, or a balanced approach that incorporates features of a variety of reading instructional strategies was not the issue. Many would believe that the methodology of teaching reading depends on the students one teaches and decisions about methodology are best decided at a local, school, and classroom level. However, understanding why RF was so controversial and why it became ensnared in scandal requires a brief examination of the decades leading up to implementation of NCLB and how the federal government became so heavily involved in reading instruction.

In 1955, Rudolf Flesch published a book entitled *Why Johnny Can't Read and What You Can Do About It*.[33] The book was an instant sensation among conservatives and libertarians, embroiled, as we have seen in chapter 2, in an assault on public schools and progressive education. In his book, Flesch excoriates the teaching profession, writing "The teaching of reading—all across the United States, in all the schools is totally wrong and flies in the face of all logic and common sense."[34] Students in public schools were being taught to read with a series of what Flesch labeled as "horrible, stupid, emasculated, pointless, tasteless little readers" and what they needed was good, solid phonics instruction.[35] The *Dick and Jane* series was widely popular in the 1950s and became the lightning rod for the conservative onslaught against what they believed to be faulty progressive reading methodology across the country.

Almost 30 years after Flesch published *Why Johnny Can't Read*, the nation was poised to deal with the perceived crisis of a failing education system, prompted by the 1983 report *ANAR*. Shortly after the publication of *ANAR*, the DOE's National Institute of Education appointed the Commission on Reading to examine research on how best to teach young children to read and begin the process of reforming education by beginning in the earliest grades. Members of this commission were emerging giants in the field of reading instruction, and their names would endure over the years leading up to the Common Core State Standards. Jeanne Chall, for example, was already a legend within the education world, highly regarded for having settled what had become known as the Reading Wars waged between phonics proponents and advocates of whole language methodology.[36] She would be joined by Dorothy Strickland, Elfrieda Hiebert, Robert Glaser, David Rumelhart, Isabel Beck, and other reading instruction luminaries.

The commission published its findings in a report entitled *Becoming a Nation of Readers: The Report of the Commission on Reading* in 1985.[37] The commissioners found, among other things, as a result of their in-depth investigation of current reading research, that phonics instruction is important in facilitating a young student's ability to identify words.[38] Based on the Commission on Reading's findings, legislative bills were introduced to Congress requiring phonics instruction in public schools. Although these bills were unsuccessful, the push for federalizing reading instruction methodology continued.

In 1989, Republican Senator William Armstrong (R-Colorado) and the Senate Republican Committee enlisted Robert Sweet, appointed by President Reagan as director of the National Institute of Education, to write a report entitled "Illiteracy: An Incurable Disease or Educational Malpractice?"—which included direct quotes from Flesch's *Why Johnny Can't Read*.[39] According to Sweet, the problem began with teacher-training institutions that refused to "admit that there is a literacy crisis" and had a "lack of knowledge about phonics teaching, negative biases toward phonics instruction, and fear that phonics advocacy equals political conservatism."[40] Echoing Milton Friedman, Sweet goes on to label the "establishment of public schools and teacher education as a monopoly."[41] He is credited with playing a role in the language for No Child Left Behind. Through Sweet's efforts, the first federal law was enacted that would require the use of SBRR methodology for teaching reading in public schools. This law would be called the Reading Excellence Act of 1997, enacted under the Clinton administration.[42]

According to Ken Goodman, early efforts to federalize reading instruction, culminating in the Reading Excellence Act, represented the politicization of the reading curriculum, pitting conservatives who favored phonics instruction against liberals who favored holistic approaches to teaching reading.[43] Conservatives would win this battle. Flesch's book would be reprinted again and again in the decades since *ANAR*. Two more federally sponsored studies of reading instruction would follow the Commission on Reading in the 1990s. In 1997, Congress commissioned the formation of the National Reading Panel under the leadership of Reid Lyon, then serving as the director of the National Institute of Child Health and Human Development (NICHD) to assess the effectiveness of reading instruction in the United States.[44] And, in 1998, the National Academy of Sciences and the U.S. Department of Education funded a study by the Committee on the Prevention of Reading Difficulties in Young Children.[45] The reports that ensued from these two organizations recommended explicit and systematic instruction in both the alphabetic principle (phonics) and phonemic awareness. Phonics proponents were busy in the years leading up to and following the implementation of the Reading Excellence Act, working with states to write standards for phonics instruction and, most important, working to develop commercial phonics programs that would be seen as the magic bullet to solve the purported literacy crisis in the United States.

By the time NCLB became the law of the land, everything was in place to implement the findings of three different distinguished panels of reading experts, which further facilitated the creation of commercial programs and ensuring that phonics would be taught in elementary schools across the country. The rush to implement RF mandates created a heady environment in which a lot of money could be made. Some careers, however, would become imperiled in the headlong rush to implement RF.

Christopher Doherty, director of the RF program, assumed his role within the DOE with a clear vision of what he thought reading instruction should look like, and he proceeded to establish guidelines to ensure that states seeking RF grants implemented programs that would reflect his vision. Doherty stacked the panels that would approve grant applications with individuals who had clear ties to the specific reading programs he favored. Dynamic Indicators of Basic Early Literacy Skills (DIBELS) became the favored assessment tool for schools seeking RF funding.[46] State officials, however, began to complain when their grant applications were turned down unless they included a very particular set of programs and excluded others. A federal investigation was ordered to examine the RF approval process and a congressional hearing was conducted to consider the findings of the investigation. As a result, Doherty was prompted to resign. The investigation did not present a flattering portrait of Doherty, finding that under his leadership the DOE appeared to violate laws that prevented the federal government from influencing curriculum in schools. Furthermore, Doherty's practice of stacking panels with members who had connections to particular programs was found to be problematic, with no consideration given to any conflicts of interest or biases toward particular programs. Reading experts Edward Kame'enui, Roland Good, and Deborah Simmons, all closely associated with DIBELS and creators of programs that were favored by Doherty, testified before Congress, and admitted that they had profited very nicely as a result of federal policies that favored their products.[47]

While the RF investigators found that the federal program created an "appearance" that they were influencing curriculum in public schools, they could not definitively conclude that a direct violation of the law had occurred. The requirement that schools had to implement SBRR programs provided a rationale for the panels to reject certain programs in favor of particular kinds of phonics-based programs. What constitutes SBRR continues to be debated. Nevertheless, as a result of RF and NCLB policies, early reading instruction has been directly impacted because of the adoption of the SBRR mantra and has been reduced in large part to a set of subskills that can be easily measured in 60 seconds and graphed to monitor progress.

In a relatively short span of a few years, RF, an essential part of NCLB legislation was found to be a failure. The Institute of Education Science (IES) released its evaluation of the RF program in 2008. All the aura and mystique associated with SBRR programs couldn't obscure the fact that a scientifically based research evaluation found that "Reading First did not produce a statistically significant impact on student reading comprehension test scores in grades one, two or three."[48]

Education reformers learned an important lesson from the RF debacle. Under the leadership of Doherty, the DOE created an *appearance* of influencing curriculum within schools. However, RF investigators could not definitively conclude that federal laws had been broken regarding federal intrusion into curriculum. The path to the Common Core would be littered with language that would skirt the legal mandates prohibiting the DOE from influencing the creation and adoption of a national curriculum. These mandates have been in place since the passage of ESEA under President Johnson and the creation of the DOE under President Carter. For example, Section 9527 of the ESEA states:

> Nothing in this Act shall be construed to authorize an officer or employee of the Federal Government to mandate, direct, or control a State, local educational agency, or school's curriculum, program of instruction, or allocation of State or any subdivision thereof to spend any funds or incur any costs not paid for under this Act.[49]

Furthermore, ESEA states:

> Notwithstanding any other prohibition of Federal law, no funds provided to the Department under this Act may be used by the Department to endorse, approve, or sanction any curriculum designed to be used in an elementary school or secondary school.[50]

When the DOE was created, more than a decade after the passage of ESEA, these federal prohibitions were further strengthened. The Department of Education Organization Act clearly states:

> No provision of a program administered by the Secretary or any other officer of the Department shall be construed to authorize the Secretary or any such officer to exercise any direction, supervision, or control over the curriculum, program of instruction, administration, or personnel of any educational institution, school, or school system, over any accrediting agency or association, or over the selection or content of library resources, textbooks, or other instructional materials by any educational institution or school system, except to the extent authorized by law.[51]

The ability to sidestep federal law would become an essential skill for those traveling along the path to the Common Core. Clinton's third way of governance would provide the map for education reformers to work within what Lofgren calls the Deep State to implement education policies that would culminate in a highly federalized education system in which Common Core State Standards would take center stage.[52]

By the end of George W. Bush's administration, it was clear that schools would not be able to live up to the overly ambitious policies of NCLB. The vast number of schools that would be forced to close or convert to charter schools would inevitably further stress the American public school system that had been officially deemed a failure since 1983. This would not deter proponents of systemic education reform, however. Arguably, they had anticipated the collapse of NCLB policies, and, far from seeing this as a problem, they had been busy developing their plan for the next phase of systemic education reform. Official federal policies were not an impediment to systemic education reformers, they were merely a framework to work around, to use when helpful, or to sidestep when possible. As Lofgren asserts, "There is another government concealed behind the one that is visible at either end of Pennsylvania Avenue, a hybrid entity of public and private institutions ruling the country according to consistent patterns in season and out, connected to, but only intermittently controlled by, the visible state whose leaders we choose."[53] Education reformers had been operating in an alternate universe, the Deep State, since 1989, when President George H. W. Bush brought the nation's governors together with corporate leaders to begin the work of systemically reforming public education in the United States.

Chapter 7

Education Reform and the Deep State: An Alternate Universe

As the educational manifestation of NCLB permeated the hallways of America's public schools during President Bush's two terms in office, an alternate universe of education reform existed. While America was trying to make sense of federal NCLB policies and many public schools were fighting for their very existence under threats of closure, a vanguard of systemic education reform advocates were busy behind the curtain of the Deep State, wielding the levers that would carry the country further down the path to the Common Core State Standards. Within this universe, individuals and groups whose allegiance to a corporate-driven free market approach to reform continued to marshal their ideas in order to finally dominate America's education landscape. For them, NCLB was a profound victory providing a bridge to their final destination. The federal government had successfully imposed on America's public schools a system in which high-stakes standardized tests became the currency to measure the worth of a school, the teachers within the school, and the students enrolled in the school.

What was needed, however, was a common standardized measurement across the 50 United States. Without a common assessment, it was impossible to determine if, for example, schools in Mississippi were performing at the same level as schools in Connecticut or California. Under NCLB, states were free to choose their own standardized tests and this was clearly not adequate. Once NCLB was in place, systemic education reformers never missed a beat. With the creation of Achieve at the 1996 Palisades Summit, a corporate mechanism was in place to continue the work of carving out the path to the Common Core.

NCLB created a framework for strengthening the curricular grip on elementary schools. The next step was to find a way to tighten the reins at the secondary level. The American Diploma Project (ADP) would serve as the road map for accomplishing what NCLB could not accomplish—a free market corporate K-12 education feeding ground and the ability to put into place common standardized assessments.

The Wellspring of CCSS: The American Diploma Project

According to the Achieve website, four organizations were instrumental in launching the American Diploma Project: Achieve, the Education Trust, the Thomas B. Fordham Foundation, and the National Alliance of Business (NAB), although the NAB soon dropped out of the project. The lead writer and often called the chief architect of the ADP was Susan Pimentel, a person who will be discussed in greater detail in chapter 8 as instrumental in creating the CCSS.[1] The stated goal of the ADP was "to help states prepare all students for success." According to Achieve, the ADP was launched in 2001, and between that year and 2004, the project "commissioned leading economists to examine labor market projections for the most promising jobs" in order to "pinpoint the academic knowledge and skills required for success in those occupations." Achieve then surveyed officials from 22 occupations, ranging from manufacturing to financial services, about the skills they believed were most useful for their employees to bring to the job. Following those conversations, Achieve worked "closely with K-12, postsecondary and business leaders" in five partner states "to identify the English and mathematics knowledge and skills needed for success in both college and work."[2] The five partner states were Indiana, Massachusetts, Kentucky, Nevada, and Texas. From 2002 to 2004, an Achieve team worked within states to develop "college and workplace benchmarks" they claimed would "offer the solid foundation upon which states can raise academic expectations and that have currency beyond 12th grade."[3]

The end result of the ADP team working within these states was a report titled "Ready or Not: Creating a High School Diploma That Counts." Achieve announced its publication in December 2004.[4] As an important aside that helps one understand the origins of the CCSS, that same month a report by the American Council of Education (ACE) entitled "The School-to- College Transition: Challenges and Prospects" was published. According to ACE, the report was "generously supported" by the Bill and Melinda Gates Foundation. The report began with the following declaration: "Within the U.S. elementary and secondary schools, the pathway to college access is marked by vast disparities in preparation for, knowledge of, and attitude toward college."[5] The report was particularly concerned about "inequitable conditions in K-12 education for low socioeconomic and racial and ethnic groups."[6] Two of the major conclusions of the ACE report were that "the barriers to college access are primarily financial and academic" and the greatest need for helping students get a college degree were in rural and urban areas of the United States where poverty was high.[7] Most important, however, to understand the origins of the CCSS, it is important to be aware that while Achieve, the National Governors Association (NGA), and the Council of Chief State School Officers (CCSSO) were engaged in an effort to systemically reform K-12 education in 2004, so was the Gates foundation.

By 2008, one year before the final push to the creation of CCSS, Gates would infuse hundreds of millions of dollars into the CCSS initiative that would then be channeled into the coffers of diverse ideological and political groups such as the more conservative ALEC, U.S. Chamber of Commerce, and the Thomas B. Fordham Institute and the more liberal Center for American Progress. Gates also funneled money to the NEA and the AFT, America's two largest teachers' unions, enticing them to join the CCSS crusade. And very importantly, as Lyndsey Layton would point out in 2014, Gates's systemic education reform dollars would also influence President Obama, "whose new administration was populated by former Gates staffers and associates."[8]

Achieve freely and proudly acknowledges that the 2004 "Ready or Not" report led to the CCSS. For example, Achieve proclaims that this "groundbreaking report—the result of over two years of research—identifies a common core of English and mathematics academic knowledge and skills, or 'benchmarks,' that American high school graduates need for success in college and the workforce."[9]

According to the "Ready or Not" report, "too many young Americans [were] graduating from high school without the skills and knowledge they need to succeed,"[10] a conclusion based on the following findings:

- More than 70 percent of high school graduates decide to go on to college, and 28 percent of these graduates need remedial help in college.
- Most college students never attain a degree.
- Most high school graduates lack basic skills in grammar, spelling, writing, and basic math.

- Most workers question the preparation that high schools provide, and these same workers rate literacy and critical thinking as much more important than job-specific or computer skills.

Based on Achieve's finding that 70 percent of high school grads go on to college and 28 percent require remedial work, it is not clear what the probability of college success for the other 30 percent that decided not to go on to college would have been. Achieve seems to want us to infer that the entire 30 percent did not go on to college because they were not properly prepared. However, an inference like this is problematic. Perhaps in some cases a student's decision not to attend college after graduating from high school was unrelated to their academic abilities at all. Many factors influence a student's decision about college attendance, including financial constraints, a desire to first serve in the military or pursue a trade or vocation, or simply a desire to postpone college for a number of reasons that may not relate to academic preparedness. As discussed in chapter 2, there was a time when some education reformers and scholars felt that only 15 to 20 percent of high school graduates had the ability to go on to college, specifically those with an IQ of 110 or higher. Nevertheless, the American system of education should be lauded for expanding opportunities for citizens to engage in postsecondary educational experiences. Community colleges and four-year institutions with open enrollment policies provide opportunities for many more citizens to earn a college diploma, unfettered by notions of who is, or is not, capable of engaging in college-level work.

Using Achieve's statistics (28 percent of the 70 percent of high school students deciding to go to college need remedial courses) actually provides a more positive picture than Achieve seems to acknowledge. For example, according to Achieve, 72 percent of all students enrolling in college did *not* need remedial courses. Looking a little closer at these percentages, even if the "entire" 30 percent of students who did not go on to college would have needed remedial work, which is highly unlikely, that still means that a little over half of "all" high school graduates were prepared to go on to some type of higher education institution. Although we need to constantly improve high schools to better meet the needs of all students, the fact that our high schools in 2004 produced as many students as they did that were capable of attaining a college degree with no remediation (according to Achieve's data) is actually quite impressive, given the fact that the United States has one of the highest poverty rates among countries that are considered to have "advanced economies."

In 2004, for example, approximately 18 percent of America's children were living in poverty after having hit a low of 12.1 percent in 2000. By 2012, according to UNICEF, the United States had 23.1 percent of its children living in poverty and ranking 34 out of 35 in countries identified as economically advanced.[11] Even in 2004, with poverty rates among children rising at a blistering rate, producing a little over 50 percent of all high school students prepared for college seems to require at least some accolades instead of complete condemnation.

Although most college students never attain a college degree, college costs, life experiences, and personal dispositions are important factors that impact college completion. Achieve infers that the reason college students do not complete their degree is because of a poor high school education. However, that inference does not accurately portray the realities of college life. For many students, the financial burden of postsecondary education for themselves and their families interrupts their ability to get an advanced degree. This, combined with other factors unrelated to academics must be considered when discussing the number of students who leave college before completion. As an interesting aside, in Finland, now often considered the personification of educational success, college tuition is free. Therefore, given the financial advantage of students in Finland, it can be reasonably inferred that if the United States followed Finland's example then college completion rates would skyrocket.

If, as noted above, a little over 50 percent of all high school graduates have the skills to be successful in college according the Achieve's statistics, then it is incorrect to proclaim that "most" high school graduates lack basic skills. It can be argued that "too many" students do lack these skills. However, this probably says more about certain high schools in certain areas of the United States rather than being an indictment of all high schools and, therefore, does not point to the need for total systemic education reform.

According to Achieve, most workers question the preparation that high schools provide and these same workers rate literacy and critical thinking as much more important than job-specific or computer skills. This makes one wonder if these workers were talking about specific literacy skills that relate to their current careers such as reading various technical manuals, reading directions for putting something together, or reading blueprints for a project or the literacy and critical thinking skills that these workers thought they could and should have gotten by reading, writing, and talking about works such as *Crime and Punishment* by Fyodor Dostoyevsky, *The Scarlet Letter* by Nathaniel Hawthorne, the historical writings of Daniel Boorstin, or *The*

Metamorphosis by Franz Kafka, which the ADP creators posited was a way to address worker literacy and critical-thinking concerns and the jobs they eventually had after high school.[12] However, teachers have always tried to explain to students how what they studied in high school would apply to their lives after high school. For some students these teachers were successful, while for others they were not for a number of reasons, including the vocational goals a student aspired to achieve that had little to do with a traditional college prep curriculum.

The final outcome of the 2004 report "Ready or Not" was based on a belief that the curricular standards that resulted from NCLB legislation were not enough. Instead, what was needed were national standards. ADP research declared that it had found "an important convergence around the core knowledge and skills that both colleges and employers—within and beyond ADP states—require." What was needed was a "high school diploma" that represented "common currency nationwide."[13] In other words, a national set of standards measured by a national test that ultimately measured a national curriculum was needed that somehow had to circumvent the fact that the federal government could not by law mandate a national curriculum. This was something that by 2014 both conservatives on the right and liberals on the left would fear.[14] A back door approach was therefore needed by Achieve, the Education Trust, and the conservative Thomas B. Fordham Foundation, and all their corporate allies, in order to negotiate these educationally treacherous federal waters. So what first needed to happen, after laying the curricular foundation that would somehow control the nation's public schools, was to create the illusion that any national curricular reform initiative would come from the states. In this way the curricular standards and subject matter that manifested these standards would not be viewed as a top-down federal approach. Instead, it could be rationalized as a bottom-up state approach.

This approach would then fit nicely into a story that went like this: If governors and states bought into these standards and the curriculum that was best able to meet these standards, then by extension the common standards and curricular exemplars would come from states that were legally responsible for public schools. This approach was, in fact, a brilliant maneuver, especially if all of these states and groups associated with this report could at the same time avoid the legalities of the ESEA. Furthermore, "Ready or Not" also declared that there was a need to "back-map standards to create a coherent, focused, grade-by-grade progression from kindergarten through high school graduation." The report explained that "high school graduation is the culmination of preparation that begins in the elementary grades. Therefore, the standards set for each grade must exhibit a clear progression of content and skills through high school completion. Unless all students are regularly exposed to a challenging curriculum in elementary and middle schools, they will forever be playing catch-up."[15] The 2004 report, in reality, began a backdoor approach using the states to create a national curriculum. For example, if all states jumped onboard the curricular ideas reflected in 2004 report, the creators of this report explained that this would lead to "creating a default curriculum for all students" something that the federal DOE was not able to create by law.[16]

The curricular results of the ADP project outlined in "Ready or Not" can now be clearly seen as a forerunner to the CCSS and were already in place and ready to go when Achieve's 2005 Education Summit convened. Many would argue, however, that there was little that was democratic about its creation and very importantly its acceptance. Arguably, this is why the only better title that could have been used for the report is "Ready or Not—Here We Come!" In other words, Achieve's 2005 summit was a mere formality in that the curricular menu was already being formulated, and all that was needed was for gubernatorial and corporate CEOs to begin taking part in the eventual feast. By the time the 2005 Education Summit took place, 13 states had already joined the ADP to form a coalition. Over the next several years the ADP Network would snowball.

Achieve

As we have seen in chapter 5, Achieve is a legal corporation, administered by a board of six governors and six corporate leaders, created as a result of recommendations for education reform that were made during the 1996 Palisades conference of corporate and gubernatorial CEOs. The officials at Achieve describe their corporation as an "independent, nonpartisan, nonprofit education reform organization dedicated to working with states to raise academic standards and graduation requirements, improve assessments, and strengthen accountability." When created, as Vinovskis explains, Achieve's goal was to "collect and disseminate standards and assessments information." Vinovskis further explains that Achieve helped "states to evaluate and improve their academic standards and assessments; creating a national standards and assessment clearinghouse; and working with the public and the business community to stress the importance of high standards and challenging assessments."[17]

Today, Achieve's website reflects the organization's long tentacles into all areas of school reform and its mission of providing a clearinghouse to help private companies sell their educational wares to schools. It seems that Achieve is the corporate education reform world's Walmart. For example, if one visits the Achieve website one will come upon the following: "Click here to visit Future Ready Projects—Achieve's one-stop advocacy resource center, designed to provide state and local college- and career-ready stakeholders with the information, strategies, messages, and tools needed to effectively make the case for the college- and career-ready agenda in their states."[18]

Even at the outset of its creation, Achieve was so powerful and influential that it was able to host the second gubernatorial and corporate CEO summit in 1999 (the 1999 National Education Summit); a third in October 2001 (the 2001 National Education Summit)—five short weeks after the 9/11 attacks; and a fourth in February 2005 (the National Education Summit on High Schools). The 2001 and 2005 education summits were particularly instrumental in creating the path to the Common Core State Standards and, therefore, require closer examination.

ACHIEVE'S 2001 NATIONAL EDUCATION SUMMIT

The 2001 National Education Summit sponsored by Achieve was cochaired by John Engler, Republican governor of Michigan, and Louis V. Gerstner, chairman and CEO of the IBM Corporation. Although only 15 governors attended the 2001 summit as a result of the terrorist attacks on New York City and Washington DC, it is interesting that the following statement preceded the final report of the 2001 summit:

> The governors, corporate leaders and educators who organized this meeting extend their deepest sympathies to those who lost loved ones in the terrorist assaults of September 11. Events of that day have profoundly affected every American. The people of the United States can draw on great reservoirs of patriotism, decency, courage and resilience as they respond to this unpardonable tragedy. The participants in this meeting, united in the belief that healthy public schools are the foundation of our democracy, dedicate this Summit to the task of building a stronger America.[19]

Of course, it should not surprise anyone that America's public schools would once again be connected to America's larger challenges, as well as its security, within the global community. Somehow corporate and gubernatorial CEOS, undoubtedly sincere in their empathy to those who suffered as a result of the attack, had now connected America's public schools to this terrorist attack, in the process making a case that public schools were an essential defense against future terrorist attacks. What was the role of American public schools in "building a stronger America" and preventing further terrorist attacks? According the Achieve, "The 2001 Summit focused on helping states address two key challenges: (1) increasing the capacity of teachers and schools to meet higher standards and (2) expanding testing and accountability systems to provide better data and stronger incentives for high student achievement."[20] The 2001 summit clearly indicates that the path to the CCSS was in the process of being paved. For example, these challenges needed to be overcome because, according to Achieve and gubernatorial and corporate CEOs, K-12 public schools were failing and the only solution was systemic education reform. In particular, K-12 public schools had created poorly educated workers and students who were not college and career ready. According to Achieve, its research had found that K-12 graduates did not have the reading, writing, speaking, and mathematical skills to be good workers and college students.[21]

What the 2001 summit also included were 21 education technology demonstrations from companies that praised their technology packages as a means to help ultimately solve all the problems in education America was facing. According to the corporate and gubernatorial CEOS, the goal of these demonstrations was to "showcase innovative education technology programs, prototypes and products that seek to help improve student achievement."[22]

In hindsight, by 2001, clearly all of these tech companies were poised to take advantage of a new education industry in which potentially hundreds of millions if not billions of dollars could become ripe for the pickings. What is now also clear was that these 21 "technology programs, prototypes, and products" heralded a huge technological cottage industry that would increasingly impact how schools needed to be run. Therefore, it is no wonder that, over the years, schools would be increasingly deluged with wave after wave of "ed tech" salespeople who would line up at the office doors of school administrators, wanting easy access to schools and school districts in order to hold out hope that if their products were purchased they would have a positive effect on a school's test scores.[23] Most important, the 2001 National Education Summit would culminate in the announcement of the creation of the ADP. At the very same time, Washington DC and the country were dealing with the anthrax terror threat and before legislators would resume negotiations before passing NCLB legislation, Achieve, operating within the Deep State, was undeterred, already laying the ground work for the next phase in systemic education reform. Even before NCLB became the federal law of the land, Achieve was immersed in the process of creating a set of national standards, which would later become the CCSS.

Achieve's 2005 National Education Summit on High Schools

The 2005 National Education Summit on High Schools was sponsored by the NGA and Achieve in partnership with the Business Roundtable, the James B. Hunt Institute, and the Education Commission of the States (ECS). As we have seen, the BRT had been deeply immersed in systemic education reform since the 1980s. Established in 2001, by 2002, the Hunt Institute had begun tutoring governors on education reform and to this day is deeply involved in facilitating the CCSS and its educational ramifications.[24] By 2012, the ECS would be working closely with the Bill and Melinda Gates Foundation as well as being engaged in tracking the progress of states in the development and implementation of Common Core strategies and policies.[25] The 2005 summit specifically focused on high schools just like *ANAR* had done 22 years earlier.

By 2005, 13 states had already formed an ADP coalition network and were encouraging other states to join. According to Achieve, this network was designed "to make college and career readiness a priority in the states." Again, Achieve also does not shirk from acknowledging that their concept of education reform could have curricular consequences on a national level. For example, in their own words, "Achieve is proud to be the leading voice for the college and career ready agenda, and has helped transform the concept of 'college and career readiness for all students' from a radical proposal into a national agenda."[26]

By 2005, it seems the education technology tsunami was also now about to swallow America's education landscape. And no better indicator of this was when Bill Gates, arguably the greatest of all technology superstars, was asked to give the opening address at the summit. In his speech, Gates declared, "Too many high school students drop out before earning a diploma, and too many of those who graduate are unprepared for the realities of the 21st century economy. This failure of our high school system has dire consequences for our economy, but even more important, it is simply wrong." Gates rightfully worried that underprivileged students were not getting the education they deserved, but, on the other hand, Gates also acknowledged that students in public schools within wealthier neighborhoods were getting an excellent education. He then explained that while his foundation was advancing equity in foreign lands by focusing on health issues, what he decided his foundation needed to focus on in America to advance equity was education.[27]

Gates went on to proclaim that American high schools were generally failing and are "obsolete." He explained, "By obsolete, I mean that our high schools—even when they're working exactly as designed—cannot teach our kids what they need to know today." Oddly enough, he then stated, "Let's be clear. Thanks to dedicated teachers and principals around the country, the best-educated kids in the United States are the best-educated kids in the world. We should be proud of that. But only a fraction of our kids are getting the best education." Gates also claimed that while teachers in wealthier districts were doing a good job, in poorer underprivileged districts teachers either felt that their students "cannot learn" or "they are not worth teaching."[28]

Gates then warned that India and China were producing more college graduates and were increasing their share of college graduates worldwide. "The percentage of a population with a college degree is important," Gates explained, "but so are sheer numbers. In 2001, India graduated almost a million more students from college than the United States did. China graduates twice as many students with bachelor's degrees as the United States, and they have six times as many graduates majoring in engineering." According to Gates, this was threatening the security of the United States, but then he contended that in a place like Kansas City great progress was being made in high school performance because of recent innovative educational approaches. Gates explained that the "Kansas City public school district, where 79 percent of students are minorities and 74 percent live below the poverty line, was struggling with high dropout rates and low test scores when it adopted the school-reform model called First Things First in 1996. This included setting high academic standards for all students, reducing teacher-student ratios, and giving teachers and administrators the responsibility to improve student performance and the resources they needed to do it. The district's graduation rate has climbed more than 30 percentage points."[29]

Gates's assertions, however, require further analysis. First, Gates never seemed to somehow bring himself to declare that America should make poverty, healthcare problems, high-crime unsafe neighborhoods, and neighborhoods with no jobs obsolete! Instead, it seems these problems could be overcome and eliminated by simply systemically reforming public schools. Gates also never mentioned the positive and complex social and economic realities in wealthier school districts that helped them produce excellent students, who, according to Gates, were "the best students in the world." According to Gates, it seems as though educational success in those wealthier schools was because teachers in those schools simply thought that their students could learn and were worth teaching, while educational failure in high-poverty schools within neighborhoods with numerous social and economic challenges was because teachers in those schools thought their students could not learn and were not worth teaching.

As far as higher education is concerned, even though Gates might have been correct when he claimed that China and India were producing more college graduates by 2005, we can simply look at realities then and now regarding higher education in these countries that were and still are inconvenient truths that Gates seemed to ignore, or perhaps just did not consider. So how were American universities doing in 2005, the year Gates made his dramatic claims about higher education in the United States when comparing their productivity to China and India? In 2005, according to the researchers at The Center for World-Class Universities of Shanghai Jiao Tong University, the United States had 53 of the top 100 universities in the world! China and India had none, however.[30]

Six years later in 2011, the *Wall Street Journal* would do an exposé on the state of India's higher education system. What the newspaper found was a system that was producing large numbers of graduates who were just not properly prepared. Corruption was rampant, standards were low, and students could pay someone to take final exams for them. Unemployment was high among India's college graduates and one employer in India bemoaned the fact that graduates lacked necessary skills.[31] Furthermore, in 2013–14, according to the United Kingdom's Times Higher Education University (THEU) findings, 30 of the top 50 institutions of higher education in the world were in the United States. Out of the top 100, 45 were in the United States, and, out of the top 200, 76 were from the United States.[32] This dominance in higher education was coming from a country with only 4.4 percent of the world's population in 2012, but with 38 percent of the top 200 universities in the world. China, on the other hand, with a 19 percent share of the world's population, had only one institution in the top 200 universities, and India, with an 18 percent share of the world's population, had no universities in the top 200. In 2013, according to the researchers at The Center for World-Class Universities of

Shanghai Jiao Tong University, the United States had eight of the top ten universities for science, six out of ten for math, eight out of ten for physics, seven out of ten for chemistry, ten out of ten for computers, and ten out of ten for engineering.[33]

As far as Kansas City's schools are concerned, Gates's proclamations of success were clearly premature. According to Bob Schaefer of the National Center for Fair and Open Testing, after ten years of NCLB goals and other supposedly innovative approaches to education like the one Gates lauded in 2005, the ACT scores among minority students indicated that they were not making educational progress. Schaefer observed, "Significant gaps remain between affluent children and their economically disadvantaged peers. Likewise, white and Asian students widened the difference between them and black and Hispanic students."[34] So with all of the educational innovations that were designed to close the achievement gap among disadvantaged groups of students, clearly, in Kansas City, its public schools alone could not solve the education challenges facing some minority groups. Larger social and economic factors needed to be overcome, factors that Gates seemed to be ignoring in his crusade to systemically reform America's public schools, when high-stakes testing became the ultimate indicator of school success.

Nevertheless, the ADP was ready to go, and its supporters would find an important road grader that would smooth America's path to the CCSS. A grand education project like the ADP, however, was not simply the result of efforts by Achieve alone. Two other groups, the Thomas B. Fordham Foundation and the Education Trust, took part in this education reform project and its curricular ramifications that would seek to dominate America's national education landscape.

THE FORDHAM FOUNDATION

The Thomas B. Fordham Foundation was created in 1959 as an organization supporting a range of philanthropic causes in Dayton, Ohio.[35] The foundation is named after industrialist Thomas B. Fordham and was created by his widow, Thelma. Its recent past president, Chester Finn, has close family ties with the Fordham family. His grandfather had been Thomas Fordham's attorney and his grandparents and parents were close friends of Thelma Fordham Pruett after her husband's death in 1945. It was not until the death of Thelma Fordham Pruett in 1995, and Chester Finn's appointment as its president, that the Fordham Foundation devoted its energies and funds to education reform. Finn explains, "because Thelma gave no clear guidance" regarding how to spend the foundation's money, the foundation board decided that they "had a free hand and soon resolved to devote this enterprise to reforming K-12 education, both nationally and in the Dayton (Ohio) area." The foundation soon adopted "the credo of the Educational Excellence Network," words that harkened back to *ANAR*. Finn, however, argues that in spite of critics at the time, the organization was not conservative, although by quickly entering into agreements with the Hudson and Manhattan Institutes this claim can be taken with a grain of salt.[36]

By 2001, the foundation jumped on board the systemic education reform bandwagon with Achieve and the Education Trust to create the ADP and its eventual report "Ready or Not." By 2002, the Fordham Foundation formed the Thomas B. Fordham Institute, which has since become the "public face" of the foundation and also a leading conservative "think tank" in the education arena.

Chester Finn has had a diverse career, primarily focusing on education reform in the United States. For example, he is a former professor of education and public policy at Vanderbilt University, is a former assistant secretary of education during the Reagan years of 1985–88, has written numerous articles and books about education, is associated with the conservative Hudson and Hoover Institutes, and holds a master of arts in teaching (MAT) degree in social studies and an EdD in education policy from Harvard. In 1991, David Kearns called Finn "one of America's most thoughtful and responsible education writers." That year, Finn, who, like many conservatives, believed America was in a state of moral and educational decay, was already calling for reforming America's public school curriculum arguing that "universal mastery of common core is what will hold us together as Americans, equalize our opportunities for happiness and prosperity, and revitalize the nation's civic, economic, and cultural life."

More than 25 years before the official starting date of the CCSS, Finn explained that one of the hardest things that needed to be overcome in systemically reforming America's public schools was not only making the nation's school curriculum more rigorous, but also defining what was meant by "competency over challenging subject matter." He then went on to say, while states can no longer simply rely on testing minimum competencies among students, "we also want our standards to be achievable by essentially all our young people, provided they work hard enough and long enough at it and then we give them enough instructional assistance."[37] According to Finn, oddly enough, this meant that on the one hand, high standards were needed that would challenge those students identified as gifted, say with an IQ of 130 or more. On the other hand, this also meant that the "high" standards and resulting rigorous curriculum had to be low enough so that they could be "essentially achievable" by other students whose academic abilities were on the other end of the education spectrum.

In his autobiography, *Troublemaker: A Personal History of School Reform Since Sputnik*, Finn describes his various roles in education: "my jobs have cycled between 'inside-action-participant' and 'outside-analyst–writer'. . . . I crave both the excitement of doing and running things, and the intellectual stimulus of trying to make sense of them. . . . I need to write books, articles, op-eds, testimony—but I also yearn for direct experience."[38] Finn's yearning for "direct experience" however, did not seem to be the kind that lends itself well to personally becoming a public school teacher. Writing about his teaching experience at Newton High School during the 1965–66 school year, Finn admits "I wasn't much good at it." He rationalized his failure by explaining that he was only 21 at the time and all his students were seniors and "mostly from the wrong side of the (Newton) tracks." According to Finn, "Newton High School was (and remains) one of America's most esteemed public schools in a predominantly upper-middle class, education-obsessed Boston suburb." Newton was also a "Conant-style comprehensive high school" with courses for bright students, as well as courses for "less able, less motivated, and less fortunate youngsters." Finn explained, "My four classes were part of 'curriculum II,' which by twelfth grade meant that my students were mostly putting in time until they could grab their diplomas and head off to work, army, or the nearby community college. . . . Many of the boys were bigger, and nearly all of them tougher, than I. The girls misbehaved less, but that didn't mean that their minds were focused on the Problems of American Democracy course that I struggled to teach."[39] Finn explained his inadequate performance as a teacher by pointing out that he had no teaching experience, and also claiming that he had no syllabus or textbook. According to Finn, his assigned "master teacher" all but ignored him. He was left to "devise his own curriculum and pedagogy." He lamented that no one "much cared what I taught or if anything, my students learned."[40]

Interestingly, in spite of Finn's lack of teaching ability as a result of his MAT degree versus one that could have been earned through a more traditional teacher education program, by 2010 he would endorse what he considered to be the innovative approach to creating teachers via Teach for America (TFA), a program that requires only a five-week training session in education before a person enters a classroom. This is a program that puts into the teaching field young recent university graduates with excellent academic records but with little training in education compared with those teachers trained in traditional teacher education programs.[41] Like Finn had been, TFA teachers are very bright young adults but have very little pedagogical training.

Finn's brief lackluster performance as a teacher led him to conclude, "I came to understand that teaching is hard and that being smart and well educated doesn't necessarily mean that one will be effective at it. . . . I also learned vividly that even the most acclaimed schools have 'kids left behind,' youngsters getting an inferior education while their age mates get a good one." Finn further concluded, "The education system that served me well as a student in Dayton just a few years earlier was mistreating these kids in Newton. Someone needed to make more of a fuss about it." Oddly enough he came to this final conclusion: "But my big discovery . . . was that retail work in the classroom was not where I belonged over the long haul. . . . If I were personally going to make a difference in American education—especially to its hoary practices, outdated assumptions, and mixed-bag performance—I would have to find a perch in the wholesale yard!"[42]

Finn's discussion of his teaching experiences at Newton High School is important when considering his role as a systemic education reformer. According to Finn, for many students Newton was doing a great job—which meant that there was no need for systemic reform. Rather, if we believe Finn's story, there was a need to reform one aspect of that school. And although Finn admitted he had gotten a good education in Dayton, at 15 he transferred to the very expensive Phillips Exeter Academy in New Hampshire. In spite of Finn's acknowledgment that "teaching is hard" and that there are social, economic, and personal issues that impact the educational lives of students, Finn would go on to use resources provided by the Fordham Foundation to engage in systemic education reform initiatives that ultimately hold teachers accountable for any low test scores in their classrooms. The Fordham Foundation would fully support the ADP and go on to become an active proponent of the CCSS.

THE EDUCATION TRUST

The Education Trust (ET) was one of the civil rights organizations Rhodes refers to as "civil rights entrepreneurs." The ET would get on the corporate bandwagon that supported school choice, vouchers, and charter schools, with all the accoutrements of high-stakes testing, in order to raise the academic achievement of minorities. The organization continues to dedicate itself to this approach. While the ET was engaged in implementing this approach in Milwaukee—an approach that would prove to be unsuccessful—it became deeply involved with Achieve and the Fordham Foundation in the creation of the ADP. The ET supported increased federal involvement in school reform as it wholeheartedly supported NCLB, rationalizing that this approach was the best way to overcome the historic underachievement of disadvantaged groups. However, when the ET threw in with Achieve and the Fordham Foundation, conservatives and corporate education reformers were able, at least to some degree, to argue that this proved that what they were doing had nothing but the best of democratic intentions. When the ET put their name on the ADP, and all of the resulting reports that ended up creating new curricular standards as well as supporting Draconian accountability and assessment measures, for lawmakers this only validated that these education reform efforts covered the entire spectrum of American society. Very importantly, as Rhodes points out, the ET was willing to "jettison their demands for the 'opportunity to learn' standards entirely."[43] In effect, this was an admission on the part of the ET that outside larger social and economic factors could ultimately be overlooked when holding public schools accountable for the success or failure of underachieving populations. In the process, the ET decided, after looking at America's failed efforts at eliminating poverty within communities in which student academic achievement was well below more affluent communities, that it was probably best to ultimately ignore all of the social and economic realities that were essential for those communities to produce education excellence.

This reality is reflected in the ET's fealty to ultimately holding public schools, and only public schools, accountable for student performance that would be measured through high-stakes tests, as well as an undying loyalty to charter schools and school choice that would help dismiss larger social and economic reasons for academic underachievement. By 2011, Adolph Reed seemed to confirm this reality as it relates to systemic education reform, when he stated, "The movement for racial justice has shifted its focus from 'inequality' to 'disparity' neatly evading any critique of structural factors such as inequality."[44] In other words, instead of directly confronting economic and social factors like poverty or segregation that have historically been and remain a root cause that impedes the opportunities and achievement of minority groups, in the case of a civil rights group, such as the ET, it decided to attack the education disparities among minorities, focusing instead on test scores as the referee for closing the achievement gap. In the process, systemic education reformers were easily able to place both the blame and solution regarding the plight of minority groups squarely on the shoulders of public schools and teachers. While the ET might have been acting with all good intentions when they decided to join the vanguard of systemic education reformers, by letting these reformers off the hook so to speak in addressing larger social and economic issues that have always been part of America's education system, the ET, wittingly or not, lent their civil rights credibility to the corporate assault on dismantling America's institution of public schools.

OUT OF MANY ONE

By 2008, ADP network membership had grown to 30 states. Earlier in November 2007, a CCSSO policy forum had addressed the need for one set of shared academic standards. In July 2008, the Achieve report "Out of Many, One: Toward Rigorous, Common Core Standards from the Ground Up" was published basically reiterating what had been said in the 2004 report "Ready or Not," but with an important addition. Now more specific high school benchmarks had been created by the ADP members. These benchmarks, as the report explicitly stated, were designed to help "states align their standards to college and career readiness."[45] By the time this report was created, 16 states had already begun the process of adopting these standards and benchmarks. Achieve and its allies discussed "the key implications of this emerging common core," triumphantly declaring, "The ADP Core is the Common Core. . . . The ADP Core has become the 'common core' as a byproduct of the alignment work in each of the states."[46]

There still was, however, a little matter of the ESEA and the fact that it was quite literally illegal to mandate a national curriculum, which is why the report stated that "while state standards from these [participating] states share a common core, they are not identical." What we therefore see developing was the mantra that states could always choose what they would do. No one, at this point was mandating that any state choose this curricular path. Achieve overtly stated the implications of their actions. "A state led movement for common core standards is feasible" they declared, and it took "a sustained coordinated effort to develop college—and career-ready standards."[47]

Achieve's role in systemic K-12 education reform was now clear. The 2008 "Out of Many" report declared the need for K-8 standards to go along with ADP high school standards. In an interesting use of language, seemingly to ensure the resulting K-12 standards would be aligned with the ADP standards and that the process would not be sidetracked by experts in K-12 education, the ADP creators made this statement: "The K-12 system can't do it alone [i.e. creating these standards]; the postsecondary and business communities must be deeply involved in order to make sure that the resulting standards reflect their expectations and are accepted by them. . . . States must now follow through and review and revise, as necessary, their K-8 standards to create a focused, clear, and rigorous set of grade-by-grade standards that provide a clear progression toward high school."[48] By 2008, Achieve's game plan was already in place and available for all to see, as it proclaimed, "Achieve is prepared to work with states collectively on this task, with the expectation that doing so will help further reinforce the emerging core of K-12 set standards in English and mathematics."[49] Within this eventual process, Achieve would hand pick a select writing team in order to make sure that those who were experts in K-8 education, let alone K-12 education, would not stand in the way of the curricular goals of Achieve and its allies.

According to the NGA, following the release of the report "Out of Many One," "the NGA Center and CCSSO convened governor's advisors and chief state school officers to gauge interest in developing a set of common, internationally benchmarked academic standards. Fifty-one states and U.S. territories signed a memorandum of understanding (MOU) committing them to participate in the development process."[50] This meeting, however, was nothing more than mere formality since it was highly unlikely the NGA and CCSSO would have abandoned their education reform course of action that had been developing since 1989. But what is most problematic is that states seemed to feel the need to sign a MOU committing to these standards. One needs to consider, however, that if these standards were really state led, then there was no need to have states make a written commitment to the standards. Was this MOU designed to simply show national unity regarding these standards in order to give them more credibility among all citizens? Or was the purpose of a MOU to signify to the federal government and the DOE that all states were fellow travelers along the path to the CCSS? As we will see in the next chapter, in order to get federal Race to the Top (RTTT) money, states would be enticed to adopt the untested CCSS.

Benchmarking for Success: Ensuring U.S. Students Receive a World-Class Education

In December 2008, during the second greatest recession in America's history caused in the main by unscrupulous hedge fund managers and questionable banking practices, another report was issued by Achieve, the NGA, and the CCSSO. The preparation of this published report, entitled "Benchmarking for Success: Ensuring U.S. Students Receive a World-Class Education," was "generously supported by the Bill and Melinda Gates Foundation and the GE Foundation."[51] Significantly, Susan Pimentel, who was the architect of the ADP and would be considered a lead writer of the CCSS, was also closely connected to the GE Foundation. An "International Benchmarking Advisory Board" was formed by the NGA, CCSSO, and Achieve to provide these "three organizations with valuable insights and help frame this bipartisan Call to Action." The group was made up of what was called "national, state, and local policy leaders."[52] The only person, however, who could have possibly been called a "local" policy leader was Beverly L. Hall, who was the superintendent of Atlanta Public Schools, a school district that was eventually scandalized with cheating on standardized tests during her tenure as superintendent.

The three cochairs of the advisory board were Sonny Perdue, Republican governor from Georgia; Janet Napolitano, Democratic governor from Arizona; and Craig R. Barnett, chairman of the board for the Intel Corporation. There were also some individuals representing already familiar groups supporting systemic reform such as Steven Baltimore, CEO of the Microsoft Corporation; Chester Finn, president of the Thomas B. Fordham Institute; James B. Hunt, chairman of the Hunt Institute; Kate Haycock, president of the ET; Janet Murguia, president and CEO of the National Council of La Raza; and Richard Riley, senior partner with EducationCounsel LLC, and the former U.S. secretary of education during the Clinton administration. The report relied a great deal on the insights regarding international education of Sir Michael Barber who would eventually become chief education strategist for the Pearson Corporation and a staunch supporter of the creation of the CCSS.[53] We will see in the coming chapters that Pearson will influence all aspects of the CCSS once in place, including the creation of high-stakes tests and in the process make huge profits.

The report was designed to further the case for the implementation of the CCSS by excoriating K-12 public schools for what the report's supporters believed was the abysmal performance of public schools within the international education arena. The report would also act as the final springboard that would help launch the CCSS. Tests associated with the Third International Mathematics and Science Study (TIMSS) and the Program for International Student Assessments (PISA) were used to make the case for complete systemic reform in America's K-12 public schools. The report claimed that "the U.S. is rapidly losing its historic edge in educational attainment," although, as we have seen, this was an argument being made for at least the last 60 or 70 years. For many decades critics of America's system of public education had been claiming public educational failure both nationally and internationally. And even though this 2008 report finally admitted that the 1983 report "*A Nation at Risk* erred in linking the recession of the early 1980s to educational stagnation," the 2008 report proclaimed that "improving education is critical to America's economic competitiveness"[54] Compared to the rest of the world, the report continued the now historical claim that America's K-12 public schools were supposedly not doing the job that was needed to give the United States the competitive edge it needed to remain the world's economic power. In particular, the report stated that "education systems in the United States tend to give disadvantaged and low-achieving students a watered down curriculum and place them in larger classes taught by less qualified teachers" which the report claimed was "exactly the opposite of the educational practices of high-performing districts."[55]

The report, however, was aware of the critics, who to this day understand the profound, debilitating effects of poverty on the lives and educational well-being of students. For this reason the report went out of its way to marginalize the impact of poverty on the educational attainment of children, arguing that the United States really did not have as many children living below the poverty level compared to some other more high-performing countries, and the only reason children living in poverty within the United States did poorly was "because its education system does a particularly poor job supporting its students and equalizing learning outcomes." Furthermore, according to the report, America really did not have any more diversity than did other countries that were performing better. The report rationalized this bizarre and illogical statement by explaining the fact that Singapore, with high PISA scores, had "three major ethnic groups" and "three-fourths of Singapore's population is Chinese, but almost a quarter is Malay or Indian." Of course, this is a far cry from the diversity seen in the United States. But what is perhaps even more bizarre and perhaps the height of educational and social chicanery, the report stated, "like the United States, Singapore experienced serious ethnic strife in the 1960s." And making sure that all its bases were covered in its quest to radically change America's entire system of education, the report also proclaimed that even America's better educated students from wealthier communities were doing poorly. So in reality, no one in the United States was getting a good education, which was why America needed new common core standards internationally benchmarked.[56]

What is perhaps the most troubling part of the December 2008 report is that it argued that somehow America's education system was so poor that pharmaceutical companies "such as Merck, Eli Lilly, and Johnson and Johnson [were] relying on India and China not only for manufacturing and clinical trials, but also for advanced research and development. As a result, scientists in those countries [were] rapidly increasing their ability to innovate and create their own intellectual property; the global share of pharmaceutical patent applications originating in India and China increased fourfold from 1995 to 2006."[57] It seems that in spite of the fact that India and China did not have generally agreed upon world-class universities, as we have already seen, somehow they were good enough for the pharmaceutical companies to use them to create drugs and impact the health and well-being of Americans.

Of course, another question that needs to be asked is: "Were these countries really producing better scientists or were they countries that produced a cheaper work force?" It also seems that for pharmaceutical companies it was a positive when India and China made their populations, many of whom were poor and illiterate, open to increased clinical trials! Of course, it can be easily argued that one reason this was appealing to the pharmaceutical companies was because India and China, for example, did not have the governmental policies in place designed to protect its citizens.[58] And in spite of China's supposedly vaunted scientific expertise, as the *China Daily/U.S.A* would report in 2014, "many Chinese companies [involved in the pharmaceutical industry] do research in American laboratories."[59] But most troubling of all is that even though China in 2014 would be relying on the expertise of American scientists to create pharmaceuticals, John P. Clark, Pfizer's chief security officer, would warn, "China is the source of some of the largest counterfeit manufacturing operations that we find globally."[60]

Nevertheless, in 2008 for all of the above reasons and more, Achieve, the NGA, and the CCSSO called for a course of action that consisted of the following five components:

1. Upgrade state standards by adopting a common core of internationally benchmarked standards for math and language arts for grades K-12.
2. Leverage states' collective influence to ensure that textbooks, digital media, **curricula** [emphasis added], and assessments are aligned to internationally benchmarked standards.

3. Revise state policies for recruiting, preparing, developing, and supporting teachers and school leaders to reflect human capital practices of top performing nations and states around the world.
4. Hold schools and systems accountable through monitoring, interventions, and support to ensure consistently high performance, drawing upon international best practices.
5. Measure state-led education performance globally by examining student achievement and attainment in an international context to ensure that, over time, students are receiving what they need to compete in the 21st century economy.[61]

The CCSS website proclaims, "The state-led effort to develop the Common Core State Standards was launched in 2009 by state leaders, including governors and state commissioners of education from 48 states, two territories and the District of Columbia, through their membership in the National Governors Association Center for Best Practices (NGA Center) and the Council of Chief State School Officers (CCSSO). State school chiefs and governors recognized the value of consistent, real-world learning goals and launched this effort to ensure all students, regardless of where they live, are graduating high school prepared for college, career, and life."[62] On paper this might be considered the official gunshot that started the CCSS and America's education race to the top. However, the official 2009 launch now can be clearly seen as a mere formality. Since at least 2001, and it might well be argued even before that year, an elaborate strategy had been employed to actually get what corporate and gubernatorial CEOs wanted all along. Something that a federal policy like NCLB, which was actually a federally reauthorized ESEA, could never give them—a nationally agreed upon set of Common Core State Standards and common assessments. But still, the federal government and the DOE needed to steer clear of any direct involvement that might infer any illegal trespass into creating a national curriculum. This was strictly forbidden by law. To make sure that all states, and by extension, all public schools within those states were on board the Common Core State Standards express, a slick and innovative approach was needed. What was needed was a carrot and stick approach that avoided federal education reform legalities but would also ensure that the goals of Achieve and its allies would be realized. Stepping up to this challenge would be the Obama administration and its newly appointed Secretary of Education Arne Duncan, with his marching orders already clearly in place.

CHAPTER 8

THE CCSS: SYSTEMIC EDUCATION REFORM WRIT LARGE

"Obama found the sweet spot with Arne Duncan," said Susan Traiman, director of educational policy at the Business Roundtable. "Both camps will be O.K. with the pick!"[1] President Obama's appointment of Arne Duncan as secretary of the DOE was certainly masterful given the education reform climate in the United States at the end of the George W. Bush administration. Two avenues of systemic education reform existed that ran parallel to each other on the eve of the Obama administration. One avenue was lined with the federal laws primarily associated with the reauthorization of ESEA as NCLB. The other avenue was populated by the organizations operating within the Deep State, which reflected the "third way" of governance that had been operating since President Clinton's administration. Clinton's third way ushered in an era in which a bipartisan spirit could be created around privatization, deregulation, and the free market that simultaneously provided the environment needed for increased corporate influence on public policy issues.[2] Although the Democrats and Republicans would remain politically polarized around many issues, on education, they had been generally united. As corporate dollars flooded the education arena, this unity has only solidified, one reason being because those who provide the biggest bucks for education reform initiatives often freely provide campaign contributions to candidates on both sides of the political spectrum.[3]

Diane Ravitch asserts that Arne Duncan's appointment as secretary of the DOE was a calculated move to appease the business community that wanted a "'real' reformer who supported testing, accountability, and choice." Linda Darling-Hammond, Obama's lead education policy advisor during his presidential transition, on the other hand, made corporate leaders nervous. She was considered too cozy with teachers' unions, too pro-teacher, and too critical of Teach for America, the darling of nontraditional teacher program advocates.[4] Duncan, however, personified the "real" reformer for proponents of systemic education reform.

Duncan's appointment was noteworthy for several reasons. As a child, he attended the Chicago Lab School, an elite private school located at the University of Chicago where Duncan's father was employed as a professor of psychology. The Chicago Lab School was founded by John Dewey, the father of progressive education, who has historically been excoriated by conservative education critics. Duncan benefited greatly from his progressive education and went on to graduate from Harvard University in 1987 with a degree in sociology. After graduating from Harvard, he spent several years playing professional basketball in Australia. In 1992, Duncan returned to Chicago and ran the Ariel Education Initiative, a nonprofit education foundation.[5] Duncan went to work for the Chicago Public School (CPS) system in 1998, first serving as the director of the district's magnet schools and later in 2000 as the deputy chief of staff of the school system.[6] When Paul Vallas resigned as the CEO of CPS in 2001, Mayor Richard Daley appointed Duncan as his successor. When Duncan was appointed secretary of the DOE by Obama, he was credited as being "the longest-serving big-city education superintendent in the country."[7]

President Obama praised Duncan's success in Chicago, beaming, "In just seven years, he's boosted elementary test scores here in Chicago from 38 percent of students meeting the standards to 67 percent." Obama went on to add, "The dropout rate has gone down every year he's been in charge."[8] Duncan's successes in reforming Chicago's public schools, however, would be challenged by his critics. According to Valerie Strauss, "The closing and reopening of schools was a signature initiative of Duncan's when he ran Chicago's schools."[9] His policies in Chicago have been criticized as disruptive to the lives of many children and teachers who would be required to reapply for their jobs once a school was closed. One of the CPS's signature programs, Renaissance 2010, a program that closed low-performing schools in order to "turn them around" by replacing staff and/or outsourcing management to a private firm, was hailed by Obama as proof of Duncan's prowess as an education reformer.[10]

Much like Rod Paige's "Texas Miracle," however, Duncan's innovative reform methods have over time proven to be less than successful. The three schools that helped "launch Duncan's signature Renaissance 2010 initiative" would, according to Becky Vevea, by 2013 be experiencing difficulties and become the focus of further scrutiny and intervention by the CPS.[11] One of these schools, Dodge Renaissance Academy, was the site chosen by President-elect Obama to announce his selection of Duncan as secretary of Education in 2008. Before being reopened as the Dodge Renaissance Academy, Dodge Elementary School was closed by Duncan in 2002 because of chronically low test scores. For the following school year its students were moved to another school. When the school reopened, it was under the management of the Academy for Urban School Leadership (AUSL), a nonprofit organization that currently manages 29 Chicago public schools and specializes in "turning around" chronically low-performing schools. Noteworthy is the fact that AUSL, while technically managing public schools and therefore receiving tax dollars, is highly funded through donors such as the Bill and Melinda Gates Foundation, Boeing, The Chicago Community Trust, The Michael and Susan Dell Foundation, and the NewSchools Venture Fund.[12]

By 2013, Chicago would announce the closing of 50 public schools in what Strauss called the "largest mass school closing in U.S. history."[13] As a result, parents staged "sit-ins" at schools targeted for closure and organized rallies, accusing Mayor Rahm Emmanuel of purposely targeting schools within black neighborhoods for closure in order to open more charter schools. "Ching, ching, that means money!" angrily declared one parent. She went on to say, "You have bullied us long enough!"[14] While all this was going on, Emanuel's children were attending the Chicago Lab School, the same progressive school a young Arne Duncan attended.[15]

The charter school movement has exploded in the years since Duncan took his formula for school reform to Washington DC. The education reform initiatives set in motion in Chicago by Duncan have become increasingly common across the country in urban areas such as New Orleans, Philadelphia, New York City, Washington DC, and Detroit.[16] A pattern is emerging in which public schools are closed and converted to charter schools, which in turn may be closed or taken over by another charter school operator. Public schools find themselves "co-occupied" by charter schools and their resources diverted to charters.[17] For those who envisioned systemic education reform as a way to "make a dime," the nationalizing of Arne Duncan's modus operandi of education reform was definitely a boon for their bottom line.

Although ESEA had not been reauthorized since 2001, it would be placed on the back burner by the Obama administration. There were more important issues to be dealt with. In particular, the American economy was on the verge of collapse. States were forced to tighten their belts, making major budget cuts across the board. In 2013, the impact of the 2008 recession was still being felt at the state level, particularly in the area of education. According to the Center on Budget and Policy Priorities, in 2013, 35 states "had K-12 funding that was below pre-recession levels when adjusted for inflation."[18]

Arne Duncan's Perfect Storm

President Obama's reaction to the economic recession he inherited was swift. On February 17, 2009, he signed into law the American Recovery and Reinvestment Act (ARRA). The purpose of the ARRA was to provide needed and immediate stimulus to the floundering economy. The entire federal stimulus package provided over $830 billion over a ten-year period to sectors of the economy most impacted by the recession. The federal DOE received $4.35 billion from the ARRA.[19] This wellspring of federal funds dramatically altered the role of the DOE because the discretionary funds provided through the ARRA would be used to implement the Race to the Top (RTTT) program.[20] During the press conference announcing RTTT on July 24, 2009, Arne Duncan proclaimed:

> From its inception in 1980 [the DOE] has traditionally been a compliance-driven agency. For most of its existence, the department has only had modest discretionary funds available for reform and innovation—and a limited ability to push for better outcomes. That's about to change. The $4.35 billion dollar Race to the Top program that we are unveiling today is a once-in-a-lifetime opportunity for the federal government to create incentives for far-reaching improvement in our nation's schools. Since the education department was created in 1980, eight of my predecessors have stood here. They fought to improve our schools, too. But none of them had the resources to encourage innovation that we have today.
>
> In fact, if you take all of the discretionary money for reform that every one of my predecessors had and then add it all together for the last 29 years in a row—it's still a much smaller money pot for reform than the $4.35 billion Race to the Top fund that we are announcing today.[21]

For Duncan, the recession had created the "perfect storm for reform."[22] "For the first time," the DOE had "the resources at the federal level to drive reform."[23]

RTTT discretionary funds were exactly what systemic education reformers needed most. Unfettered by ESEA restrictions or oversight, these funds could be mined more easily by private industry. By the time the RTTT program was announced, venture capitalists were already lined up to take advantage of Duncan's "money pot," and had a strong ally already in place at the DOE. In May 2009, Duncan had appointed Joanne Weiss to lead the development of the RTTT program and serve as its director.[24] Weiss had secured her credentials to oversee the $4.35 billion RTTT budget by working for the NewSchools Venture Fund for eight years. NewSchools was created in 1998, linking venture capitalists with entrepreneurs seeking to implement innovative ideas in education. Weiss's appointment to oversee RTTT was also a coup for *Friedmanomic* free market devotees. The economic recession had created the requisite crisis, and, not without a little irony, big government had provided a ready bundle of capital to enable the free market to swoop in and re-create a school system ripe for the pickings.

The NewSchools Venture Fund continues to provide a match.com service to marry venture capitalists with groups ready to start charter schools, sell education technology, provide consulting, and have the ready answer for schools on the verge of being shut down for failing to meet NCLB mandates. The NewSchools's website has a link for education entrepreneurs that spotlights the individuals and groups who were able to use the organization to find the right "match" with venture capitalists who would invest in their ideas. NewSchools provides impressive lists of possible investors for nonprofit or for-profit ventures, as well as links to consultants and resources to help individuals "pitch" their ideas.[25] Joanne Weiss was a lead player in NewSchools Venture Fund, and that's who Arne Duncan chose to oversee the $4.35 billion RTTT program.

Instead of Race to the Top, the Obama administration's education reform initiative could well have been called "Race to the Trough." While the average citizen may have heard the president's statements announcing the RTTT program in July 2009 as a standard run of the mill press release, corporate America heard an open invitation. For example, Obama stated that RTTT education reform "will take business leaders asking what they can do to invest in education in their communities."[26] And if the business leaders weren't quite sure how to cash in on RTTT funds, the president explained that he had "encouraged states to lift caps on the number of charter schools that are allowed."[27] And then, in the true spirit of the free market, the president made sure to explain that RTTT funds were competitive and states that had fewer or no limits on charter schools had a better chance to get these funds.

The president also gave a nod to the tech industry, letting them know that he wasn't leaving them out, stating, "And businesses can follow the examples of Intel and Microsoft by developing the software tools and cutting-edge technologies that prepare today's students to be tomorrow's teachers." And there were other opportunities as well. "Thoughtful assessments" needed to be developed as well as electronic data storage and reporting systems.[28]

What was the role of teachers in RTTT? Their role was absolutely essential. States would have to demonstrate that its teachers' effectiveness was based primarily on the test scores of the students they taught. President Obama declared, "Any state that makes it unlawful to link student progress to teacher evaluations will have to change its ways if it wants to compete for a [RTTT] grant."[29] So while the business community would see RTTT as an amazing opportunity, for teachers, RTTT reflected a tightening of the noose that had already been put in place with NCLB. And teachers who taught in low-performing, high-poverty schools in urban and rural areas would be doubly impacted. Under NCLB, which would remain in place, persistent low test scores could result in the closing of their schools and/or the replacement of all teachers. With RTTT, teacher evaluations would now be directly linked with their students' test scores. With all the existing research demonstrating the correlation between high poverty and low academic achievement, however, one has to wonder how this could possibly incentivize teachers to seek employment in high-needs areas. But RTTT proposed a solution for that as well, requiring states to "expand preparation and credentialing options and programs" for producing effective teachers.[30] Clearly, traditional colleges of education that were producing certified teachers were inadequate. Programs like Teach for America would, therefore, also benefit greatly from Obama's education reform initiative.

Arguably, the various stakeholders who would be affected by the RTTT initiative perceived the announcement in very different ways. Governors and state officials would envision an influx of cash that would bolster states' economies and basically keep the school doors open. Corporate America would envision a way to make a lot of money in the education sector through charter school ventures, educational technology, assessment development, and numerous other schemes for providing resources within the educational arena. Teachers, on the other hand, would understand that their professional livelihood would become inextricably linked to standardized test scores.

The RTTT program focuses on four core education reform areas:

1. Adopting standards and assessments that prepare students to succeed in college and the workplace and compete in the global economy;
2. Building data systems that measure student growth and success, and inform teachers and principals about how they can improve instruction;
3. Recruiting, developing, rewarding, and retaining effective teachers and principals, especially where they are needed most; and
4. Turning around our lowest-achieving schools.[31]

Each of these four core areas would prove to be a quagmire that deepened with each year of RTTT implementation. For example, while many American citizens, and in particular many parents, by 2014 would express their consternation over the CCSS and related assessments, each of these four areas would, in fact, serve to provide a feeding frenzy for free market entrepreneurs and, at the same time, serve as a weapon for undermining and destroying the public school system.

RTTT and CCSS

While RTTT would later become directly linked to the CCSS, in its earliest days, President Obama and Secretary Duncan referred to academic standards in more generic terms. For example, Obama simply called for a set of "rigorous and challenging standards."[32] Duncan, however, was a little more specific, describing a set of "common, internationally-benchmarked K-12 standards."[33] The RTTT grant application further extended the definition of what the DOE expected of states as they developed standards, stating that "the common set of K-12 standards means a set of content standards that define what students must know and be able to do and that are substantially identical across all States in a consortium."[34] In November 2009, therefore, when the RTTT grant application was announced, the language did not seem to indicate any demand that states were required to adopt the CCSS.

What was not made clear to most American citizens, however, was that the CCSS were already being written by a team that had been formed by Achieve. The Deep State already had a well-articulated systemic education reform initiative in place and they had not missed a step along the way. The federal government, operating in the public arena, carefully orchestrated the presentation of education policy to the American citizens. However, they withheld any disclosure to the public that education policy was actually being made in the private sector. Therefore, it is no wonder that within a few short years, when RTTT was fully in place and corporate America's influence could be felt, the American public would become alarmed and begin to resist federal intrusion in education policy.

In case there was any misunderstanding, however, regarding the intentions of the DOE to fully implement a national set of standards, Duncan and the Obama administration would clarify the message by mid-2011 with the release of the updated ESEA Flexibility guidelines. States seeking waivers from NCLB mandates were required to demonstrate that they were, indeed, implementing all the mandates outlined in the RTTT program. However, now the language shifted from discussions of state educational standards common within a consortium of states to more specific language. The DOE was very clear in their expectations regarding the adoption of standards in order to qualify for the much needed waivers, stating: "Over the past few years, Governors and Chief State School Officers have developed and adopted rigorous academic content standards to prepare all students for success in college and careers in the 21st century. . . . To support States in continuing the work of transitioning students, teachers, and schools to a system aligned to college and career ready expectations, this flexibility would remove obstacles that hinder that work."[35]

Writing the CCSS: Never Let a Crisis Go to Waste

The CCSS website declares that "the state-led effort to develop the Common Core State Standards was launched in 2009 by state leaders, including governors and state commissioners of education from 48 states, two territories and the District of Columbia, through their membership in the National Governors Association Center for Best Practices (NGA Center) and the Council of Chief State School Officers (CCSSO)."[36] These are, however, carefully chosen words since we now know this broad education reform effort is much more accurately described as a long-evolving example of government and corporate mutualism. The creation of national standards was simply another step in the process of systemically reforming education within the third way of Deep State governance.[37]

By 2009, Achieve had already been collaborating with gubernatorial and corporate CEO's in spearheading the creation of national standards. In 1998, the same year Weiss's organization, NewSchools

Venture Fund, was created, Achieve had already begun its Academic Standards and Assessments Benchmarking Pilot Project. Corporate funding had certainly also fortified and invigorated Achieve's education reform efforts along the way.[38] Bill Gates and his foundation, for example, had provided tens of millions of dollars to Achieve, as well as the NGA, CCSSO, and Student Achievement Partners.[39]

At an April 2009 meeting in Chicago, the NGA, CCSSO, and their education policy advisors officially discussed the creation of the CCSS initiative, a meeting that now seems to have been nothing more than an exercise in formality. The timeline found on the CCSS website explains that the 2009 meeting resulted in the NGA and CCSSO inviting states to participate, and, based on the interest of the states, work began to develop the CCSS. A better way to understand the CCSS developmental process, however, is to actually think of the April 2009 meeting as the final push to an education reform initiative that was long in the making. During the development process of the CCSS, the standards would be divided into two categories that reflected a two-stage process. **During Stage 1**, general college- and career-readiness standards (CCRS) would be developed that addressed what students are expected to know and understand by the time they had graduated from high school. The CCRS (stage 1) were standards largely based on the American Diploma Project. **During Stage 2**, more specific grade-by-grade "K-12 standards, which address expectations for elementary school through high school" would be created.[40]

Although it is rather difficult, if not impossible, to get a detailed timeline as to the real discussions that took place regarding the creation of the CCSS among its writers and collaborators, in May 2009, a Development Work Group was formed that began the final push to develop college- and career- readiness standards (CCRS). Following that work, an initial Feedback Group would be given the first draft of the CCRS for review. At the time, however, the list of individuals who made up these groups was secret, which naturally caused suspicion.[41]

In July 2009, the NGA Center and CCSSO, under increasing public pressure, finally announced the "names of the experts serving on the Common Core State Standards Development Work Group and Feedback Group."[42] By that month, however, it seems that the initial work of both of these work groups had been completed. Unfortunately, not all members of America's supposedly democratic press were all that concerned about the secretive process that had taken place prior to the announcement of these groups. For example, Anthony Cody pointed out on July 6, 2009, that the *San Francisco Chronicle* had written "that secrecy in this project is . . . a wise decision." As Cody went on to explain, the newspaper felt that "a truly open process would result in the experts being lobbied by countless interest groups, and—given the still-controversial nature of the standards—it could torpedo the plan altogether." Cody's consternation over this statement was clear when he caustically quipped, "Heaven forbid 'interest groups' such as teachers, parents, and students should be given the opportunity to muck up these standards."[43]

CCRS Development Work Group and Feedback Group

The CCRS Development Work Group was made up of two subgroups, mathematics and English language arts (ELA). When the makeup of the CCRS Work Group was revealed, there were 15 members on the mathematics subgroup and 14 members on the ELA subgroup. However, five members were on both subgroups, so, in fact, only a total of 24 different people were on the Development Work Group that would initially decide what it would mean to be properly educated after going through America's K-12 public education system. Of the 24 different members on both groups, 16 represented Achieve, ACT, Inc., or the College Board.

Two other members, David Coleman and Jason Zimba, were listed as connected to Student Achievement Partners (SAP). According to Coleman, one of 2007 founders of the company, SAP is an "organization that assembles leading thinkers and researchers to design actions to substantially improve student achievement."[44] The SAP website also points out that Zimba and Susan Pimentel (ADP architect) were cofounders of the company, and all three are now credited with being the lead writers of the CCSS. After the CCSS became finalized, SAP would be at the education reform money-trough, for example, creating professional development modules aligned with the CCSS. One of the things that causes concern among CCSS critics is that these writers had no real full-time K-12 teaching experience or advanced knowledge about child development. SAP would become connected at the hip with large corporate foundations such as the GE Foundation and the Bill and Melinda Gates Foundation. For example, in 2012, SAP would receive an $18 million grant from GE and two grants worth 6.5 million from Gates.[45]

Two members of this CCSS Work Group worked for America's Choice at the time. The company describes itself as follows: "America's Choice provides school designs and instructional systems to help low performing schools raise their performance. America's

Choice partners with states, districts, and schools to deliver solutions to improve results for all students by providing high-quality materials, professional development, and technical assistance that bring increased rigor to instructional programs."[46] On August 3, 2010, just two months after the final version of the CCSS was released, the Pearson Group acquired America's Choice.[47]

The CCRS Development Feedback Group would consist of two subgroups, with 19 members on the mathematics subgroup and 18 on the ELA subgroup. There was only one real K-12 teacher on these two subgroups, a math teacher from a Virginia Middle School. Overwhelmingly, these two subgroups were made up of university professors still practicing in higher education, although the now-familiar Chester Finn had somehow been appointed to the ELA group.

THE CCSS VALIDATION COMMITTEE

On September 24, 2009, an announcement available on the NGA website states, "The NGA Center and CCSSO today released the names of the members of the Validation Committee (VC) for the Common Core State Standards Initiative (CCSSI)." The report, "Reaching Higher: The Common Core State Standards Validation Committee," published in June 2010 by the NGA added a bit more clarity to the creation of this committee and the period of time it began initially working when the report explained, "The VC (Validation Committee) was appointed in September 2009, and first met in Washington, D.C., in December 2009."[48] The September 24 announcement stated that this 29 member committee would be "immediately tasked with reviewing and verifying the standards development process and the resulting evidence-based college- and career-readiness standards." It was explained that "the standards are intended to be research and evidence-based, aligned with college and workforce training expectations, reflective of rigorous content and skills, and internationally benchmarked." One of the most important things to keep in mind is that according to the NGA Center and CCSSO, the essential task of the committee members was to "validate the sufficiency of the evidence supporting each college- and career-readiness standard." The announcement went on to explain that each member of the committee would be "asked to determine whether each standard has sufficient evidence to warrant its inclusion."[49]

According to a statement by the NGA and CCSSO, however, "A draft of the common core standards (CCRS-stage 1) was available for public comment between September 21 and October 21, 2009."

Within this statement, the NGA and CCSSO explained that after the initial two stages were complete "a validation committee **provides** [emphasis added] advice to the entire process and the products of the initiative."[50] It seems, therefore, as though the public might have been given a product to comment upon even before the VC had completed their initial work regarding the CCRS. At least three simple questions can be logically asked to help clarify what actually happened, therefore: (1) Was the draft of the CCRS (stage 1) that was put forth for public comment actually validated by the VC? (2) Had the VC, established in September 2009, been able to work so rapidly to validate the initial CCRS so that all the VC comments and suggestions could be then properly incorporated into the CCRS in time for a September 21 release? And (3) Was the VC actually envisioned by the creators of the CCSS as a rubber stamp group, whose comments, if given serious consideration, might only slow down the process of creating the CCSS? These questions, and many more, need to be answered. Nevertheless, without further clarification and answers to questions such as these, critics of the CCSS can make a valid claim that the creation of the Common Core was a hasty process moving forward at breakneck speed in order to take advantage of the economic crisis that was impacting America so that America's public school system could become another drop in a bucket of free market adventurism.

K-12 Standards Work and Feedback Groups

On November 10, 2009, the NGA Center and CCSSO announced the individuals who would develop the K-12 standards for ELA/literacy and mathematics as part of stage 2.[51] However, these individuals had been working on these K-12 standards since at least August 2009. This apparently happened after the "career and readiness standards Work Groups" (CCRS, stage 1) had finished their initial work in July 2009, but well before the Validation Committee was formed and actually "validated" the CCRS upon which the K-12 standards were to be based. The K-12 Work Group would write what would turn out to be the larger of the two parts (stages 1 and 2). What is interesting, in other words, is that in September 2009, the VC was formed and then began their work of "validating" the CCRS (stage 1)—but at the same time the K-12 group was working on specific grade-by-grade standards. On the face of it, this seems problematic, since it would seem logical that before work was begun regarding specific

K-12 grade-by-grade standards, the first stage (CCRS) needed to be first validated in order to have a "valid" footing upon which to base the K-12 standards. Apparently, however, when the VC began "validating" CCRS stage 1 in September 2009, the K-12 group was already working on their "stage 2" K-12 standards, in spite of the fact that the "stage 1" CCRS had not been validated.

Clearly, the stage 2 K-12 group had a large task to perform. The stage 1 CCRS had been developed in only three months. The NGA claimed that the specific K-12 standards "also will be research and evidenced-based, aligned with college and workforce program expectations, reflective of rigorous content [which on the face of it seems to infer that these standards require a specific curriculum] and skills and internationally benchmarked." Again, this stage 2 process seems to have begun in August 2009, after stage one was initially completed but without validation.

In November 2009, the CCRS (stage 1) were incorporated into the K-12 Standards (stage 2). This combined package became known as the "K-12 grade by grade college and career readiness standards."[52] By December 2009, the VC had already been given a draft of the now combined package, and had been able to swiftly provide edits and feedback to this draft.[53] If this was the case, then the public deserves a good deal more information on how these large K-12 Work Groups and the VC were able to so quickly accomplish their task. For example, who was actually writing the standards and how did the rest of the group go about contributing to the task? Were these standards really being written in stages (one follows the other)—or did they actually become simultaneously created by the time the VC entered the picture in September 2009? It seems that the latter is true, however, and that there was a juggling act going on between writing groups and the VC.

The process of writing the CCSS appears to have been an exercise in obfuscation. Very importantly, two things are certain. This complex writing process regarding a profound educational issue was happening at breakneck speed, and, as we will see, would eventually be severely criticized by some members of the VC as well as others. However, perhaps Rahm Emanuel in 2008 when he was chief of staff for President-elect Obama had already explained the approach that was being taken by the writers of the CCSS when America was in the midst of its worst economic crisis since the Great Depression. In an address before the *Wall Street Journal* CEO Counsel, Emanuel, analyzing the state of America and taking a page from the *Friedmanomics* playbook as far as how this crisis applied to different aspects of society including education, proclaimed, "Never let a serious crisis go to waste. And what I mean by that, it's an opportunity to do things you think you could not do before."[54]

In January 2010, one short month after the VC gave their insights regarding K-12 standards that were supposedly seriously considered, in a first-rate example of corporate efficiency, a draft was ready to be reviewed for further feedback by individual groups. One month after this, in February 2010, another newly "revised version of the K-12 standards" was quickly trotted out and "distributed to the states." Then in March 2010, the states had worked in such a thorough and efficient manner that allowed for another new draft to be written and approved for public scrutiny. In fact, this draft was made available online to the public for comment on March 10, 2010.[55]

According to the NGA, CCSSO, and writers of the CCSS, ten thousand comments were received as a result of the March 2010 posting. On June 2, 2010, the NGA and CCSSO announced the final completion of the CCSS. Apparently, in only three months, all of the comments had been seriously considered, rejected, accepted, and used to properly inform the final product. While one might question the swiftness of the process, the following statement within the summary report of "CCSS public comments" suggests the writers of the CCSS viewed these public comments rather dismissingly:

> On March 10, 2010, a draft of the K-12 standards was posted online for public feedback. This offered the public an opportunity to provide input on the draft standards to the writing teams. **By design** [emphasis added], this was not a scientific, representative survey, and the results are **not necessarily predictive of general public opinion** [emphasis added]."[56]

It seems that in retrospect, truer words were never spoken. While everything that the creators of the CCSS did to develop these standards was supposedly based on sound scientific research and evidence-based findings, this same standard could not be trusted to be applied to the insights, beliefs, and will of the American public when it came to reforming their public schools. For CCSS creators, the regular citizen could just not be trusted to do the right thing when it came to education. In spite of all these supposedly "bottom up" systemic education reform efforts, this approach to education reform seemed to be rather unsuccessful if one believes that it was intended to be a truly democratic process when reforming America's public schools, since a 2013 PDK/Gallup poll indicated that 62 percent of the American public still knew nothing about the CCSS.[57]

THE VALIDATION COMMITTEE AND THE MINORITY DISSENT

The June 2010 report "Reaching Higher: The Common Core Validation Committee" would set off a firestorm that continues to this day. Somehow the number of individuals on the original VC had shrunk from 29 to 24. In fact, five members of the VC refused to sign off on the CCSS final draft. The five were Alfinio Flores from the University of Delaware; R. James Milgram, emeritus professor at Stanford University; Sandra Stotsky, endowed chair in Teacher Quality at the University of Arkansas's Department of Education Reform; Dylan William, director, Learning and Teaching Research Center at the Education Testing Service; and Barry McGaw, professor and director at Melbourne Education Research Institute, University of Melbourne, and director of education for OECD.[58] At this point, the most vocal validation committee dissenters have been Stotsky and Milgram.

For example, on September 9, 2013, at a conference at the University of Notre Dame, Stotsky claimed that the CCRS (stage 1) "Feed Back Group members' suggestions were frequently ignored, according to one English professor on this group, without explanation." But what is perhaps most troubling, Stotsky explains that "in theory, the Validation Committee should have been the fail-safe mechanism for the standards." However, according to Stotsky, "It quickly became clear that the VC existed as window-dressing—to rubber stamp, not improve, whatever standards were declared as college- and career-readiness and grade level standards."[59]

Not surprisingly, her comments would not go unchallenged by numerous supporters of the CCSS and would reflect the current turmoil over the standards that now rages in America. Just one example came from Michael Petrilli, a long-time supporter of the CCSS and executive vice-president for the Fordham Institute. Testifying before the Ohio House Education Committee in November 2013, he called Stotsky's criticism of the CCSS and its creation "Balderdash!"[60]

Stotsky would testify before a number of state legislative groups criticizing the CCSS and its creation. Her testimony in Wyoming, for example, reflects comments that are made in other states such as Ohio, Wisconsin, and Pennsylvania. Stotsky criticized the notion that the creation of these standards was state led, instead arguing that "it is by now well-known that three private organizations in Washington D.C. were in charge of the initiative—the National Governors Association (NGA), the Council for Chief State School Officers (CCSSO), and Achieve, Inc.—all heavily funded by another private organization, the Bill and Melinda Gates Foundation." She went on to explain that she did not believe that "the people who wrote the standards represent the relevant stakeholders. Nor were they qualified by experience to draft standards in English language arts and mathematics. And the Validation Committee that was created to put the seal of approval on the drafters' work was useless if not misleading, both in its membership and in the procedures they had to follow."[61]

Stotsky criticized the fact that most of the actual standards writers were connected to Achieve, ACT, Inc., the College Board, and America's Choice, a for-profit project of the National Center for Education and the Economy (NCEE). She went on to explain that in her mind "the absence of relevant professional credentials in the two grade-level standards-writing teams helps to explain the flaws in the two sets of standards these private organizations produced." She was also very critical because, in her words,

> the "lead" writers for the grade-level ELA standards, David Coleman and Susan Pimentel, had never taught reading or English in K-12 or at the college level. Neither has a doctorate in English, nor has either of them ever published serious work on K-12 curriculum and instruction. Neither has a reputation for literary scholarship or research in education; at the time they were appointed, they were virtually unknown to English educators and higher education faculty in rhetoric, speech, composition, or literary study."[62]

Stotsky did explain that "two of the lead grade-level standards-writers in mathematics had no K-12 teaching experience but did have relevant academic credentials for the subject." Jason Zimba was a physics professor at Bennington College at the time, while William McCallum was (and remains) a mathematics professor at the University of Arizona. The only member of this three-person team of lead writers with teaching experience, Phil Daro, had majored in English as an undergraduate; he was also on the staff of NCEE America's Choice. "None had ever developed K-12 mathematics standards before." Stotsky also explained that both she and Milgram were concerned with the mathematics standards since these standards really did not prepare students for STEM-related careers, something that Zimba would later confirm. What was also very troubling for her was that the VC members were required to sign an agreement to never discuss what had taken place at their meetings. For Stotsky, this lack of "sunshine" destroyed an important part of any democratic process. It is for all these reasons, and more, as her testimony indicated, that she could not sign off on the final draft of the CCSS.[63]

Milgram also shares Stotsky's views. Milgram, commenting in March 2014, observed that "a number of the people who led the (CCSS) writing project are now in very high positions. For example, one of them (David Coleman) is the head of the College Board, which controls a whole group of exams." Milgram has made his feelings known, arguing, "These people have not been very forthcoming. They've been very careful in what they say—and I don't think they have given the public any real idea of what's actually going on." He calls his experience in the creation of the CCSS a "weird odyssey into education." Milgram is also troubled by the gag order placed on the VC, and he is very troubled that the concerns of a rather significant percentage of the committee were not allowed to be made public in a minority report. When this happened, according to Milgram, "this allowed the claim that was made that everyone approved and they (the standards) are internationally benchmarked."[64]

Many other critics of the CCSS have also appeared since its creation, as any Internet search of the phrase "CCSS criticism" will confirm. The film "Building the Machine" created through the sponsorship of the Home School Defense Association, and easily accessed on the Internet, provides insight into CCSS criticisms. For example, Jim Stergois, executive director of the Pioneer Institute, explains that there was some public comment, but, in his view, "extensive public hearings and testimonials" did not happen. He feels that the list of comments "put forth by the writers of the CCSS" was "a very truncated list with vague general comments. There was no clear response to these comments. These kinds of things trouble me." Stergois also mentioned that when Massachusetts developed its academic standards that are considered quite excellent, it took a couple of years of numerous and intense public forums to finally arrive at a publicly agreed upon set of standards. Neil McCluskey, associate director of the Cato Institute for Educational Freedom states, "When you hear that the NGA and CCSSO did it—what the Common Core supporters will say is this shows states are doing it. And then this assumes what the NGA and CCSSO do, reflects the will of the people in states. That is an extremely tenuous assertion. First of all that assumes that when I vote for governor in my state, one of the things I'm thinking about is what's he going to do in the NGA."[65]

Andrew Hacker, professor emeritus in the Department of Political Science at Queens College pondered, "I'm trying to think of something analogous to this that slipped through so easily on a national basis - and I really can't. That's why I called it radical—it's a real change from the past." Ze-ev Wurman, a former DOE official under

George W. Bush, points out what he feels is the absurdity of claiming these standards can create a student mass that is both college **and** career ready. Wurman believes that no single set of standards that are measured by a single test can do this. The result will be standards either too high for "career readiness" after high school, or too low for college readiness.[66] This makes sense when one simply asks, "What kind of career is a student ready for armed with only a high school degree?" As an important aside, most of the countries that are being held up as having superior public education systems compared to the United States have at least a two-tiered education system; one track for students identified as heading to college versus another track that is vocational in nature.

Critics of the CCSS and its implementation are also now appearing among some members of Congress. In February 2014, Republican Congressman Jeff Duncan of South Carolina introduced H. Res. 476, which denounced "the use of federal coercion to lure states into adopting Common Core academic standards," and stressing "the importance of returning education to the states." Forty-two Republican House members signed on to Congressman Duncan's resolution. The congressman states, "Common Core is one of the most frequent concerns I hear from parents when I'm traveling across the district. Parents and teachers alike are alarmed by this top-down approach to education that wrongly ties education money for states to the adoption of academic standards that do not fully reflect the values of South Carolina. Beyond the most important constitutional issues with federal education standards, many education leaders have been raising concerns with the content of the standards themselves."[67]

Coleman, Pimentel, and Zimba: The Architect and the Lead Writers of the CCSS

David Coleman is now called the lead architect of the CCSS and also a lead writer for the ELA/literacy standards. He along with Zimba and Pimentel founded Student Achievement Partners (SAP), in 2007, and were in a very strategic position to advantageously become involved with the creation of the CCSS and the money to be had in multifaceted ways during its implementation, all in the name of positive systemic education reform. SAP explains that "it reserves no right to intellectual property, does not compete for federal, state or district contracts, and does not accept money from publishers." The company also proudly proclaims, "Student Achievement Partners' independence is essential to our work."[68] However, SAP does accept millions of dollars from corporate entities, which means that the company's independence is dependent on corporate interests.

Coleman was a product of the New York City public school system during the 1970s and 1980s when *A Nation at Risk* made education headlines. The educational foundation Coleman received in these New York City public schools enabled him to earn a BA in philosophy from Yale and a Rhode's Scholarship in 1991. In 1994, he was awarded a degree in English literature from Oxford and an advanced degree in ancient philosophy from Cambridge. One source explains that he intended to return to the United States and teach high school English, but instead became a consultant at McKinsey and Company,[69] a company that describes itself as a "global management consulting firm . . . and a trusted advisor to the world's leading businesses, governments, and institutions."[70] Another source, however, explains that "upon returning to New York, Coleman applied for a high school teaching position and was turned down."[71] Coleman would go on to cofound the Grow Network with Zimba, a company that provided testing assessment analysis for parents, teachers, and students, as well as learning guides for students. In 2005, McGraw-Hill acquired the Grow Network, and Coleman became the chief executive officer and cofounder of Grow Network/McGraw-Hill.[72]

Coleman, in his devotion to systemically reforming America's public school system, has been lauded for his education reform efforts by those who support the CCSS. Nevertheless, he has always been suspect for these same efforts by his critics and seems to have now become almost infamous after delivering the keynote address at the Institute for Learning (IFL) Senior Leadership Meeting in December 2011. Although he may have been making this statement "tongue-in-cheek" when he described the education reform efforts of his colleagues at SAP in the following manner, for his critics, "in jest, there was truth." Coleman stated, "All you need to know about us are a couple of things. One is we're comprised of that collection of unqualified people who were involved in developing the common standards. And our only qualification was our attention to and command of the evidence behind them."[73] Less than a year later, in October 2012, Coleman became the president of the College Board, the creators of the SAT.

Jason Zimba is the lead writer for the mathematics standards of the CCSS and has been a close associate of Coleman for quite some time. They met when both were Rhodes Scholars in England, Zimba studying mathematics and physics. Zimba's academic credentials are excellent. He holds a BA from Williams College with a double major in mathematics and astrophysics; an MSc in mathematics from Oxford; and a PhD in mathematical physics from the University of California at Berkeley. According to Achieve, "As a researcher, Dr. Zimba's work has spanned a range of fields, including astronomy, astrophysics, theoretical physics, philosophy of science, and pure mathematics. His academic awards include a Rhodes scholarship and a Majorana Prize for theoretical physics."[74]

Zimba is a dedicated supporter of the CCSS but has become embroiled with critics of the mathematics standards, in particular, VC members Milgram and Stotsky, and Ze-ev Wurman, a 2014 visiting scholar at the Hoover Institute and an expert in developing mathematics standards for the State of California. Critics became particularly concerned about the mathematics standards when Zimba was questioned by Stotsky at a meeting of the Massachusetts Board of Elementary and Secondary Education on March 23, 2010. Serious concerns about the mathematic standards intensified when Zimba confirmed that the "mathematics standards aren't designed to prepare students for STEM (science, technology, engineering, and math) studies," but also "that they're not designed to get a student into any selective college," even in non-STEM disciplines. During the meeting, Zimba explained, "The standards (for math) were a minimal definition of college readiness." These mathematics standards, according to Zimba, "were not for STEM."[75] This means these standards were not designed for students planning to go into STEM-related occupations, something Bill Gates had claimed was a major reason why the CCSS was needed in order to create engineers and scientists that could compete with those being produced in larger numbers from universities in countries like China and India. The debate over these mathematics standards continues.

Susan Pimentel holds a BS in early childhood education and a law degree from Cornell University. She has a long career in the world of education standards writing, cofounding Standards Work in 1991, as well as SAP in 2007. She is now vice-chair of the National Assessment Governing Board (NAGB), which is responsible for NAEP testing. After attaining her law degree, she entered the world of education reform when she began working with the Maryland state legislature. She was also a counselor for Lamar Alexander when he was secretary of education for George H. W. Bush before cofounding Standards Work. Standards Work has a long history connected to education reform efforts after the publication of *A Nation at Risk*, which included the promotion of America 2000.[76]

What is very fascinating, and for some very troubling, is that Coleman is now president of the College Board, which controls the creation of education tests like the SAT, and Pimentel is vice-chair of the NAGB Executive Committee, which controls NAEP testing. One can certainly speculate, with a good degree of confidence, that corporate and government education reformers are now well positioned to finally make the CCSS the "educational gorilla in the room" that could finally take complete control away from locally controlled public schools and dominate all aspects of education within the United States. This is something to which Representative Duncan and his congressional supporters might agree.

Chapter 9

CCSS: The Gorilla in the Room for Free Market Education Reform

While the CCSS is the essential component of the RTTT program, the assessments associated with them form the engine that gives the standards real power. Almost immediately upon publication of the standards and even prior to full implementation, CCSS assessments were being created and field tested across the United States. According to the Educational Testing Service's (ETS) K-12 Center, six multistate consortia were established to develop CCSS assessments.[1] At the top of the list is the Partnership for the Assessment of Readiness for College and Careers (PARCC) consortium and the Smarter Balanced Assessment Consortium. CCSS assessments were intended to be the antidote for problems resulting from the bubble-in, multiple-choice standardized tests that have dominated K-12 classrooms in recent decades. Newly developed CCSS assessments would be computer driven, requiring students to engage in a deeper analysis of texts, and include constructed responses in order to demonstrate critical-thinking skills.

Like every other aspect of RTTT, however, these assessments have proven to be highly problematic. CCSS test development has been financed through $330 million RTTT funds, with the Pearson Company awarded lucrative state contracts by states to administer the assessments.[2] However, no amount of public relations efforts or promotions have been effective in selling parents and schools on the worthiness of these assessments. Reports have emerged about the multitude of errors on the assessments and their developmental inappropriateness. As a result, parents across the United States have begun a grassroots "opt-out movement," refusing to allow their children to take the field tests being administered by PARCC and Smarter Balanced during the 2013–14 school year.[3] The "opt-out movement" arose as parents began questioning the CCSS in general and the curriculums that were being generated as a result of standards implementation. Anti-CCSS sentiment has created an unprecedented alliance among disparate groups against the CCSS. Some parents aligned with the conservative right decry the standards as liberal propaganda to indoctrinate children in the Marxist ideology that represents further encroachment of the federal government into the lives of American citizens. Other parents aligned with the progressive left see the CCSS as a one-size-fits-all approach to education that squeezes the arts out of the curriculum while being driven by high-stakes standardized testing under the influence of corporate-led school reformers.[4] These concerns remind one of Chester Finn's comment in 1997 when the Clinton administration proposed a plan for national testing. Finn had stated that "liberals . . . hate the word 'testing' and 'conservatives' . . . hate the word 'national.'"[5]

Criticisms of the CCSS from factions within both the political right and the political left are becoming a formidable force, however. A simple Internet search of "parents and anti-common core" reveals the myriad of blogs and Facebook pages devoted to parents fighting implementation of the CCSS and CCSS tests.[6] In New York, for example, one of the first states to adopt the CCSS and field test PARCC assessments, angry parents confronted education superintendent John King at an open forum that was intended to build consensus among parents in support of the standards. The meeting was so heated that King canceled future meetings.[7] As the firestorm grew across the state unabated, Arne Duncan issued a statement that would further fuel the fire, stating at a meeting of the Council of Chief State School Officers, "It's fascinating to me that some of the pushback is coming from, sort of, white suburban moms who—all of a sudden - their child isn't as brilliant as they thought they were and their school isn't quite as good as they thought they were."[8]

RTTT and Data Systems

According to Achieve, "A seamlessly integrated, accessible **P-20** [emphasis added] longitudinal data system with college and career readiness as its central driver should be a linchpin of any state's effort to maximize the impact of its RTTT strategy."[9] The concept of longitudinal data systems was not a new concept within the DOE, however. The department already had in place a grant program to facilitate the creation of statewide data systems with the authorization of the 2002 Educational Technical Assistance Act and began awarding grants to states in 2005.[10] RTTT opened the door, however, for private consulting groups, such as the Public Consulting Group (PCG), to profit from federal education reform.

PCG was established in 1986, providing a wide range of services for private and public entities. Within the public arena, the consulting firm has assisted state and local governments in analyzing policies and services that run the gamut from Medicaid to social services and public welfare. PCG's education division would be expanded to assist states trying to meet increased federal demands for standardized testing data management systems since implementation of NCLB. However, its involvement in the education system further expanded after RTTT implementation. According to its website, "PCG Education's school data systems are customized to target and solve your 'real world' education problems, from at-risk student identification to state and federal reporting."[11] By 2013, PCG was working with 22 state governments, providing consulting services on a range of issues from establishing longitudinal data systems to assisting in "turning around" failing schools. The consulting firm has important partners that also enable them to have a seat at the table when states seek assistance in meeting federal mandates. According to their website, PCG has four business partner organizations: (1) the Council of Chief State School Officers; (2) the National Literacy Project; (3) the Partnership for 21st Century Skills; and (4) Pearson Education.[12]

Other private consulting firms would enter the education data market as well. However, as the American citizenry became increasingly aware of intentions to harvest children's educational data beginning in preschool and extending throughout their college education, public alarm caused this burgeoning data-mining industry to hit the pause button. After all, federal laws are in place to protect students' privacy. In particular, the Family Educational Rights and Privacy Act (FERPA) has been in place since 1974 to protect students' privacy and to ensure that their records cannot be accessed by individuals without their parents' consent if the student is under 18 or student consent if they are over the age of 18.[13] FERPA presented a challenge for private consulting groups engaged in developing and maintaining large-scale longitudinal data systems because the law prohibited third parties from accessing confidential student information.

In December 2011, the DOE met this challenge by reinterpreting FERPA regulations to enable third parties to access personal student data. In February 2012, the Electronic Privacy Information

Center (EPIC) filed a lawsuit challenging the DOE's reinterpretation of FERPA, arguing that the federal government had exceeded its statutory authority. In September 2013, however, EPIC's lawsuit was dismissed because the court found that the organization did not "have standing to bring the claims asserted in the complaint." It became legal, therefore, for school districts and states to provide confidential student data to private third party consulting firms without the students' or parents' permission. And, most important, the DOE was able to reinterpret and amend FERPA without congressional approval.[14]

But even before EPIC's lawsuit was dismissed, the free market was prepared to take advantage of their access to the mother lode of student data ready to be mined, thanks to the newly created inBloom Inc. According to Stephanie Simon, writing for Reuters, inBloom resulted from a joint project of the Bill and Melinda Gates Foundation (which provided most of the funding), the Carnegie Corporation, and Amplify Education (a division of Rupert Murdoch's News Corp).[15] Working with school officials from several states, the group developed a database of student information ready to be harvested by private corporations. inBloom unveiled their innovation at the SXSWedu Conference they sponsored in Austin, Texas, in March 2013. Attendees at the conference were giddy with the prospect of having access to a wealth of data to use in marketing their wares. According to Simon, one attendee, a product manager for CompassLearning, proclaimed, "This is going to be a huge win for us." This was certainly not an understatement. In the span of three months, inBloom had already amassed a treasure trove of student data. Simon reported:

> In operation just three months, the database already holds files on millions of children identified by name, address and sometimes social security number. Learning disabilities are documented, test scores recorded, attendance noted. In some cases, the database tracks student hobbies, career goals, attitudes toward school—even homework completion.[16]

Of course, enthusiasm for inBloom's database was not shared by many, including parents. According to Simon, "While inBloom pledges to guard the data tightly, its own privacy policy states that it 'cannot guarantee the security of the information stored . . . or that the information will not be intercepted when it is being transmitted.'"[17] Upon learning about inBloom's database, parents began contacting their state officials with concerns about their children's privacy, and groups such as the American Civil Liberties Union and the Parent-Teacher

Association became involved in discussions about possible misuse of student data.

It became clear that the creation of longitudinal data systems was not merely useful as a way to assess the quality of teaching or the effectiveness of schools. For venture capitalists, inBloom provided a gold mine of information to use in the pursuit of profit. According to Simon, "The [education] sector is undeniably hot; technology startups aimed at K-12 schools attracted more than $425 million in venture capital last year" as reported by the NewSchools Venture Fund. In addition to the Gates Foundation's $100 million investment in the inBloom database, it also "pledged $70 million in grants to schools and companies to develop personalized learning tools."[18]

The Orwellian notion of a huge database containing all the personal and confidential data of every school child in America made available to private corporations was troubling to many. In fact, it violated American individualism and privacy much like the NSA scandal would do in 2013–14. The audacity of inBloom in compiling such a database was further compounded by the fact that, while the original nine states that provided student data were not charged a fee, according to the Education Action Network, the organization planned to charge school districts between $2 and $5 for the "privilege of participating in the student data collection scheme."[19]

As word spread about inBloom's intentions, however, thanks largely to the growing number of blogs and parent groups protesting RTTT policies, inBloom found themselves in an untenable position. By April 2014, they closed the doors of their company, issuing a public letter from inBloom's Chief Executive Officer, Iwan Streichenberger, which stated, "We have realized that this concept is still new, and building public acceptance for the solution will require more time and resources than anyone could have anticipated. Therefore, in full alignment with the inBloom Board of Directors and funders, I have made the decision to wind down the organization over the coming months."[20]

Power to the people! Of all the lessons learned along the path to the CCSS, this aspect of the RTTT initiative has been the most potent. While the federal government has been pushing the limits of its statutory power through the third way and the Deep State of education policy making, the federal government's acquiescence of control to the private sector has proven to be toxic. But when the corporate-owned and -controlled television media failed to expose inBloom's data-mining scheme, the blogosphere relentlessly pursued the story and parents, teachers, and a few school administrators continued the campaign to stop the exploitation of their children by private corporations. Americans fought back and they won the battle—at least with inBloom. That in itself is no small feat.

RTTT and Effective Teachers

For many educators, the election of Obama as president offered hope. During his presidential campaign he seemed to understand the detrimental impact of NCLB policies on the teaching profession. He hit all the right notes on the campaign trail. He was committed to early childhood education because he understood that a "world-class education" begins on the day a child is born and continues until the child graduates from college. And the key to closing the achievement gap is an investment in early childhood education. Obama pledged to fix the "broken promises of No Child Left Behind. . . . We all want high standards," said Obama on the campaign trail. "We all want a world class education;" and "we all want highly qualified teachers in the classroom."[21] Obama asserted, "Labeling a school and its students as failures one day and then throwing your hands up and walking away from them the next is wrong." He went on to declare, "And don't tell us that the only way to teach a child is to spend most of the year preparing him to fill in a few bubbles on a standardized test." This declaration won Obama applause and cheers from his supporters.[22] Obama seemed to be supportive of teachers and seemed to understand that they were as invested in the notion of education excellence as policy makers and proponents of education reform. He seemed to understand that the overemphasis on standardized testing was having a detrimental impact on education and that the achievement gap was not the result of teachers who don't care about their students.

After Obama was elected president and appointed Arne Duncan as secretary of the DOE, however, the message seemed to change, particularly with regard to teachers and the role of standardized testing in teacher accountability. His speech announcing the RTTT initiative sounded more like previous presidents who believed that teachers needed greater scrutiny, and the best way to determine the worth of a teacher was to examine the test scores of their students. Obama asserted, "We should use tests as just one part of a broader evaluation of teachers' performance." Nevertheless, he went on to say, "But let me be clear. Success should be judged by the results, and data is a powerful tool to determine results. We can't ignore facts. We can't ignore data." Thus, he further established the primacy of testing data in evaluating teachers when he warned, "Any state that makes it unlawful to link student progress to teacher evaluations will have to change its ways if it wants to compete for a [RTTT] grant."[23]

In addition to the stringent teacher accountability measures proposed by President Obama, RTTT also proposed a plan to attract other "highly qualified individuals" to the teaching market. States had to demonstrate that they provided alternate routes for teacher certification. Alternative routes for teacher certification would help ensure that teachers struggling to teach in urban and rural areas plagued by high poverty rates could be replaced by teachers certified through alternative routes.

The group that would most profoundly benefit from RTTT's mandate for alternative routes would be Teach for America (TFA). In 2008, the organization had nearly twenty-five thousand applicants. By 2012, that number had nearly doubled to forty-eight thousand five hundred, and in 2013 more than fifty-seven thousand college seniors applied to join the ranks of TFA teachers.[24] Less than 15 percent of TFA applicants are selected to enter the teaching profession for a two-year stint through this alternate route for teacher certification. TFA has become a formidable force and, thanks to the RTTT initiative, has experienced tremendous growth in the education arena. And thanks to millions of corporate and philanthropic dollars flowing into its coffers, TFA is thriving. For example, the organization has become a favored recipient of donations from organizations such as the Bill and Melinda Gates Foundation, the Broad Foundation, and the Walton Family Foundation. This reality prompted one former TFA teacher, Chad Sommer, to write, "Today, having completed the two-year program and seeing how it operates from inside, I'm convinced that TFA now serves as a critical component of the all-out-effort by corporate elites to privatize one of the last remaining public institutions of our country: our public schools."[25] Diane Ravitch writes, "We live in an age of public relations and perception. And the TFA brand is a winner."[26]

TFA presents a compelling story. The organization is the brainchild of Wendy Kopp who developed the idea while a student at Princeton University as her undergraduate thesis in 1989. The concept is elegantly simple and based on the zeitgeist in America that public schools were generally failing and in need of systemic reform and that, most important, there was a critical shortage of high-quality teachers, particularly in impoverished rural and urban communities. Kopp's thesis suggested a solution to the problem: Recruit some of the nation's top graduates to work for two years as teachers in high-needs school districts that were having difficulties recruiting certified teachers. TFA would be comparable to the Peace Corps and attract bright, well-educated students to perform community service in the poorest communities and schools across America. According to Ravitch, "Even before a single new teacher had entered a single classroom, major publications such as *The New York Times*, *Newsweek*, and *Time* lauded TFA, and corporations offered millions of dollars to launch the new program."[27]

Arguably, TFA's appeal is twofold. First, Wendy Kopp positions herself as a crusader following in the footsteps of civil rights leaders. For Kopp, her TFA idea was a germ that "exploded into a movement" and "magnetized thousands of people—including college students, experienced educators, and philanthropists."[28] Who could possibly criticize an organization that sends idealistic young Americans to serve in impoverished communities while foregoing lucrative careers in the business sector or earn MBAs and law degrees for two years? TFA recruits are hailed as noble, unselfish, and the best and the brightest. And many TFA recruits are just that. They are good people, wanting to do good work and make a difference in the lives of people less privileged than themselves. Some, however, may join the ranks of TFA teachers because they have not landed their first high-paying job right after college—a common phenomenon during the economic recession. TFA is, indeed, a good way to beef up resumes and graduate school applications. Nevertheless, for the most part, TFA applicants are "good souls" ready to embark on a two-year missionary journey into a world far different than the middle-class existence from which most come.

Second, TFA's appeal is also rooted in Kopp's own ideology regarding education, an ideology that mirrors the no-excuses policies of Bill Clinton and George W. Bush. According to Kopp, there is no need to address poverty in order to close the achievement gap. In her book, *A Chance to Make History*, she asserts that "many assumed that fixing education would require fixing poverty first."[29] According to Kopp, in the years since she began TFA, America had learned that it wasn't necessary to "fix poverty" in order to "dramatically improve educational outcomes for underprivileged students."[30] This declaration is music to the ears of conservatives who have cried foul at every attempt to positively intervene in the lives of impoverished Americans through federal initiatives since the days of Franklin Roosevelt's New Deal policies and Lyndon Johnson's War on Poverty policies. It also fits in nicely with the ideas of systemic education reformers who have promoted stringent accountability measures with standardized testing as the primary arbiter of student, teacher, and school success. President

Clinton's speech at Palisades in 1996 and George W. Bush's accusation that the education profession was promoting the "soft bigotry of low expectations" also aligned nicely with Kopp's way of thinking regarding the impact of poverty on children.

Ironically, TFA appeals to idealistic college students to participate in what she deems as a new civil rights struggle within low-income communities, but then positions poverty as inconsequential in improving academic achievement. This isn't to say that Kopp doesn't acknowledge that poverty has a devastating impact on the lives of families and children. However, she clearly posits that America doesn't need to "fix poverty"; instead, America needs to "fix schools." Ravitch, on the other hand, queries, "What civil rights leader would say that? What civil rights leader would assert that we can 'fix' the schools instead of improving jobs, health care, and housing?"[31]

If TFA has become the ideal model for RTTT's expectations for an alternate route to teacher certification, then what does their model look like? College graduates who are accepted into the TFA program receive five weeks of training during the summer before their first school year. During this five-week training session, TFA recruits work with K-12 students who have been assigned to attend summer school. TFA teachers also attend a series of professional development training sessions throughout the school year and are offered assistance by TFA staff members assigned to their region. Upon completion of their two-year commitment, "TFAers" are fully certified and have the same teaching credentials as graduates of four-year teaching programs from accredited colleges of education. Some TFAers stay in the teaching profession, but most do not. Some use their TFA experience to join the ranks of systemic education reform proponents and go on to open or manage charter schools. As a matter of fact, the founders of the Knowledge Is Power Program (KIPP), an early model of the charter schools that have proliferated across America, was founded by two TFA alums.[32] Other TFA alums go on to serve in influential positions within state governments. Michelle Rhee, for example, infamously ran the Washington DC school district before an investigation into allegations of cheating on standardized tests forced her to resign in 2010. Rhee's tenure as chancellor of the DC schools was controversial, marked by her firing of hundreds of teachers and administrators and the closing of numerous schools.[33] She remained a leading figure within systemic reform circles, however. In 2010, Rhee founded the StudentsFirst organization that promotes, among other policies, teacher evaluations based on test scores, the elimination of teacher tenure, and school choice.

John White, another TFA alum, went on to serve as the state superintendent of education for Louisiana and is credited with spearheading efforts to privatize education in the state. Serving under Governor Bobby Jindal, according to Ravitch, White radically implemented privatization policies by "diverting money dedicated by the state constitution to the support of public elementary and secondary schools, not only to charters and vouchers, but to for-profit online businesses and private vendors of every kind."[34] Another TFA alum, Kevin Huffman was appointed in Tennessee to promote a teacher accountability system based on students' standardized test scores and to expand charter schools within the state.

Not all TFA alums, however, remain supporters of the organization after their two-year stint. Like Chad Sommer, who saw TFA as a tool of corporate America in dismantling the public school system, Gary Rubinstein, who would use his TFA credentials to become a career teacher of mathematics, is highly critical of the organization he was part of in its early years in the 1990s. His critique is primarily aimed at TFA alums who have joined the ranks of systemic reformers, using their power to destroy public schools. According to Rubinstein, "These leaders are some of the most destructive forces in public education. They seem to love nothing more than labeling schools as 'failing,' shutting them down, and blaming the supposed failure on the veteran teachers. The buildings of the closed schools are taken over by charter networks, often with leaders who are TFA alums and who get salaries of $200 thousand or more to run a few schools."[35]

Olivia Blanchard, who left her TFA position after the first year, challenges the underlying presumption of the organization that TFA is an antidote for what is wrong with public schools. Blanchard cites an email she received during her five-week training session, which stated that the schools provided "a system of students who have simply not been taught. . . . That's really what the achievement gap is—for all the external factors that may or may not add challenges to our students' lives - mostly it is that they really and truly have not been taught and therefore are years behind where they need to be." According to Blanchard, "The subtext is clear: Only you (TFAers) can fix what others screwed up."[36] Not without irony, Blanchard points out that one of her TFA trainers in Atlanta left in the middle of the training session when she was implicated in the Atlanta test cheating scandal. In discussing the difficulties she had during her one-year TFA experience, Blanchard believes that five weeks was simply not enough time to prepare a new teacher for the rigors of teaching, particularly in a school wracked with problems.

As a model of alternate routes to teacher certification, it would seem that TFA would have a proven record of positively impacting student achievement. Empirical evidence does not, however, support TFA effectiveness. According to Ravitch, research demonstrates that TFA teachers get "about the same test score results as other new and uncertified teachers."[37] While some studies indicate that TFA teachers are able to produce "small but significant" increases in math scores, there is no improvement in reading scores. TFA critics claim that not only do TFA teachers fail to substantially improve student achievement, but the nature of a program that becomes a revolving door of young inadequately trained and inexperienced teachers is disruptive to schools and students.[38]

Critics also point out that the program is expensive for school districts already burdened with shrinking budgets and few resources. Districts pay a $2–$5 thousand fee to TFA for each recruit, plus a full salary for the teacher.[39] While this may have been a good investment when there was an authentic teacher shortage in the early 1990s, it seems like an exorbitant amount of money that could be better invested in existing schools and teachers. However, for advocates of free market reform who, like Milton Friedman, consider the public education system a government monopoly dominated by teachers' unions, TFA fees are a small price to pay in the campaign to privatize education. Systemic education reformers have successfully established a system in which federal policies dictate that poor performing schools are closed, entire teaching staffs can be fired, and private charter schools can be opened and staffed with nonunion TFA recruits.

Critics have also asserted that in 2013, as the Chicago Public School system announced the closing of 49 traditional unionized schools, TFA was working closely behind the scenes with a number of private charter school operators to open 52 nonunion charter schools heavily staffed by TFA recruits.[40] New Orleans, the city that Milton Friedman hailed as the perfect site for implementing free market reform after being devastated by Hurricane Katrina, would be inundated by TFAers. A key feature of the charter schools that replaced the public schools closed after the hurricane has been the number of TFA recruits they employ.[41] Former TFAer Hannah Sadtler was remorseful after she began teaching in a New Orleans school. She had been told that the reason TFA teachers were needed in New Orleans was because of a teacher shortage. Once in New Orleans, however, she learned the ugly truth. There was, in fact, no teacher shortage at all. As a matter of fact, shortly after Katrina, the city's seven thousand teachers were placed on "disaster leave without pay" and subsequently fired.[42] Unwittingly, Sadtler found herself a pawn in the free market scheme to privatize New Orleans public schools, taking a job that rightfully belonged to a certified teacher who had strong ties to the community. In January 2014, the Louisiana appeals court found that the teachers had been fired illegally and were awarded back pay.[43]

Value-Added Measurement

In spite of President Obama's recognition that "there's a concern among some that a teacher won't be judged fairly when we start linking students' performance to the performance of their teachers,"[44] the application for RTTT grants clearly favored states that used students' standardized test scores which "take into account data on student growth . . . as a significant factor."[45] In fact, a model for evaluating teacher effectiveness based on their students' test scores had been in place for a number of years. William Sanders, the statistician credited with creating the "value-added model" (VAM) of teacher assessment, identifies *A Nation at Risk* as the point of origin for this model and, even more specifically, George H. W. Bush's 1989 summit of governors and business leaders. This summit, according to Sanders, called for "greater accountability linked to assessment of educational outcomes."[46]

The Tennessee Value-Added Assessment System (TVAAS) was developed in response to Tennessee's 1992 Education Improvement Act (EIA), which increased education funding through higher taxes in the state. At the time, there was bipartisan demand within the state legislature for "a strong accountability provision to be included in the act to ensure that the new monies would be spent to improve student academic achievement."[47] The TVAAS, referred to in the EIA as the "Sanders model," was the "methodology designated to ascertain the effectiveness of school systems, schools, and teachers in producing academic growth in Tennessee students, thereby linking student outcomes to educational evaluation for the first time." Although it became a cornerstone of Tennessee's accountability system, even its creator asserts, "It cannot be the only source of data in a teacher's evaluation."[48]

Nevertheless, the Sanders model, or VAM, has become widely accepted as the preferred model in states seeking RTTT funds as a means to demonstrate to the DOE that student test scores are a "significant factor" in evaluating teacher effectiveness. As a matter of fact, a state's failure to implement an evaluation system that relies heavily on student test data can have financial implications for states requesting NCLB/ESEA waivers from the DOE. In April 2014, Arne Duncan sanctioned the state of Washington for not implementing a system of teacher accountability that uses test data to differentiate among teachers (and principals) who have "made significantly different contributions to student learning growth."[49] And as further evidence of the Obama administration's stance regarding VAM, in April 2014, the administration announced the appointment of Robert Gordon as assistant secretary for planning, evaluation, and policy development for the DOE. Gordon has been a strong proponent of VAM, having coauthored a paper entitled "Identifying Effective Teachers Using Performance on the Job" in 2006 for the Brookings Institute—a paper credited with renewing interest among policy makers in Sander's VAM model.[50]

Sanders' model was designed to be a means for determining the "value added" by a teacher (or, as Duncan refers to it—the teacher's contribution) to the educational achievement of a child. Although it is based on a complex statistical calculation, the concept appears on face value to be quite simple. The concept, however, is an oversimplification. In essence, the underlying notion of the VAM model is that a teacher's effectiveness can be determined by comparing her or his students' academic growth, as measured by their test scores, with their academic growth during their previous years in school, as well as with the growth of other students in the same grade. By examining student growth in this way, the impact of other factors such as socioeconomic status or other social factors are supposedly minimized. In other words, if a student experienced significant growth in a previous year when assigned to another teacher, that student should, according to a VAM model, continue to make comparable growth the following year with a different teacher. If that student does not make comparable growth, it is obviously because the teacher did not add enough value to that student's educational experience.

As H. L. Mencken asserted, however, "There is always a well-known solution to every human problem—neat, plausible, and wrong."[51] In April 2014, the same month that Duncan withdrew Washington's NCLB/ESEA waiver and the Obama administration appointed a VAM advocate to the DOE, the American Statistical Association published the "ASA Statement on Using Value-Added Models for Educational Assessment," stating:

> Research on VAMs has been fairly consistent that aspects of educational effectiveness that are measurable and within teacher control represent a small part of the total variation in student test scores or growth; most

> estimates in the literature attribute between 1% and 14% of the total variability to teachers. This is not saying that teachers have little effect on students, but that variation among teachers accounts for a small part of the variation in scores. The majority of the variation in test scores is attributable to factors outside the teacher's control such as student and family background, poverty, curriculum, and unmeasured influences.[52]

The American Education Research Association and the National Academy of Education issued a similar statement in 2011 entitled "Getting Teacher Evaluation Right: A Brief for Policymakers." In this statement, caution is urged with regard to teacher evaluation systems that rely heavily on VAM measures:

> With respect to value-added measures of student achievement tied to individual teachers, current research suggests that high-stakes, individual-level decisions, or comparisons across highly dissimilar schools or student populations, should be avoided. Valid interpretations require aggregate-level data and should ensure that background factors—including overall classroom composition—are as similar as possible across groups being compared. In general, such measures should be used only in a low-stakes fashion when they are part of an integrated analysis of what the teacher is doing and who is being taught.[53]

RTTT policies that insist on teacher evaluations based on test score data have already had a devastating effect on teachers across the country. In 2010, the *Los Angeles Times* published the VAM rankings based on their own analysis of the almost twelve thousand teachers within the Los Angeles Unified School District (LAUSD),[54] and the newspaper has continued to do so each year in an online data base. In 2012, the LAUSD attempted to protect their teachers, by changing teacher ID numbers and withholding teachers' names and schools. As a result, the *LA Times* filed a lawsuit asking the courts to demand the release of all requested information.[55] In November, 2013, Ravitch stated, "The *Times* doesn't care whose career or reputation they blight," recalling the suicide of an inner-city school teacher in Los Angeles after the 2010 release of the *LA Time's* teacher rankings. In spite of his dedication and esteem among students and families for being an impressive and caring teacher, the *LA Times* rated him "less effective" than his peers. According to his family, the teacher was depressed about his rating posted on the newspaper's website. [56]

In 2014, legal attempts to stop a Florida newspaper from publishing VAM ratings of school teachers failed.[57] As the full impact of VAM teacher evaluation systems are beginning to be felt across the country, lawsuits are also beginning to emerge challenging systems that reward or withhold merit pay based on this questionable model. By the close of the 2014 school year, teachers in New York, Tennessee, and Texas had filed lawsuits and it is speculated that this is just the beginning.[58] As an important aside, TFA teachers, who only sign on for two years are unaffected by VAM models of teacher effectiveness. If they receive a negative score based on VAM, they may feel badly, but they have not signed on for the long haul. They can go on to lucrative careers regardless of their effectiveness as a teacher. And since they are not usually a part of the community in which they teach, their names will be long forgotten by the parents who access the ratings to assess their child's teacher.

RTTT: Turning Around the "Lowest-Achieving Schools" as Charter Schools

Four school intervention models for turning around lowest-achieving schools are provided in the RTTT program: (1) a turnaround model; (2) a restart model; (3) a school closure model; or (4) a transformation model. NCLB already provided a provision for failing schools to be transformed into charter schools. The RTTT's restart model, therefore, further delineates a state's ability to convert a school or close and reopen "a school under a charter school operator, a charter management organization (CMO), or an education management organization (EMO)." A CMO is described as "a non-profit organization that operates or manages charter schools by centralizing or sharing certain functions and resources among schools." An EMO is described as a "for-profit or non-profit organization that provides 'whole-school operation' services." And to ensure that the DOE's clarion call to prochoice education reform advocates was heard loud and clear, the Obama administration added a provision to RTTT that would make absolutely sure that the free markets were open in the educational arena, finally busting the supposed education monopoly that had previously hindered those who envisioned the education sector as a way to profit from the schooling of America's children.[59]

States that have laws that prohibit or "effectively inhibit increasing" the number of charter schools jeopardized their ability to receive RTTT funds.[60] In other words, any state that demonstrates its dedication to the idea of public schools by limiting the incursion of charter schools, CMOs, and EMOs need not apply for RTTT cash. This is an open declaration by the DOE of their alignment with free market, prochoice advocates in the spirit of Milton Friedman. According to the Friedman Foundation for Educational Choice, schooling options within choice models include private schools, charter schools, homeschooling, and online learning.[61] RTTT was therefore a resounding victory for prochoice advocates. Friedman's original school reform idea may have been the use of tax dollars to fund school vouchers. However, the shifting of language from school vouchers to school choice that had occurred during the Reagan administration, and the subsequent iteration of school choice to include charter schools, enabled free market reform advocates to push forward their agenda of school privatization.

In 2005, Nick Gillespie called Milton Friedman "the father of modern school reform."[62] In 2007, Eric Hanushek explained that, while Friedman's voucher concept had not yet been fully embraced, the belief that parents tended to prefer nongovernment schools when given the option, "has led to the growth of charter schools."[63] On Friedman's one hundredth birthday, July 31, 2012, free market advocates celebrated his legacy. Lindsey Burke, a fellow at the conservative Heritage Foundation, cited Friedman's assertion that the free market has the power to reform education "by privatizing a major segment of the educational system - i.e., by enabling a private, for-profit industry to develop that will provide a wide variety of learning opportunities and offer effective competition to public schools." Burke went on to say, "Today, we have a growing number of innovative school choice options—charters, vouchers, tax credits, online learning, and education savings accounts, to name a few. These options were conceived in the mind of Friedman and are being brought to life by reform-oriented governors and legislators across the country."[64]

By 2011, just two years after RTTT implementation and one year after the creation of the CCSS, school choice through its various options had permeated America's education landscape so much so that the *Wall Street Journal* dubbed 2011, "the year of school choice." Part of the expansion in school choice is due to the lifting of state caps on charter schools. According to the *Wall Street Journal*, school choice is critical in reforming schools, due in large part to its power to "erode[s] the union-dominated monopoly that assigns children to schools based on where they live." The newspaper also asserted that teacher tenure needs to be eliminated and teacher effectiveness must be measured against student performance.[65]

The Obama administration, however, did not need to celebrate Milton Friedman's one hundredth birthday in 2012. They had already honored him with an expensive monument—a free market monument that would be paid for by Americans and their children that enabled school tax dollars to flow into private industry coffers profiting from the RTTT program under the banner of school choice and charters. Unfortunately, far from being the panacea for what systemic education reformers perceive to be a failing education system, charter schools largely remain an untested, unproven experiment. What research exists on charter schools does not demonstrate that they have the ability to improve student achievement any more than traditional public schools. In fact, according to the Center for Public Education, research reveals that at the high school level, charter school students underperform in the areas of math and reading compared with their peers in traditional public schools. A Stanford University study found that overall, only 25 percent of charter school students had better reading test scores than public school students and 19 percent of charter schools produced lower reading test scores than public schools in their community. Amazingly, in 56 percent of all charter schools, there was no difference in their achievement compared with public schools. In math, 29 percent of the charter schools performed better, but 31 percent performed worse, and 40 percent performed at the same level as public schools.[66]

For the percentage of charter schools that do outperform public schools, questions have been raised about the reasons behind their superior performance. Charter schools, for the most part, operate in much the same way as private schools. In short, they get to choose their students. They do not have to tolerate badly behaved students and they find ways to kick out poorly performing students. Teachers, parents, and students sign charter school contracts, agreeing to do all the things necessary to promote educational growth among the student body. According to a sample KIPP contract, for example, teachers agree to work longer hours, on some Saturdays, and often in the summer, to always make themselves available to students and parents, and to "do whatever it takes for our students to learn."[67]

Parents agree, in short, to be good parents and support their children, ensuring that they are at school, have done their homework, dress according to the dress code, and follow the rules. Students agree to be, in general, good kids, do their homework and call their teacher if they need help, dress properly, and follow the rules. The driving force behind a charter school's academic achievement, arguably, are the rules, and not necessarily because kids who follow the rules do better in school academically. The reality is that the rules serve as an exit or termination clause in the contract. The KIPP sample contract is very clear in its language stating that students who fail to adhere to commitments outlined in the contract risk losing various privileges or, as a last resort, being forced to return to a traditional public school. Teachers, likewise, understand that if they fail to work the extended hours or are unwilling to be on-call seven days a week for students or parents, they may be removed from the school. Charter school jobs are, after all, nonunion jobs.

Charter schools have established a predictable pattern. There are so many rules and behavior expectations that there are a myriad of ways to kick out lower performing students. Suspension rates in charter schools are alarmingly high when compared with public schools. And, when students rack up enough demerits for anything from chewing gum to speaking out of turn or not walking in a straight line down the hall, then the result is that they can have their contract terminated for noncompliance and suffer the ultimate penalty—having to return to a traditional public school. By the time schools administer standardized tests, charter schools can sufficiently weed out their low scorers by sending them back to the traditional public schools. So not only are charter schools able to game the system in order to raise their own test scores, they are also able to lower public school test scores by sending low-performing students back to them. Another pattern is emerging, too, that indicates that charter schools tend to serve fewer numbers of students with disabilities and fewer English language learners.[68]

It would seem that this gaming of the system, then, would enable charter schools to excel. According to the DOE's Institute of Education Science's (IES) analysis of charter schools' academic achievement ratings, overall mathematics performance in charter schools was lower than public schools; and in reading, "there was no measurable difference" in 2003.[69] In a follow-up study, the IES controlled for variables such as student population characteristics. According to this study, "After adjusting for student characteristics, charter school mean scores in reading and mathematics were lower, on average, than those in public non-charter schools."[70] Furthermore, if, as Arne Duncan asserts, education and education reform is a civil rights issue, then the drastic increase in the number of charter schools across America is absolutely the wrong approach. According to a study conducted by UCLA's Civil Rights Project, "The charter school movement has been a major political success, but it has been a civil rights failure." The impact of charter schools has been a drastic increase in racial segregation and isolation for the minority students they overwhelmingly serve.[71] According to Myron Orfield, director of the University of Minnesota's Institute on Race and Poverty, "charters are an engine of racial segregation."[72]

In spite of the fact that there is a lack of empirical evidence that charter schools generally outperform traditional public schools, and there is evidence that charter schools are rolling back the 1954 *Brown v. Board* decision, it does seem counterintuitive for the DOE to continue to promote charter schools as an effective education reform initiative. Arguably, the lure of charter schools has more to do with a total allegiance to free market principles, and the promotion of charters by those who see the movement as a boon to profit-seeking entrepreneurs, than it does with actually improving the lives of K-12 students.

While the CCSS is problematic to be sure, it represents the gorilla in the room that ushered in an entire host of policies that threaten the institution of public education. Each one of the RTTT policies seem made to order for advocates of free market education reform. Each one of these policies on its own chips away at the foundation of public education. Together, however, all wrapped up in the expensive RTTT package presented to corporate America, these policies have the potential to completely dismantle public education in the United States, and, in the process, have allowed the free market to become public education policy.

Conclusion

Speaking Truth to Power: Reclaiming the Politics of Education Reform

There is a price on the head of every child in America. As the free market theories of Milton Friedman became the driving force behind public policy in the United States, beginning with the Reagan administration, public schools would inevitably become ensnared in the dragnet of entrepreneurs who envisioned public education as a burgeoning market. In the post-Reagan years, however, free markets would become a new esprit de corps among Democrats and Republicans emboldened by the Clinton administration's "third way" of governance that manifested a bipartisan spirit through corporate partnerships in many public policy arenas.

Reagan's presidency was a resounding victory for a conservative movement that had been coalescing since the end of WWII. This conservative wellspring had a long history of anti-public school sentiment. For public education, the Reagan years produced a toxic environment. First, the cacophony of public education critics reached a fevered pitch resulting in the publication of *A Nation at Risk*, which purposefully used inflammatory language in asserting that the U.S. public education system was responsible for the economic woes of the nation. Second, *Friedmanomics* was lauded as the panacea for every sector of American life. There was no sacred public ground.

For the most part, the American public failed to notice the steady encroachment of the corporate world in the education arena. Milton Friedman's assertion of public schools as a government monopoly that needed to be privatized through voucher systems seemed shrill and inconsequential in the decades leading up to the Common Core. Corporate superstars such as Lou Gerstner and David Kearns seemed benevolent, wise, and generous as they engaged in systemic education reform efforts based on what seemed to work in the corporate world. Since Total Quality Management principles had worked in turning around Xerox and IBM, surely they could work in public schools. The National Governors Association courted corporate leaders, and the Department of Education wholeheartedly embraced the business model, even inviting Kearns to serve within the department during the George H. W. Bush administration.

The steady drumbeat of corporate encroachment into the education arena was there the entire time. However, its cadence was so steady and natural that, like cicadas at sunset, the noise went almost unnoticed by too many Americans. The idea that the nation's public school system was a failure had become an unquestioned zeitgeist by a burgeoning number of critics who jumped on board the anti–public school bandwagon. Those on both the political right and the political left seized every opportunity to point to the need to systemically reform public education. It became the one issue that could unite conservatives and liberals in Washington DC, regardless of who was in the White House or which party controlled the legislature. However, the very need for total systemic education reform has been predicated on a set of faulty conclusions reached by the National Council on Education Excellence, the committee that authored *A Nation at Risk*. In fact, the committee investigated secondary education, and their assertions about the systemic failure of public schools were primarily based on the realities of urban schools serving predominantly minority students living in poverty. And at the same time the country was reckoning with the scurrilous attacks on its public education system, the Department of Education was awarding "Blue Ribbons" to successful schools. It was no wonder, then, that when the Sandia Report researchers submitted their findings to the Department of Education during the George H. W. Bush administration they were met with animosity and their report was buried. Education policy makers simply could not tolerate research findings that discredited the need for total systemic education reform. In 1991, Sandia researchers asserted that "much of the current reform agenda, though well intentioned, is misguided" and "based on a 'crisis mentality, many proposed reforms do not property focus on actual problems." However, by now the corporate world was solidly at the table in discussions of federal education reform, with former Xerox CEO David Kearns ensconced in the federal DOE.

The Clinton administration became an important nexus in which federal legislative education initiatives became irretrievably intertwined with corporate education reform initiatives. Ironically, during the Reagan administration, the need for systemic education reform was based on the floundering economy that existed in the early 1980s. However, when the economy surged during the Clinton years, there was no abatement in the assertions that public schools were failing, much less any suggestion that public schools had in any way contributed to the economic surge of the 1990s. If anything, the merging of corporate and gubernatorial CEOs around education reform that occurred in the years following the Reagan administration became energized and even radicalized, with corporate superstar Lou Gerstner declaring that corporate funds should be used for "arming the insurgents." Therefore, when President Clinton gave a "shout out" to Bill Gates at the 1996 Palisades Education Summit, it didn't signal the beginning of the Draconian overreach of the corporate world in education reform. Gates was simply following in the footsteps of other corporate superstars in the education arena.

By the time George W. Bush became president in 2001 and began the work to reauthorize ESEA as NCLB, a great deal of the infrastructure was in place for developing the CCSS. Achieve, the organization that would lead the charge in creating these standards, had been formed during the Clinton administration as a result of the 1996 Palisades summit. By 1998, Achieve began working on its Academic Standards and Assessments Benchmarking Pilot Project. It is, however, during the George W. Bush administration when we see the fruition of the third way of governance and its impact on education policy. While the federal government turned its attention to the reauthorization of ESEA in 2001, which resulted in the far-reaching NCLB initiative, another powerful set of players was busy within the private sector pursuing systemic education reform within what Michael Lofgren calls the Deep State. For those working within the Deep State, federal laws were almost inconsequential—something to be worked around, exploited, or simply ignored. Therefore, while the nation's schools were trying to acclimate themselves to a new era of high-stakes testing in which schools operate under the constant threat of sanctions and ultimate closure based on low test scores, within the Deep State, organizations like Achieve were growing fat from corporate dollars. Unfettered by legislative oversight, Deep State operators worked in plain sight marketing systemic education reform, first developing college and career ready standards under the banner of the American Diploma Project and then almost seamlessly morphing those standards into the Common Core State Standards.

The CCSS, however, is only one component of efforts to systemically reform education, although it has become the gorilla in the room of education policy. While resistance to the standards dominates the discourse, the CCSS is the unwieldy beast that carries with it other reform initiatives that seem "made to order" for free market proponents who envision education as a burgeoning market in which everyone from small entrepreneurs to major corporations and hedge fund managers can "make a dime." Therefore, it is understandable that while there is a growing consensus among American citizens on the political right and the political left that the CCSS are untenable, those who reject the standards posit very different reasons for their complaints. Policies that originate within the Deep State create confusion among citizens attempting to identify who exactly is responsible for the quagmire. On one hand, the obvious villains for conservative small government free market advocates are those seated in Washington DC. Obviously, for them, the Obama administration is responsible for extending the Bush administration's federal overreach into education policy. On the other hand, for more progressive liberals, the obvious villains are the hedge fund managers and corporate leaders with deep pockets who use federal education policies to exploit a ready market in which all children represent tax dollars and a source for federally funded, shovel-ready projects that carry the potential for huge profits.

Discourse about the CCSS is complicated by the reality that RTTT policies were not merely about a set of standards. Defeating the CCSS may be the desired outcome for critics of federal overreach into education policies; however, the real money for corporate reformers lies within the different aspects of the RTTT initiative. There is no money to be had in publishing and marketing the standards alone. The real money is in the curriculums that will be created and marketed based on the standards, the huge testing industry that is emerging to test the standards, the technology that is required to implement the tests and analyze the data, and the databases that will be developed to warehouse all the information about students from preschool through college. And, as can be seen in recent years, when RTTT required states to lift any limits on charter schools, the market for privately managed for-profit and nonprofit charter schools exploded. No amount of public proclamations that charter schools are public schools can overcome the reality that charter schools represent the move to privatize education in the United States. Milton Friedman's own foundation claims the charter school movement as a victory for the free market.

Most important, what should be of great concern to America's citizenry is that all of these policies require the attenuation, if not the outright elimination, of locally controlled public school governing boards. In 2008, Matt Miller, a senior advisor for the global management company, McKinsey and Company (the company that employed CCSS architect David Coleman early in his career), boldly declared in the *Atlantic*, "First, Kill All the School Boards!" That same year, corporate superstar Lou Gerstner wholeheartedly endorsed this idea in the *Wall Street Journal.*

It is, however, not too late for American citizens to take back their public schools. America's system of public education has served the nation well, reflecting the ideals that undergird its democratic society. America's public schools have played a major role in helping create scientists, doctors, lawyers, business people, trades people, and just plain hardworking citizens, who have helped the United States achieve so much in so little time. Public schools have historically been contested democratic sites for breaking down barriers of race and places that helped diverse immigrant groups enter American society. America's public schools have been honored places where local communities, representing the diverse and multifaceted nature of a pluralistic society, could come together in an interactive democratic manner and impact the community's most prized possession—its children. America's public schools have always been the one institution that could mold and unite a culturally diverse society. At the same time, however, public schools were able to nurture that unique democratic American spirit of individualism within students while also empowering marginalized groups. Decision making, where individuals interacting within their community schools in conjunction with individual states being guided by these local communities about what its children needed in order to become properly educated, reflected a process that has been an important part of the American democratic experience.

The creation and sustainability of America's system of public education, however, has not become a reality without challenge. For the last half of the twentieth century, and now well into the twenty-first, this challenge has only intensified. Far from being a bastion of democracy where individual citizens acting in a democratic communal manner have their voices and ideas impact the educational lives of their children, conservative critics of America's system of public education have labeled this system an appendage of an authoritarian socialistic state. For these critics, the one sure solution to this problem was to dismantle the public school system and turn it over to the free market. Although the free market may be good for some industries, and competition may be an effective mechanism for keeping prices low as well as improving the quality of a raft of products including technological paraphernalia, the role of public schools and complex social and cultural challenges these schools are required to meet, requires a public discourse that allows individual citizen inclusion, not exclusion.

For the citizens, speaking truth to power is essential in protecting their public school system from further encroachment by corporate-led systemic education reformers. That being the case, what are some things a citizen needs to know and do when engaging in education reform?

I. When politicians or pundits begin a discussion with an assertion that the entire American public school system is a failure, it is a clear indication that (A) they have blindly accepted the assertions of *A Nation at Risk* that were clearly misleading; (B) they are largely uninformed about the realities of American public schools that have, for the most part, served our society very well; and (C) they would rather target public schools for reform than engage in a meaningful discussion about how to eliminate poverty and larger social issues that are at the root of low academic achievement in some communities in America.

II. Insist on transparency with regard to education policies at the local, state, and federal level. Follow the money trail. This is not always easy. However, it shouldn't come as a surprise when hedge fund managers, special interest groups, or foundations fund political campaigns and simultaneously use their money to fund corporate education reform initiatives.

III. Place American children above political affiliation. Republicans will always blame unions. That will not change. Understand that teachers' unions and associations are not the problem. As a matter of fact, in this current era of Deep State education reform, the unions have endorsed many Deep State initiatives before reconsidering their positions. More progressive liberal Democrats will always focus attention on issues of equity and equality. That will not change. But understand that this devotion to social issues has helped promote the privatization of public schools through the co-option of civil rights discourse to promote charter schools and high-stakes testing. Public school critics use unions, teacher tenure, and the plight of urban schools to bolster their arguments. These are, however, straw men arguments. For example, in a state like Mississippi that has no teacher tenure protection, test scores are among the lowest in the country, while in a state like Massachusetts with teacher tenure, test scores are high. And to argue that charter schools are the answer to low-performing schools in urban areas is to ignore the systemic social problems that created the neighborhoods that are served by those schools.

IV. Insist that the federal legislature assume its proper role in education policy. By law the Elementary and Secondary Education Act (ESEA) must be reauthorized every five years. This has not occurred since 2001. This is unacceptable. Although we Americans have a voice through our duly elected senators and representatives, we have squandered our opportunity to stop the abuses associated with high-stakes testing and sanctions that result in school closures. RTTT does not supersede ESEA. RTTT resulted from an unprecedented windfall of "discretionary funds" made available to venture capitalists as a result of the American Recovery and Reinvestment Act. Insist that Congress revise and reauthorize ESEA, this time with the well-being of children and public schools as its cornerstone.

V. Demand federal oversight and regulation of all schools. In June 2014, the Bill and Melinda Gates Foundation suddenly called for a two-year moratorium on high-stakes decisions based on assessments aligned with the CCSS. Why is this coming from the corporate world? Isn't this the proper role of our elected officials? At the very least, it would seem that the time is right for a congressional investigation into the use of RTTT funds to promote national standards, and, by extension, a national curriculum, actions prohibited by federal law.

VI. Maintain the autonomy of your local school boards and hold your elected leaders accountable. Citizens have incredible power. However, one has to be diligent. Cities and communities across the United States have seen the erosion of local control over schools, with citizens learning about changes after the fact.

VII. Stop allowing the closing of public schools. You cannot reform or improve a school that has been closed. Charter school operators promote themselves as shining beacons of hope for children who otherwise would have to attend their neighborhood public schools. However, there is no data that demonstrates that students attending charter schools outperform their counterparts in traditional public schools. Therefore, communities should reject the notion that closing a public school and reopening it as a charter school, often under the management of highly paid administrators from outside the community, is a viable and sustainable reform initiative.

VIII. Vote on behalf of your children and the American children of the future. Vote for politicians who support public schools. Don't just vote in national elections. Your vote is equally important at the local and state levels.

IX. Make your voice heard. American citizens defeated inBloom through their informal and formal collective voices. Don't tolerate the exploitation of children. It's one thing to tolerate a private business that tracks your purchases in order to post advertisements on your Internet search provider. It's another matter entirely to allow the private information about children to be trafficked by corporations or anyone clever enough to hack the data bases. Parents have the power to advocate for their children, who have no vote and little voice in matters of education policy. Sometimes that means simply saying no, without rancor or ill will for your child's school. The opt-out movement continues to grow across the country and is becoming a formidable force. Parents who choose to opt their children out of CCSS high-stakes testing are exercising an important American right and protecting their children from the overreach of the corporate world into their private lives. Most important, parents are asserting the American ideal of an upwardly mobile society in which data does not determine destiny.

X. Understand that collective voices are powerful. Form coalitions and be actively involved. Bridge the gap between the right and the left, unifying over our common ground—our children. Advocates for the CCSS are intent on making opposition to the CCSS a Tea Party issue. It is not. It is an American issue.

For American citizens, if there is only one thing to remember about their public schools it is this: Public schools are not government schools, nor are they corporate free market schools. Public schools belong to the public. Public schools are citizen schools, and it is now up to citizens to reclaim what is theirs!

Notes

Chapter 1

1. Ronald Reagan, "First Inaugural Address" (January 20, 1981). Ronald Reagan Presidential Library and Museum. http://www.reagan.utexas.edu/archives/speeches/publicpapers.html.
2. Ronald Reagan, "Republican National Convention Acceptance Speech" (July 17, 1980). Ronald Reagan Presidential Library and Museum. http://www.reagan.utexas.edu/archives/speeches/publicpapers.html.
3. D. T. Stallings, "A Brief History of the United States Department of Education: 1979–2002." (Center for Child and Family Policy, Duke University, 2002), 3.
4. David Carleton, *Landmark Congressional Laws on Education: Student's Guide to Landmark Congressional Laws.* (Westport, CT: Greenwood Publishing Group, 2001), 193–204.
5. Jimmy Carter, "Department of Education Organization Act Statement on Signing S.210 into Law" (October 17, 1979). The American Presidency Project. http://www.presidency.ucsb.edu/ws/?pid=31543.
6. Ibid.
7. Mary Dalheim, "Shirley Hufstedler—ED's New Head: Who Is She? What Can She Do for Education?" *Instructor* 90, no. 4 (1980): 42–48.
8. Patricia Albjerg Graham, *Schooling America: How the Public Schools Meet the Nation's Changing Needs* (New York: Oxford University Press, 2005), 156.
9. Terrel H. Bell, *The Thirteenth Man: A Reagan Cabinet Memoir* (New York: The Free Press, 1988), 1.
10. Ibid., 92–96.
11. Ibid., 52–66.
12. Ibid., 116.
13. Ibid.
14. Ibid., 117.
15. The National Commission on Excellence in Education (NCEE), "A Nation at Risk: The Imperative for Educational Reform" (April, 1983), v.
16. Annette Y. Kirk, "Annette Kirk on Leadership." (speech at the March Meeting of Luncheons with Leaders, The Russell Kirk Center for Cultural Renewal, Grand Valley State University, March 3, 2010).
17. Darrin Moore, "The Prophet of Conservatism: Russell Kirk." *The Imaginative Conservative.* 2012. http://www.theimaginativeconservative.org/2012/02/prophet-of-conservatism-russell-kirk.html.

18. Curtis Good, "A Nation at Risk: Committee Members Speak Their Mind," in *American Educational History Journal,* J. Wesley Null (ed.), 37, no. 1 and 2, (2010): 373.
19. Bell, 118–19.
20. NCEE.
21. Lawrence C. Stedman, "The NAEP Long-Term Trend Assessment: A Review of Its Transformation, Use, and Findings," A Paper Commissioned for the 20th Anniversary of the National Assessment Governing Board: 1988–2008 (Washington DC: National Assessment Governing Board, March, 2009), 2.
22. David C. Berliner and Bruce J. Biddle, *The Manufactured Crisis: Myths, Fraud, and the Attack on America's Public Schools* (Reading, MA: Addison-Wesley Publishing Company, Inc., 1995), 24–26; Gerald W. Bracey, *The War Against America's Public Schools: Privatizing Schools, Commercializing Education* (Boston, MA: Allyn and Bacon, 2002), 23–24.
23. Bell, 136.
24. Stedman, 2.
25. Ibid., 3.
26. L. A. Munday, "Declining Admissions Test Scores," ACT Research Report No. 71 (Iowa City, IA: The Research and Development Division of The American College Testing Program, February, 1976), 14.
27. Bell, 137.
28. Benjamin M. Superfine, *Equality in Education Law and Policy, 1954–2010* (Cambridge, UK: Cambridge University Press, 2013), 37–67.
29. Jonathan Kozol, *Death at an Early Age: The Destruction of the Hearts and Minds of Negro Children in the Boston Public Schools* (Boston, MA: Houghton Mifflin, 1967). Other books by Jonathan Kozol include: *Amazing Grace: The Lives of Children and the Conscience of a Nation* (1995); *Savage Inequalities: Children in America's Schools* (1991); and *The Shame of the Nation: The Restoration of Apartheid Schooling in America* (2005).
30. Munday, 14.
31. Ibid.
32. Ibid., 22–23.
33. Ibid., 23.
34. John J. White, "College Boards," in *Encyclopedia of Education Reform and Dissent* (Thomas C. Hunt, James C. Carper, Thomas J. Lasley II, and C. Daniel Raisch, eds.), (Thousand Oaks, CA: Sage Publications, 2010), 181; Nancy Ordover, *American Eugenics: Race, Queer Anatomy, and the Science of Nationalism* (Minneapolis, MN: University of Minnesota Press, 2003), 26; Phillip F. Rubio, *A History of Affirmative Action, 1619–2000* (Jackson, MS: The University of Mississippi Press, 2001), 75.
35. Bracey, 58.
36. College Entrance Examination Board, "On Further Examination: Report of the Advisory Panel on the Scholastic Aptitude Test Score Decline," College Entrance Examination Board (Princeton, NJ: College Board, 1977).

37. Ibid., 13.
38. Ibid., 17.
39. Ibid., 13.
40. Ibid., 16.
41. Ibid.
42. Ibid., 14.
43. Ibid., 18–31.
44. Ibid., 37.
45. Ibid., 31–32.
46. William A. Turnbull, "Student Change, Program Change: Why the SAT Scores Kept Falling," Educational Testing Service College Board Report No. 85–2, ETS RR No. 85–28 (New York: College Entrance Examination Board, 1985), 4.
47. Ibid., 1.
48. Ibid., 5.
49. Ibid., 6.
50. Ibid., 7.
51. College Entrance Examination Board, 19–20. In Turnbull, 7.
52. Turnbull, 7.
53. Berliner and Biddle, 23.
54. NCEE, Appendices B-E, 42–61.
55. NCEE, Appendix B, 42–43.
56. Ibid.
57. Ibid., 44–48.
58. Ibid., 5.
59. David Pierpont Gardner, Interview with Harry Kreisler, "Leadership in Education: Conversation with David Pierpont Gardner" *Conversations with History* (University of California Berkeley: Institute of International Studies, 1998). http://globetrotter.berkeley.edu/conversations/Gardner/.
60. Ibid.
61. Glenn Seaborg, "A Nation at Risk Revisited," *Glenn Seaborg: His Life and Contributions, Part I* (Berkeley, CA: University of California, Lawrence Berkeley National Laboratory, 1993). http://www2.lbl.gov/Publications/Seaborg/risk.htm.
62. Good, 378.
63. "Themes and Discussion Points from A Nation at Risk Summit" (Washington DC: The Center for Education Reform, April 3, 1998, 1). http://www.edreform.com/edreform-university/resource/themes-discussion-points-from-a-nation-at-risk-summit-1998/.
64. Good, 378.
65. Ibid., 375.
66. Jay M. Sommer, "The Excellence Commission and the Humanities," in *Challenges to the Humanities*, Chester E. Finn, Jr., Diane Raitch, and P. Holley Roberts, eds. (New York: Holmes and Meier Publishers, Inc., 1985), 175.
67. NCEE, 14.

68. Paul Copperman, *The Literacy Hoax: The Decline of Reading, Writing, and Learning in the Public Schools and What We Can Do about It.* (New York: William Morrow and Company, 1978); in NCEE, 19.
69. NCEE, 18–19.
70. Ibid., 19–21.
71. Ibid., 21–22.
72. Ibid., 22–23.
73. Ibid., 24–27.
74. Ibid., 27–29.
75. Ibid., 29–30.
76. Ibid., 30–31.
77. Ibid., 32–33.
78. Ibid., 29–30.
79. Ibid., 30.
80. College Entrance Board Examination, 14; Turnbull, 5.
81. NCEE, 1.
82. Good, 384.
83. Ibid., 375.
84. NCEE, 14.
85. Ibid., 62–63.
86. "Blue Ribbon Schools Program," (Washington DC: U.S. Department of Education, 1982). http://www2.ed.gov/programs/nclbbrs/list-1982.pdf.
87. Bell, 149.
88. NCEE, 62.
89. Bell, 123.
90. Kirk, 5
91. Kirk, 6
92. Ronald Reagan, "Remarks on Receiving the Final Report of the National Commission on Excellence in Education."
93. Graham, 154.
94. Bell, 130–31.
95. Ibid.
96. Ibid., 144–49.
97. Ibid., 155.

Chapter 2

1. Kim Philips-Fein, *Invisible Hands: The Making of the Conservative Movement from the New Deal to Reagan* (New York: W. W. Norton and Company, Inc., 2009), 261.
2. Ibid., 261.
3. "About Russell Kirk," *The Russell Kirk Center for Cultural Renewal,* accessedJanuary25,2014,http://www.kirkcenter.org/index.php/about-kirk/.

4. Murray N. Rothbard, *Education: Free and Compulsory* (Auburn, AL: Ludwig von Mises Institute, 1999), vi. Ryan made this statement in the preface of this book. The text within this book, however, was originally published in 1971 in the *Individualist Magazine*.
5. Russell Kirk, *The Conservative Mind*, 7th revised ed. (Washington DC: Regency, 1985), 371.
6. Albert Jay Nock, *The Theory of Education in the United States* (Auburn, Alabama: The Ludwig von Mises Institute, 2007), 31. This book is based on a series of lectures delivered in 1931 published as a book that year.
7. Ibid., 53.
8. Richard Gamble, ed., *The Great Traditions: Classic Readings on What It Means to Be an Educated Human Being* (Wilmington Delaware: ISI Books, 2007).
9. Nock, 151.
10. Ibid., 120.
11. Ibid. 13.
12. Ibid., 34.
13. Ibid., 36–37.
14. Ibid., 35–37.
15. Ibid., 38–39.
16. Ibid., 40.
17. Ibid., 42–46.
18. Steven Tozer, Guy Senese, and Paul C. Violas, *School and Society: Historical and Contemporary Perspectives*, 7th ed. (New York: McGraw Hill, 2013). In particular see, Chapter 9 "Literacy and Today: Contemporary Perspectives." This chapter is a good place to begin understanding the different interpretations of what literacy means and the educational ramifications of the different meanings. The chapter also helps guide the reader to numerous authors who focus on the different aspects of the topic. In addition, one can begin to search on the Internet for terms such as conventional, functional, cultural, and critical literacy that can be effective guides to more in-depth analyses of these terms.
19. Nock, 45.
20. Ibid., 19–20.
21. "The von Mises Institute," accessed January 20, 2014, http://mises.org/Literature/Author/731.
22. George H. Nash, *The Conservative Intellectual Movement since 1945* (New York: Basic Books, 1976), 15.
23. Educational Policies Commission, *The Purposes of Education in American Democracy* (Washington DC: National Education Association of the United States, 1938), 39–124.
24. Andrew Hartman, *Education and the Cold War: The Battle for the American School* (New York: Palgrave Macmillan, 2008), 96, 142. Hartman's book is an excellent in-depth analysis of the impact of the Cold War on American public schools that also gives important insights into the

relationship between conservatism and public schools through the lens of Cold War rhetoric and hysteria.

25. Clarence J. Karier, *The Individual, Society, and Education: A History of American Educational Ideas* (Urbana, IL: University of Illinois Press, 2nd ed., 1986), 278. Karier's book is essential reading for those who want to probe deeply into the educational ideas of individuals such as Mann, Dewey, Babbitt, Counts, Brameld, Rousseau, Barzun, and Bestor, to name only a few.
26. Lawrence A. Cremin, *The Transformation of the School: Progressivism in American Education, 1876–1957* (New York: Knopf, 1961), 236.
27. Karier, 281.
28. John Dewey, *Democracy and Education (1916)* in "The Middle Works of John Dewey, 1899–1924, Vol. 9, Jo Ann Boydston, ed. (Carbondale: Southern Illinois University Press, 1985), 93
29. Ibid, 93–94.
30. Robert B. Westbrook, *John Dewey and American Democracy* (Ithaca, NY: Cornell University Press, 1991), 339–41.
31. Lanny Ebenstein, *Milton Friedman: A Biography* (New York: Palgrave Macmillan, 2007), 142–43. See also "The von Mises Institute."
32. F. A. Hayek, *The Road to Serfdom Text and Documents; The Definitive Edition*. Edited by Bruce Caldwell (London: University of Chicago Press, 2007). Caldwell has written an excellent introduction in which he helps further analyze Hayek's monumental work. Therefore, we will be specific when alluding to "Caldwell's introduction" and also cite sources he has used.
33. Caldwell, Introduction, 23–24. Quoted from, Letter, John Maynard Keynes to Hayek, June 28, 1944, reprinted in John Maynard Keynes, *Activities 1940–46. Shaping the Post-War World: Employment and Commodities,* ed. Donald Moggridge, vol. 27 (1980) of *The Collected Writings of John Maynard Keynes*. London: Macmillan [for the Royal Economic Society], p. 385.
34. Ibid., 386.
35. Hayek, 85.
36. Ibid., 86.
37. Ibid., 87.
38. Caldwell, Introduction, 20. Quoted from F. A. Hayek, "Planning and 'The Road to Serfdom': Friedrich Hayek Comments on Uses to Which His Book Has Been Put," *Chicago Sun Book Week*, May 6, 1945.
39. Ibid., 20. Quoted from "The Road to Serfdom, an Address before the Economic Club of Detroit," April 23, 1945, 6. Caldwell explains that "a transcript to the address may be found in the Hayek Papers, box 106, folder 8, Hoover Institute Archives."
40. Hayek, 40–44.
41. Ibid., 142.
42. For in-depth analyses that looks specifically at the relationship between the Cold War and education, see, for example, Stuart J. Foster, *Red Alert:*

Educators Confront the Red Scare in American Public Schools, 1947–1954 (New York: Peter Lang, 2000), and Hartman.

43. As quoted in Westbrook, 487.
44. See, for example: (1) Harry S. Truman, "Education Our First Line of Defense: Learning Alone Can Combat the Tenets of Communism" (speech delivered at Rollins College, Winter Park, FL, March 8, 1949). Harry S. Truman Library and Museum, *Public Papers of Truman, 1945–53.* (2) James B. Conant, *Education and Liberty* (Cambridge, MA: Harvard University Press, 1953), 62. Conant proclaimed, "If the field of Waterloo was won on the playing field of Eton, it may well be that the ideological struggle with Communism in the next fifty years will be won on playing fields of the public high schools of the United States. That this may be so is the fervent hope of all of us who are working to support and improve these characteristic American institutions." (3) Hyman G. Rickover, *Education and Freedom* (New York: E. P. Dutton, 1959), 38. Rickover claimed "education is America's first line of defense." Both Conant and Rickover, however, felt that only those students with an IQ of 115 or over, or in other words the top 15 to 20 percent of all students based on IQ tests, had the academic talent to go on to college.
45. Hartman, 103.
46. Newton, Michael. *The Ku Klux Klan in Mississippi A History* (Jefferson, NC: McFarland and Company, 2010), 102.
47. For a more detailed account of the social, economic, and political issues impacting the Pasadena situation see, David Hubbard, *This happened in Pasadena* (New York: Macmillan, 1951).
48. Time Magazine, "Pasadena Revisited," May 7, 1951.
49. National Education Association, *The Pasadena Story: An Analysis of Some Forces and Factors That Injured a Superior School System: Report of an Investigation by the National Commission for the Defense of Democracy through Education of the National Education Association of the United States* (Washington, DC: National Association of the United States, 1951).
50. Foster, 3.
51. Foster, 138–39.
52. As quoted by Cremin, 342–43.
53. John T. Flynn, "Who Owns Your Child's Mind?" in *Public Education under Criticism: Presenting penetrative articles from leading magazines and educational journals dealing with criticism of our public schools,* C. Winfield Scott and Clyde M. Hill, eds. (New York: Prentice-Hall, 1954), 158–59.
54. John T. Flynn, *The Road Ahead: America's Creeping Revolution* (New York: Devon-Adair Company, 1949), 9–12. See also Chapter 9, "The War on the South." In the 1949 hard copy edition he had originally included "to socialism" on the front cover.
55. John E. Moser, "The Ideological Odyssey of John T. Flynn," accessed January 26, 2014, http://personal.ashland.edu/~jmoser1/flynn.html.

For greater detail regarding Flynn's life see, John E. Moser, *Right Turn: John T. Flynn and the Transformation of American Liberalism* (New York: New York University Press, 2005).

56. David Harvey, *A Brief History of Neoliberalism* (New York: Oxford University Press, 2005). 64.
57. Mortimer Smith, *And Madly Teach: A Layman Looks at Public School Education* (Chicago: Henry Regnery Company, 1949), vii.
58. Cremin, 239–40.
59. Karier, 313.
60. Arthur Bestor, *Educational Wastelands: The Retreat from Learning in Our Public Schools*, 2nd ed., (Urbana, IL: University of Illinois Press, 1985), 6.
61. Ibid., 7.
62. Ibid., 111–12, 118.
63. Bestor, 157–59.
64. Ibid., 122–24.
65. Clarence Karier, "Retrospective One," in Bestor, 250.
66. Hartman, 13.
67. Hyman Rickover, *Education and Freedom*, (New York: E. F. Dutton, 1959). This book is a collection of essays he had written criticizing public schools.
68. Russell Kirk, *The Conservative Mind: From Burke to Eliot*, 7th revised ed., (Washington, DC: Regnery Publishing, 1985). The original text printed in 1953 was titled *The Conservative Mind: From Burke to Santayana.*
69. "RIP Irving Louis Horowitz," The Russell Kirk Center for Cultural Renewel. Accessed January 26, 2014, http://www.kirkcenter.org/index.php/news/.
70. "Ten Conservative principles," The Russell Kirk Center for Cultural Renewel. Accessed January 26, 2014, http://www.kirkcenter.org/index.php/detail.
71. Nash, 71.
72. Ibid., 15.
73. Kirk, 363.
74. Ibid., 365.
75. Ibid., 365.
76. Nash, 16.
77. Frank Chodorov, *Fugitive Essays: Selected Writings of Frank Chodorov* (Indianapolis: Liberty Press, 1980), 237, 74.
78. Ibid., 239.
79. Chodorov, "A Solution of Our Public School Problem (brought up to date)," *Human Events*, XI (20), May 19, 1954.
80. Ibid., 1–3.
81. Nash, 24.
82. Douglas Martin, "William F. Buckley Is Dead at 82," *The New York Times*, February 27, 2008.

83. William F. Buckley Jr., "Our Mission Statement," *The National Review Online*, accessed February 2, 2014, http://www.nationalreview.com/articles/223549/our-mission-statement/william-f-buckley-jr.
84. William F. Buckley, *God and Man at Yale: The Superstitions of "Academic Freedom"* (Washington, DC: Regnery, 1986), 23. First published in 1951.
85. William F. Buckley Jr., "Mr. Eisenhower's Decision and the Eisenhower Program," *National Review*, 1(18) March 21, 1956, 10.
86. Allan J. Lichtman, *White Protestant Nation: The Rise of the American Conservative Movement* (New York: Atlantic Monthly Press, 2008), 201.
87. Buckley, "Mr. Eisenhower," 10.
88. Buckley, "Why the South Must Prevail," *National Review*, IV (7) August 24, 1957, 14
89. Ibid., 149.
90. Anthony Harrigan, "The South Is Different," *National Review*, March 8, 1958, 1.
91. Ibid., 2.
92. J. B. Martin, "The Deep South Says Never," *Saturday Evening Post*, CCXIX, June 15, 1957, 23.
93. Neil R. McMillen, *The Citizens' Council: Organized Resistance to the Second Reconstruction*, 1954–64 (Chicago: University of Illinois Press, 1971), 138–55.
94. Ibid., 37.
95. Ibid., 190–91.
96. Association of Citizens' Councils of Mississippi. 2nd Annual Report, August 1956, 1.
97. James F. Byrnes, "The Supreme Court Must Be Curbed," (Greenwood, MS: Association of Citizens' Councils, 1956). Originally published in *U.S. News and World Report*, May 18, 1956.
98. James C. Cobb, *The Most Southern Place on Earth: The Mississippi Delta and the Roots of Regional Identity* (New York: Oxford University Press, 1992), 211.
99. Tom P. Brady, *Black Monday: An Address Made to the Indianola Citizens Council*, (Winona, Mississippi: Association of Citizens Council, 1955).
100. Brady, Foreword.
101. Brady, 56.
102. Cremin, 102.
103. John A. Andrew, *The Other Side of the Sixties: Young Americans for Freedom and the Rise of Conservative Politics* (New Brunswick, NJ: Rutgers University Press, 1997), 178–84.
104. Matthew Avery Sutton, *Jerry Falwell and the Rise of the Christian Right: A Brief History and Documents* (Bedford, NY: St. Martin's Press, 2012).
105. James D. Koerner, *Who Controls American Schools?—A Guide for Layman*, (Boston: Beacon Press, 1968).

106. Nock, 15.
107. Koerner, vii.
108. Ibid., 180.
109. Ibid., 121.
110. Murray N. Rothbard, *Education: Free and Compulsory*, (Auburn, AL: Ludwig von Mises Institute, 2010), 19.
111. Ibid., 9.
112. Ibid., 6–7.
113. Ibid., 8.

CHAPTER 3

1. Lanny Ebenstein, *Milton Friedman: A Biography* (New York: Palgrave Macmillan, 2007), 208.
2. Milton and Rose Friedman, *Free to Choose: A Personal Statement* (Orlando, FL: Harcourt Press, 1990), 154.
3. Milton Friedman and Anna Jacobson Schwartz, *A Monetary History of the United States, 1867–1960* (Princeton, NJ: Princeton University Press, 1963); Milton Friedman, *Capitalism and Freedom* (Chicago: University of Chicago Press, 1962), 37–55.
4. Ebenstein, 121.
5. Brian Snowdon and Howard R. Vane, *Conversations with Leading Economists: Interpreting Modern Macroeconomics* (Cheltenham, UK: Edward Elgar, 1999), 134.
6. Milton and Rose Friedman, *Two Lucky People: Memoirs* (Chicago: University of Chicago Press, 1998), 50.
7. Friedman, *Capitalism and Freedom*, 50.
8. George L. Perry (ed.), *Economic Events, Ideas, and Policies: The 1960s and After* (Washington DC: Brookings Institution Press, 2000), xi–xiv.
9. Joseph E. Stiglitz, *Globalization and Its Discontents* (New York: W. W. Norton and Company, 2003), 78.
10. Friedman, *Capitalism and Freedom*, 2.
11. Friedman, "Fiscal Responsibility," *Newsweek* 7, August 7, 1967, http://0055d26.netsolhost.com/friedman/pdfs/newsweek/NW.08.07.1967.pdf; in Ebenstein, 176.
12. Bruce Bartlett, "Tax Cuts and 'Starving the Beast,'" *Forbes*, May 7, 2010, http://www.forbes.com/2010/05/06/tax-cuts-republicans-starve-the-beast-columnists-bruce-bartlett.html.
13. Ebenstein, 198–99.
14. Milton Friedman, "The Role of Government in Education" in Robert A. Solo (ed.), *Economics and the Public Interest* (New Brunswick, NJ: Rutgers University Press, 1955); The Friedman Foundation for Educational Choice, http://www.edchoice.org/The-Friedmans/The-Friedmans-on-School-Choice/The-Role-of-Government-in-Education.aspx.
15. "Milton Friedman on Vouchers," (CNBC Interview, March 24, 2003). Friedman Foundation for Educational Choice, accessed February 3,

2014, http://www.edchoice.org/The-Friedmans/The-Friedmans-on-School-Choice/Milton-Friedman-on-Vouchers.aspx.

16. Deroy Murdock, "Friedman: Call Them Government Schools," *National Review Online*, August 1, 2012, http://www.nationalreview.com/corner/312879/friedman-call-them-government-schools-deroy-murdock.
17. Friedman, "The Role of Government in Education."
18. Frank Chodorov, "A Solution of Our Public School Problem," *Human Events,* May 19, 1954.
19. Milton and Rose Friedman, *Free to Choose*, 136–37.
20. Ibid., 164–65.
21. Ibid., 164.
22. Ibid., 170.
23. Milton Friedman, "Selling School Like Groceries: The Voucher Idea," *New York Times Magazine,* September 23, 1975, The Friedman Foundation for Educational Choice, http://www.edchoice.org/The-Friedmans/The-Friedmans-on-School-Choice/Selling-School-like-Groceries--The-Voucher-Idea.aspx.
24. Judith Areen and Christopher Jencks, "Education Vouchers: A Proposal for Diversity and Choice," *Teachers College Record* 72, no. 3 (1971), 327–36.
25. Friedman, "The Role of Government in Education."
26. Friedman, "Selling School Like Groceries."
27. James T. Patterson, *Brown v. Board of Education: A Civil Rights Milestone and Its Troubled Legacy (Pivotal Moments in American History edition)* (New York: Oxford University Press, 2002), 86–118.
28. Friedman, *Capitalism and Freedom*, 117.
29. Ibid., 117.
30. Neil R. McMillen, *The Citizens' Council: Organized Resistance to the Second Reconstruction, 1954–64* (Urbana, IL: University of Illinois Press, 1994), 15–40.
31. Jeffrey Raffel, *Historical Dictionary of School Segregation and Desegregation: The American Experience* (Westport, CT: Greenwood, 1998), 114.
32. Constance Curry. *Silver Rights* (Chapel Hill, NC: Algonquin Books of Chapel Hill, 1995), 208.
33. Ibid., 25.
34. John Dittmer, *Local People: The Struggle for Civil Rights in Mississippi* (Urbana, IL: University of Illinois Press, 1994), 390.
35. Joseph Crispino, *In Search of Another Country: Mississippi and the Conservative Counterrevolution* (Princeton, NJ: Princeton University Press, 2007), 241.
36. Beverly Browne, Pamela Kinsey-Barker, and Direka Martin, "Vouchers: An Initiative for School Reform?" *Issues Challenging Education, Horizon Site* http://horizon.unc.edu/projects/issues/papers/Voucher.html.
37. Ebenstein, 169–70.

38. James Boyd, "Nixon's Southern Strategy: 'It's All in the Charts,'" *New York Times* 25, May 17, 1970, 105–108.
39. Gary Orfield, Susan E. Eaton, and the Harvard Project on School Desegregation, *Dismantling Desegregation: The Quiet Reversal of Brown v. Board of Education*. (New York: The New Press, 1996), 9–13.
40. Areen and Jencks, 335–36.
41. Milton and Rose Friedman, *Free to Choose*, 172–73.
42. Alex Molnar, "School Vouchers: The Law, the Research, and Public Policy Implications," *Center for Education Research, Analysis, and Innovation* (Milwaukee, WI: University of Wisconsin–Milwaukee, 2001), 3.
43. Richard Nixon, "Special Message to the Congress on Education Reform" (speech before Congress, Washington DC, March 3, 1970), The American Presidency Project, http://www.presidency.ucsb.edu/ws/?pid=2895.
44. Ibid.
45. Ibid.
46. Ibid.
47. Ibid.
48. Ebenstein, 208.
49. Crispino, 1.
50. David C. Berliner and Bruce J. Biddle, *The Manufactured Crisis: Myths, Fraud, and the Attack on America's Public Schools* (Reading, MA: Addison-Wesley Publishing Company, Inc., 1995), 175.
51. Lou Cannon, *President Reagan: The Role of a Lifetime* (New York: Public Affairs, 1991), 459–60; Crispino, 239.
52. Molnar, 3.
53. Kevin J. Dougherty and Lizabeth Sostre. "Minerva and the Market: The Sources of the Movement for School Choice," Peter W. Cookson (ed.), *The Choice Controversy* (Newbury Park: CA: Corwin Press, 1992), 24–45. In Berliner and Biddle, 175.
54. Milton Friedman, "Selling School Like Groceries."
55. Marge Scherer, "On Savage Inequalities: A Conversation with Jonathan Kozol," *Educational Leadership* 50, no. 4 (December 1992–January 1993), 4–9.
56. Michael Mintrom. *Policy Entrepreneurs and School Choice, American Governance and Public Policy Series*. (Georgetown University Press, 2000), 182–208.
57. Diane Ravitch, *The Death and Life of the Great American School System: How Testing and Choice are Undermining Education* (New York: Basic Books, 2010), 8.
58. John E. Chubb and Terry M. Moe, *Politics, Markets, and America's Schools* (Washington, DC: The Brookings Institution, 1990), 2, 12; Ravitch, *The Death and Life*, 119.
59. "Federal Education Policy and the States, 1945–2009: A Brief Synopsis" *States' Impact on Federal Education Policy Project* (Albany, NY: New York State Archives, January 2006, revised November 2009).

60. Ravitch, *The Death and Life*, 17.
61. Terry M. Moe, *Schools, Vouchers and the American Public* (Washington DC: The Brookings Institution, 2002), 36.
62. Diane Ravitch, *Reign of Error: The Hoax of the Privatization Movement and the Danger to America's Public Schools* (New York: Alfred A. Knopf, 2013), 20–21.
63. Ravitch, *The Death and Life*, 121.
64. Ravitch, *Reign of Error*, 211.
65. Ibid., 21.
66. Ibid., 307–308.
67. Ibid., 208–209.
68. Ibid., 210.
69. Ibid., 210–11.
70. Ibid., 209.
71. Ibid., 213.
72. Milton Friedman, "The Promise of Vouchers," *The Wall Street Journal* (December 5, 2005).
73. Naomi Klein, *The Shock Doctrine: The Rise of Disaster Capitalism* (New York: Picador, 2007), 7.
74. Ibid., 7.
75. Ibid., 518.
76. Lyndsey Layton, "New Orleans Leads Nation in Public Charter School Enrollment," *Washington Post*, December 10, 2013, http://www.washingtonpost.com/local/education/new-orleans-leads-nation-in-percentage-of-public-charter-school-enrollment/2013/12/10/cb9c4ca6-61d6-11e3-bf45-61f69f54fc5f_story.html.
77. Moe, 346.
78. Dick M. Carpenter II, "School Choice Signals: Research Review and Survey Experiments, The Friedman Foundation for Educational Choice, January, 2014, http://www.edchoice.org/Research/Reports/School-Choice-Signals--Research-Review-and-Survey-Experiments.aspx.
79. Diane Ravitch, "How Embarrassing for the Friedman Foundation," Diane Ravitch's Blog. January 9, 2014. http://dianeravitch.net/2014/01/09/how-embarrassing-for-the-friedman-foundation/.

CHAPTER 4

1. David A. Garvin, "How the Baldrige Award Really Works." *Harvard Business Review* 69, no. 6 (November–December, 1991), 80–96. See also "Baldrige Performance Excellence Program." *Baldrige Performance Excellence*, accessed March 3, 2014, http://www.baldrigepe.org/.
2. Gerhard Gschwandtner, "David T. Kearns." *Selling Power Magazine*, accessed March 3, 2014, http://www.sellingpower.com/content/article/?a=3395/david-t-kearns&page=5.
3. John Jay Bonstingl, "The Quality Revolution in Education" *Improving School Quality* 50, no. 3 (November, 1992): 4–9.

4. Ibid., 4.
5. Ibid.
6. Ibid., 5–6.
7. Ibid.
8. Louis V. Gerstner Jr., with Roger D. Semerad, Denis Philip Doyle, and William B. Johnston. *Reinventing Education: Entrepreneurship in America's Public Schools.* (New York: The Penguin Group, 1994), 117.
9. Leanna Landsmann and Mary Harbaugh. "Education's Entrepreneurs. (include comments by chief executive officers on education) (Educating America: An Entrepreneurial Approach). *Forbes* (October 14, 1991). *Highbeam Business*, accessed March 5, 2014, http://business.highbeam.com/392705/article-1G1-11303756/education-entrepreneurs.
10. Larry Cuban. *The Blackboard and the Bottom Line: Why Schools Can't Be Businesses.* (Cambridge, MA: Harvard University Press, 2007), 91.
11. Thomas Heath. "Louis V. Gerstner Jr. Lays Out His Post-IBM Life. *The Washington Post* June 7, 2013, http://www.washingtonpost.com/business/economy/louis-v-gerstner-jr-lays-out-his-post-ibm-life/2013/06/07/04e9da2a-cd42-11e2-8845-d970ccb04497_story.html.
12. "About IBM." IBM, accessed March 14, 2014, http://www.ibm.com/ibm/us/en/; "Fast Facts." *National Center for Education Statistics. Institute of Education Sciences*, accessed March 21, 2014, http://nces.ed.gov/fastfacts/display.asp?id=372; "Occupational Outlook Handbook." Bureau of Labor Statistics, accessed March 21, 2014, http://www.bls.gov/ooh/management/elementary-middle-and-high-school-principals.htm.
13. Alain Jehlen. "ESEA at 45." *National Education Association*, accessed March 24, 2014, http://www.nea.org/home/38860.htm.
14. Diane Ravitch. *Reign of Error: The Hoax of the Privatization Movement and the Danger to America's Public Schools* (New York: Alfred A. Knopf, 2013), 175.
15. Gerstner, et al., xii.
16. Ibid., 8.
17. Ibid., x.
18. Ibid., 13.
19. Daniel Tanner. "A Nation 'Truly' at Risk." *Phi Delta Kappan* 75, no. 4 (December, 1993): 288–97.
20. Ibid.
21. "About Sandia." *Sandia National Laboratories*, accessed March 12, 2014, www.Sandia.gov.
22. Tanner, 288–97.
23. Ibid.
24. Lawrence C. Stedman. "The Sandia Report and U.S. Achievement: An Assessment." *Journal of Educational Research* 87, no. 3 (January–February, 1994): 133.
25. Ibid.

26. Tanner, 288–97.
27. Gerald W. Bracey. *The War against America's Public Schools: Privatizing Schools, Commercializing Education* (Boston, MA: Allyn and Bacon, 2002), 53.
28. Julie A. Miller. "Report Questioning 'Crisis' in Education Triggers an Uproar." *Education Week*, October 9, 1991, http://www.edweek.org/ew/articles/1991/10/09/06crisis.h11.html.
29. Tanner, 288–97.
30. Ibid.
31. Ibid.
32. Ibid.
33. Ibid.
34. Ibid.
35. Ibid.
36. Bracey, 53.
37. Tanner, 288–97.
38. Bracey, 53.
39. Gerald Bracey. "Righting Wrongs." The Huffington Post, December 3, 2007, http://www.huffingtonpost.com/gerald-bracey/righting-wrongs_b_75189.html.
40. "Perspectives on Education in America." *Journal of Educational Research* 86, no. 5 (May–June, 1993): 269.
41. Ibid., 272.
42. Ibid., 270.
43. Ibid., 272.
44. Ibid.
45. Ibid., 272.
46. Ibid., 263
47. Ibid.
48. Ibid., 265.
49. Ibid., 275.
50. Ibid., 293–94.
51. Ibid.
52. Ibid., 290.
53. Ibid., 279–82.
54. "Blue Ribbon Schools Program," (Washington DC: U.S. Department of Education, 1982). http://www2.ed.gov/programs/nclbbrs/list-1982.pdf.
55. Kathy Emery. "The Business Roundtable and Systemic Reform: How Corporate-Engineered High-Stakes Testing Has Eliminated Community Participation in Developing Educational Goals and Policies." (Dissertation, University of California, Davis, 2002).
56. Archie B. Carroll and Ann K. Buchholtz. *Business and Society: Ethics and Stakeholder Management*, 7th ed. (Mason, OH: South-Western Cengage Learning, 2009).
57. Ibid., 8.

58. Ibid.
59. Ibid.
60. Ibid.
61. Ibid.
62. Ruth F. Kolb and Robert P. Strauss. "State Laws Governing School Board Ethics." (Presentation at American Education Finance Association Conference 1999 Research Conference, Seattle, WA, March 19, 1999), 3.
63. Kathy Emery and Susan Ohanian. *Why Is Corporate America Bashing Our Public Schools?* (Portsmouth, NH: Heinemann, 2004), 33.
64. "History of Business Roundtable." *Business Roundtable*, accessed March 20, 2014, http://www.businessroundtable.org/about/history.
65. Joseph Beckham and Barbara Klaymeier Wills. "Duties, Responsibilities, Decision-Making, and Legal Basis for Local School Board Powers." *Education Encyclopedia*, accessed March 20, 2014, http://education.stateuniversity.com/pages/2391/School-Boards.html.
66. Matt Miller. "First, Kill All the School Boards: A Modest Proposal to Fix the Schools." *The Atlantic*, January 1, 2008, http://www.theatlantic.com/magazine/archive/2008/01/first-kill-all-the-school-boards/306579/.
67. Louis V. Gerstner. "Lessons from 40 Years of Education 'Reform:' Let's Abolish Local School Districts and Finally Adopt National Standards." *The Wall Street Journal*, December 1, 2008, http://online.wsj.com/news/articles/SB122809533452168067.
68. Diane Ravitch. (Keynote Speech, Network for Public Education First Annual Conference, Houston, TX, March 2, 2014).
69. American Legislative Exchange Council (ALEC), accessed June 2, 2014, http://www.alec.org/about-alec/history/.
70. Ibid.
71. Ibid.
72. Ibid.

Chapter 5

1. Leslie Larson. "Former First Lady Barbara Bush: Bill Clinton Thinks of George H.W. Bush Like the Father He Didn't Have. *Daily News*, January 21, 2014, http://www.nydailynews.com/news/politics/lady-barbara-bush-love-bill-clinton-article-1.1586676.
2. Brent Budowsky. "Bill Clinton's Rescue Ride." *The Hill*, February 26, 2014, http://thehill.com/opinion/brent-budowsky/199368-brent-budowsky-bill-clintons-rescue-ride.
3. Diane Ravitch. *The Death and Life of the Great American School System: How Testing and Choice are Undermining Education* (New York: Basic Books, 2010).
4. David Osborne and Ted Gaebler. *Reinventing Government: How the Entrepreneurial Spirit Is Transforming the Public Sector from Schoolhouse to Statehouse, City Hall to the Pentagon.* (Reading, MA: Addison-Wesley Publishing Company, Inc., 1992).

5. Jesse H. Rhodes. *An Education in Politics: The Origin and Evolution of No Child Left Behind.* (Ithaca, NY: Cornell University Press, 2012), 103.
6. Ibid., 104.
7. Ibid., 102.
8. Ibid., 107.
9. Ibid., 108. See alsoBusiness Roundtable, *The Essential Components of a Successful Education System: Putting Policy into Practice.* (New York: The Business Roundtable, 1992), 2.
10. Rhodes, 199.
11. Ibid.
12. Ibid., 109.
13. Ibid., 111.
14. Ibid., 112.
15. Improving America's Schools Act of 1994 (IASA), Part C, Sec. 10301. http://www2.ed.gov/legislation/ESEA/toc.html.
16. *Goals 2000:* Educate America Act, http://www2.ed.gov/legislation/GOALS2000/TheAct/index.html.
17. Michael M. Heise. "Goals 2000: Educate America Act: The Federalization and Legalization of Educational Policy," *Fordham Law Review*, 63, (1994), 345, 358: http://ir.lawnet.fordham.edu/flr/vol63/iss2/2.
18. Ibid., 358.
19. "The Clinton Years: Improving America's Schools Act." Federal Education Policy and the States, 1945–2009. States' Impact on Federal Education Policy. New York State Education Department, accessed June 3, 2014, http://www.archives.nysed.gov/edpolicy/research/res_essay_clinton_iasa.shtml.
20. Diane Ravitch. "50 States, 50 Standards: The Continuing Need for National Voluntary Standards in Education." Brookings Institution, Summer 1996, http://www.brookings.edu/research/articles/1996/06/summer-education-ravitch.
21. Rhodes, 131.
22. William J. Clinton. "Statement on Signing the School-to-Work Opportunities Act of 1994. The American Presidency Project, May 4, 1994, http://www.presidency.ucsb.edu/ws/?pid=50105
23. Louis V. Gerstner Jr. "Remarks of Louis V. Gerstner Jr., Chairman and CEO—IBM Corporation at the National Governors' Association Annual Meeting" (speech, National Governors Association Annual Meeting, Burlington, VT, July 30, 1995), 5.
24. Ibid., 1.
25. Ibid., 3–4.
26. Ibid., 5.
27. Ibid., 13.
28. Sybil Eakin. "Forum: National Education Summit." *Technos Quarterly* 5, no. 2, Summer 1996, http://www.ait.net/technos/tq_05/2eakin.php.
29. "A Review of the 1996 National Education Summit." Achieve. Accessed March 29, 2014, http://www.achieve.org/summits.

30. Denis P. Doyle. "A Personal Report from the Education Summit: What Does It Mean for Educational Reform?" The Heritage Lectures, no. 564. (Washington DC: The Heritage Foundation, May 21, 1996), 4.
31. Ibid.
32. "A Review of the 1996 National Education Summit," 3.
33. Doyle, 3.
34. Ibid.
35. William J. Clinton. "Remarks to the National Governors' Association Education Summit in Palisades, New York, March 27, 1996." The American Presidency Project: Document Archive: http://www.presidency.ucsb.edu/ws/index.php?pid=52594.
36. Ibid.
37. Ibid.
38. David Hursh. "Dr. David Hursh on Neoliberalism and 'Reform,'" Diane Ravitch's Blog, posted March 13, 2014, http://dianeravitch.net/2014/03/13/full-youtube-video-for-dr-david-hursh-on-neoliberalim-and-reform/.
39. Doyle, 1.
40. Ibid., 3.
41. Louis V. Gerstner Jr. "Lessons from 40 Years of Education Reform."
42. Doyle, 2.
43. Ibid., 4.
44. "Achieve and the American Diploma Project." Achieve, accessed March 15, 2014, http://www.achieve.org/files/About%20AchieveADP-Apr2012.pdf.
45. Sidney M. Milkis and Michael Nelson. *The American Presidency: Origins and Development, 1776–2011.* 6th ed. (Thousand Oaks, CA: CQ Press, 2011) 396.
46. William J. Clinton. "Address Before a Joint Session of the Congress of the State of the Union." The American Presidency Project, January 19, 1999. http://www.presidency.ucsb.edu/ws/?pid=57577.
47. Maris A. Vinovskis. *From a Nation at Risk to No Child Left Behind: National Education Goals and the Creation of Federal Education Policy.* (New York: Teachers College Press, 2009), 140–52.
48. Vinovskis, 150. See also, Rhodes, 143.
49. Vinovskis, 151.
50. Vinovskis, 151.
51. Julian Vasquez Heilig. "Billionaires Co-Opt Minority Groups into Campaign for Education Reform." *Cloaking Inequity*, March 7, 2014, http://cloakinginequity.com/2014/03/07/billionaires-co-opt-minority-groups-into-campaign-for-education-reform/.
52. Rhodes, 17–20.
53. "Resolution on Charter Schools." National Association for the Advancement of Colored People (NAACP), http://naacp.3cdn.net/ec6459eda5247ea257_d1m6bxsf6.pdf.

54. Valerie Strauss. "Key Flaw in Market-Based School Reform: A Misunderstanding of the Civil Rights Struggle." *The Washington Post*, August 5, 2013, http://www.washingtonpost.com/blogs/answer-sheet/wp/2013/08/05/key-flaw-in-market-based-school-reform-a-misunderstanding-of-the-civil-rights-struggle/.
55. Denisha Jones. "Beware of Education Reformers Who Co-Opt the Language of the Civil Rights Movement. *emPower*, February 27, 2014, http://www.empowermagazine.com/beware-education-reformers-co-opt-language-civil-rights-movement/.
56. Mike Lofgren. "Anatomy of the Deep State." *Moyers and Company*, February 21, 2014, http://billmoyers.com/2014/02/21/anatomy-of-the-deep-state/.
57. Ibid.
58. Ibid.
59. David T. Kearns and David A. Nadler. *Prophets in the Dark: How Xerox Reinvented Itself and Beat Back the Japanese*. (New York: HarperCollins Publishers, 1992).
60. Chester Finn. "Speech at a Meeting of the Georgia Policy Foundation." October 8, 1996, https://www.youtube.com/watch?v=v_M_JNOxQ8A.
61. Peter Applebome. "Lure of the Education Market Remains Strong for Business." *The New York Times*, January 31, 1996, http://www.nytimes.com/1996/01/31/us/lure-of-the-education-market-remains-strong-for-business.html.
62. Douglas Dewey. "How to Separate School and State: A Primer." *The Freeman*, July 1, 1996, http://www.fee.org/the_freeman/detail/how-to-separate-school-and-state-a-primer

CHAPTER 6

1. "Bush Calls Education 'Civil Rights Issue of Our Time.'" *CNN Inside-Politics*, January 19, 2002, http://edition.cnn.com/2002/ALLPOLITICS/01/19/bush.democrats.radio/index.html.
2. Jonathan Parker. "No Child Left Behind: The Politics and Policy of Education Reform." In *Assessing the George W. Bush Presidency: A Tale of Two Terms*, Andrew Wroe and Jon Herbert eds. (Edinburgh, UK: Edinburgh University Press, 2009), 185.
3. "Glossary of Terms Frequently Used in Federal Education Discussions." Children's Defense Fund, March 2011, http://www.childrensdefense.org/child-research-data-publications/data/education-glossary-of-terms.pdf.
4. Marian Wright Edelman. "The Courage and Vision of Medgar Evers." The Huffington Post, February 8, 2013, http://www.huffingtonpost.com/marian-wright-edelman/the-courage-and-vision-of_b_2649092.html.

5. Marian Wright Edelman. "Revisiting Marks, Mississippi." The Huffington Post, March 25, 2011, http://www.huffingtonpost.com/marian-wright-edelman/revisiting-marks-mississi_b_840786.html.
6. Peter Edelman. *Searching for America's Heart: RFK and the Renewal of Hope*. (Boston, MA: Houghton Mifflin Company, 2001), 51–54.
7. "The Poor People's Campaign." Children's Defense Fund, accessed April 4, 2014, http://www.childrensdefense.org/about-us/our-history/poor-peoples-campaign.html.
8. "Board of Directors Emeriti." Children's Defense Fund, accessed April 4, 2014, http://www.childrensdefense.org/about-us/board-of-directors/emeritus.html.
9. Barbara Vobejda and Judith Havemann. "2 HHS Officials Quit over Welfare Changes." *The Washington Post*, September 12, 1996, http://www.washingtonpost.com/wp-srv/national/longterm/welfare/quit.htm.
10. Peter Edelman. "The Worst Thing Bill Clinton Has Done." *The Atlantic Monthly* 279, no. 3, 43–58.
11. See Peter Edelman. *So Rich, So Poor: Why It's So Hard to End Poverty in America*. (New York: The New Press, 2012).
12. "Child Poverty in America 2010." Children's Defense Fund, September, 2011, http://www.childrensdefense.org/child-research-data-publications/data/child-poverty-in-america-2010.pdf.
13. H. Luke Schaefer and Kathryn Edin. "Extreme Poverty in the United States, 1996 to 2011." Policy Brief #28. National Poverty Center, University of Michigan. Gerald R. Ford School of Public Policy, accessed April 12, 2014, http://www.npc.umich.edu/publications/policy_briefs/brief28/.
14. Garrett Albert Duncan. "The Pitfalls of No Child Left Behind." *Viewpoint, Washington University in St. Louis Magazine*, Winter 2005, http://magazine-archives.wustl.edu/winter05/Viewpoint.htm.
15. Rhodes, 150.
16. Ibid., 151.
17. Ibid., 151–52.
18. Maris A. Vinovskis. *From a Nation at Risk to No Child Left Behind: National Education Goals and the Creation of Federal Education Policy*. (New York: Teachers College Press, 2009), 168.
19. Ibid.
20. Ibid., 169.
21. Ibid.
22. Patrick B. McGuigan and Stacy Martin. "Schools approach No Child Left Behind Deadline; Feds Say Nation's Schools Cannot Meet It." *CapitolBeatOK*, April 3, 2011, http://capitolbeatok.com/reports/schools-approach-no-child-left-behind-deadline-feds-say-nations-schools-cannot-meet-it; "Duncan Says 82 Percent of America's Schools Could 'Fail' under NCLB This Year." U.S. Department of Education, March 9, 2011, https://www.ed.gov/news/press-releases/duncan-says-82-percent-americas-schools-could-fail-under-nclb-year.

23. Rebecca Leung. "The Texas Miracle: 60 Minutes Investigates Claims That Houston Schools Falsified Dropout Rates." *CBS News*, January 6, 2004, http://www.cbsnews.com/news/the-texas-miracle/.
24. Ibid.
25. Julian Vasquez Heilig and Linda Darling-Hammond. "Accountability Texas-Style: The Progress and Learning of Urban Minority Students in a High-Stakes Testing Context." *Educational Evaluation and Policy Analysis* 30, no. 2, 75–110.
26. Larry Copeland. "School Cheating Scandal Shakes Up Atlanta." *USA Today*. April 14, 2013, http://www.usatoday.com/story/news/nation/2013/04/13/atlanta-school-cheatring-race/2079327/; Greg Toppo, "Memo Warns of Rampant Cheating in DC Public Schools." *USA Today*, April 11, 2013, http://www.usatoday.com/story/news/nation/2013/04/11/memo-washington-dc-schools-cheating/2074473/.
27. Greg Toppo, "Education Chief Calls Teachers Union 'Terrorist Organization.'" *Washington/Politics*, February 23, 2004, http://usatoday30.usatoday.com/news/washington/2004-02-23-paige-remarks_x.htm.
28. Robert Pear. "Education Chief Calls Union 'Terrorist,' Then Recants." *The New York Times*, February 24, 2004, http://www.nytimes.com/2004/02/24/us/education-chief-calls-union-terrorist-then-recants.html; "Education Chief's 'Terrorist' Remark Ignites Fury: Paige's Apology Does Little to Mollify Teacher's Union." *CNN Online*, February 24, 2004, http://www.cnn.com/2004/EDUCATION/02/24/paige.terrorist.nea/index.html?iref=mpstoryview.
29. Rod Paige. *The War against Hope: How Teachers' Unions Hurt Children, Hinder Teachers, and Endanger Public Education* (Nashville, TN: Thomas Nelson, 2006).
30. "About Us." *Chartwell Education Group LLC*, accessed April 13, 2014, http://www.chartwelleducation.com/pages/about-us.php.
31. "Rod Paige Joins Board of Fordham Foundation." *Education Week*, May 3, 2005, http://www.edweek.org/ew/articles/2005/05/04/34fed-3.h24.html.
32. Nancy E. Bailey. *Misguided Education Reform: Debating the Impact on Students* (Lanham, Maryland: Rowman and Littlefield Publishers, 2013), 60.
33. Rudolf Flesch. *Why Johnny Can't Read and What You Can Do About It* (New York: Harper and Row Publishers, Inc., 1955).
34. Ibid., 2.
35. Ibid., 4.
36. Jeanne S. Chall. *Learning to Read: The Great Debate*, 3rd ed. (Belmont CA: Wadsworth Publishing Company, 1995).
37. Richard C. Anderson, Elfrieda H. Hiebert, Judith A. Scott, and Ian A. G. Wilkinson. *Becoming a Nation of Readers: The Report of the Commission on Reading* (Urbana, IL: University of Illinois, 1985).
38. Ibid., 57–58.

39. S. W. Armstrong. "Illiteracy: An incurable disease or educational malpractice?" (Washington, DC: Senate Republican Policy Committee, 1989).
40. Robert W. Sweet Jr. "Illiteracy: An Incurable Disease or Education Malpractice?" *The National Right to Read Foundation*, 1996, http://www.nrrf.org/essay_Illiteracy.html.
41. Ibid.
42. "The Science of Reading Instruction and No Child Left Behind." Civic Bulletin, No. 49, September 2007. Bulletin adapted from a transcript of a Manhattan Institute forum in New York City, May 22, 2007, http://www.manhattan-institute.org/html/cb_49.htm.
43. Ken Goodman. "Comments on the Reading Excellence Act (U.S.) (HR 2614, Senate- passed version). An Invited Contribution. International Reading Association, December, 1998. Reading Online, http://www.readingonline.org/critical/act.html.
44. National Institute of Child Health and Human Development. (2000). *Report of the National Reading Panel. Teaching Children to Read: An Evidence-Based Assessment of the Scientific Research Literature on Reading and Its Implications for Reading Instruction* (NIH Publication No. 00–4769). Washington, DC: U.S. Government Printing Office.
45. National Research Council. *Preventing Reading Difficulties in Young Children*. (Washington, DC: National Academy Press, 1998).
46. "DIBELS Data System. Our History." University of Oregon, accessed April 20, 2014, https://dibels.uoregon.edu/about/#history.
47. Diana Jean Schemo. "Justice Dept. Is Asked to Investigate Reading Plan." *The New York Times*, April 21, 2007, http://www.nytimes.com/2007/04/21/us/21reading.html?_r=0. Complete coverage of the "Reading First Program Oversight" hearings is available on the *C-SPAN* website: http://www.c-span.org/video/?197699-1/reading-first-program-oversight-part-1.
48. U.S. Department of Education. "Reading First Impact Study. Executive Summary," Institute of Education Sciences. National Center for Education Evaluation and Regional Assistance, November, 2008, http://ies.ed.gov/pubsearch/pubsinfo.asp?pubid=NCEE20094038
49. ESEA Elementary & Secondary Education Act of 1965 (ESEA) (P.L.89–10) Sec. 604, Federal Control of Education Prohibited.
50. Ibid.
51. Department of Education Organization Act (Public Law 96–88, October 17, 1979) Sec. 103, Federal—State Relationships.
52. Mike Lofgren.
53. Ibid.

Chapter 7

1. "Susan Pimentel." GE Foundation, accessed April 23, 2014, https://sites.google.com/site/gefoundation2011a/sue- pimentel.
2. Achieve, Inc., the Education Trust, and the Thomas B. Fordham Foundation. "Ready or Not: Creating a High School Diploma That Counts"

(Washington, DC: American Diploma Project, 2004). 105. See also, Achieve, "Ready or Not," http://www.achieve.org/ReadyorNot, 4.

3. Achieve, "Ready or Not." 2.
4. Ibid.
5. Patricia M. McDonough, "The School-to-College Transition: Challenges and Prospects." *National Association of State Student Grant and Aid Programs*, 2004, http://www.nassgap.org/index.aspx.
6. Ibid., 18.
7. Ibid., 7, 13.
8. Lyndsey Layton, "How Bill Gates Pulled off the Swift Common Core Revolution." *The Washington Post*, June 7, 2014, http://www.washingtonpost.com/politics/how-bill-gates-pulled-off-the-swift-common-core-revolution/2014/06/07/a830e32e-ec34-11e3-9f5c-9075d5508f0a_story.html.
9. "Our History." Achieve, accessed April 14, 2014, http://www.achieve.org/history-achieve.
10. Achieve, Inc., "Ready or Not." 3.
11. Ayana Douglas-Hall and Heather Koball. "The New Poor: Regional Trends in Child Poverty since 2000." National Center for Child Poverty, Mailman School of Public Health, Columbia University, Aug. 2006, http://www.nccp.org/publications/pdf/text_672.pdf; 3; Washington Post Foreign Staff, "How 35 Countries Compare on Poverty (the United States is ranked 34th)." *The Washington Post*, April 15, 2013, http://www.washingtonpost.com/blogs/worldviews/wp/2013/04/15/map-how-35-countries-compare-on-child-poverty-the-u-s-is-ranked-34th/.
12. Achieve, "Ready or Not," 38–40.
13. Ibid., 4.
14. Jonathan Martin, "Republican See Wedge in Common Core," *The New York Times*, April 19, 2014, http://www.nytimes.com/2014/04/20/us/politics/republicans-see-political-wedge-in-common-core.html?_r=1.
15. Achieve, "Ready or Not," 8.
16. Ibid., 10.
17. Maris A. Vinovskis. *From a Nation at Risk to No Child Left Behind: National Education Goals and the Creation of Federal Education Policy.* (New York: Teachers College Press, 2009), 133.
18. Achieve, "Future Ready Project," accessed April 14, 2014, http://www.achieve.org/future-ready.
19. Achieve, "2001 National Education Summit," accessed April 14, 2014, http://www.achieve.org/files/2001NationalEducationSummitBriefing%20Book.pdf, 2.
20. Achieve. "Summits." accessed April 14, 2014, http://www.achieve.org/summits
21. Achieve, "2001 National Education Summit," accessed April 15, 2014, http://www.achieve.org/files/2001NationalEducationSummitBriefing%20Book.pdf, 10–11.
22. Ibid., 41.

23. Glenn McCandless, "Positioning Your Company for Ed-Tech Platform Leadership." From *Selling to Schools. Our Expertise. Your Success*, accessed June 13, 2014, http://www.sellingtoschools.com/education-marketing-strategies-for-platform-leadership; See also, for example, Jessica Stillman, "A Lesson in Hustle: How an Edtec Startup Got Their Product into 3000 Schools in a Year." *Women 2.0*, October 28, 2013, http://women2.com/lesson-hustle-edtech-startup-got-product-3000-schools-year/; Paula Maylahn and Pat Walkington, "Six Steps to Plan for Success in the K-12 Education Market." *Selling to Our Schools. Our Expertise. Your Success*, accessed June 13, 2014, http://www.sellingtoschools.com/articles/plan-sales-success-k-12-sales-education-market.
24. "2002 Governors Education Symposium Report." The Hunt Institute, December 1, 2002, http://www.hunt-institute.org/knowledge-library/articles/2002-12-1/2002-governors-education-symposium-report/.
25. "Bill Gates: Education Commission of the States Annual Conference." Bill and Melinda Gates Foundation, July 11, 2012, http://www.gatesfoundation.org/media-center/speeches/2012/07/bill-gates-education-commission-of-the-states-annual-conference.
26. Achieve, "About Us."
27. "Bill Gates: Education Commission of the States Annual Conference."
28. Ibid.
29. Ibid.
30. "Academic Rankings of World Universities." The Center for World-Class Universities (CWCU) of Shanghai Jiao Tong University, accessed April 29, 2014, http://www.shanghairanking.com/index.html.
31. Geeta Anand, "India Graduates Millions, but Too Few Are Fit to Hire," *The Wall Street Journal*, April 5, 2011, http://online.wsj.com/news/articles/SB10001424052748703515504576142092863219826.
32. "World University Rankings, 2013–14" (Sponsored by Reuters) *Times Higher Education*, accessed April 29, 2014, http://www.timeshighereducation.co.uk/world-university-rankings/2013-14/world-ranking.
33. "Academic Rankings of World Universities."
34. Joe Robertson, "Scores on ACT point to many disparities," *Kansas City Star*, August 21, 2013, http://www.kansascity.com/2013/08/21/4424263/scores-on-act-point-to-many-disparities.html. See also, Joe Robertson and Dawn Bormann, "ACT Is Sobering News on School Performance," *The Kansas City Star*, August 22, 2013, http://www.kansascity.com/2012/08/21/3772904/act-is-sobering-news-on-school.html.
35. "About Us." Thomas B. Fordham Institute, accessed May 1, 2014, http://www.edexcellence.net/about-us.
36. Chester E. Finn, *Troublemaker: A Personal History of Education Reform since Sputnik* (Princeton, NJ: Princeton University Press, 2008), 225.
37. Chester E. Finn Jr., *We Must Take Charge: Our Schools and Our Future* (New York: The Free Press, 1991), 254. Kearns proves an introductory statement to Finn's 1991 book.

38. Finn, *Troublemaker*, 224.
39. Ibid., 26.
40. Ibid., 26.
41. Diane Ravitch, *Reign of Error*, 134. For a more in-depth analysis of the Teach for America initiative, see Chapter 14, "The Problem with Teach for America," 133–45.
42. Finn, *Troublemaker*, 27.
43. Rhodes, 20.
44. Adolph Reed Jr., "Nothing Left: The Long Slow Surrender of American Liberals." *Harpers* 328, no. 1966, March 2014, 29.
45. Achieve, "Out of Many, One: Toward Rigorous Common Core Standards from the Ground Up." July 2008, http://www.achieve.org/files/OutofManyOne.pdf, 4.
46. Achieve, "Out of Many, One," 11, 16.
47. Ibid., 21.
48. Ibid.,
49. Ibid., 22.
50. Tabitha Grossman, Ryan Reyna, Stephanie Shipton. "Realizing the Potential: How Governors Can Lead Effective Implementation of the Common Core State Standards," National Governors Association, October 2011, http://www.nga.org/files/live/sites/NGA/files/pdf/1110CCSSIIMPLEMENTATIONGUIDE.PDF,4. This report was made possible by the Bill and Melinda Gates Foundation, the Ewing Marion Kauffman Foundation, and the William and Flora Hewlett Foundation.
51. Achieve, the National Governors Association, and the Council of Chief State School Officers. "Benchmarking for Success: Ensuring U.S. Students Receive a World-Class Education," (Washington, DC: National Governors Association, 2008), 2.
52. Ibid., 3.
53. Ibid., 19, 27, 28. See also Donald Zancanella and Michael Moore. "The Origins of the Common Core: Untold Stories." *Language Arts* 91, no. 4 (March, 2014), 273–79.
54. Ibid., 21.
55. Ibid., 6.
56. Ibid., 20.
57. Ibid., 10.
58. See, for example, "Without Consent: How Drug Companies Exploit Indian 'Guinea Pigs." *The Independent*, May 6, 2014, http://newamericamedia.org/2011/08/us-pharmaceutical-companies-testing-drugs-on-indias-poor.php; "U.S. Pharmaceutical Companies Testing Drugs on India's Poor," *New America Media*, August 1, 2011, http://www.independent.co.uk/news/world/asia/without-consent-how-drugs-companies-exploit-indian-guinea-pigs-6261919.html; Gardiner Harris. "Medicines Made in India Set Off Safety Worries," *The New York Times*, February 14, 2014, http://www.nytimes.com/2014/02/15/world/asia/medicines-made-in-india-set-off-safety-worries.html?_r=0.

59. Zhao Yanrong. "Chinese Pharmaceuticals Testing the US Drug Market," *The China Daily/USA,* October 28, 2011, http://usa.chinadaily.com.cn/business/2011-10/28/content_13997107.htm.
60. Gardiner Harris. "Medicines Made in India Set Off Safety Worries." *The New York Times,* February 14, 2014, http://www.nytimes.com/2014/02/15/world/asia/medicines-made-in-india-set-off-safety-worries.html?_r=0.
61. Achieve et al., "Benchmarking for Success," 6.
62. "Development Process." *Common Core State Standards Initiative: Preparing America's Students for College and Career*, accessed May 4, 2014, http://www.corestandards.org/about-the-standards/development-process/.

CHAPTER 8

1. Sam Dillon. "Schools Chief from Chicago Is Cabinet Pick." *The New York Times*, December 15, 2008, http://www.nytimes.com/2008/12/16/us/politics/16educ.html?_r=0.
2. *The Death and Life of the Great American School System: How Testing and Choice are Undermining Education* (New York: Basic Books, 2010), 21. See also Mike Lofgren. "Anatomy of the Deep State." *Moyers and Company*, February 21, 2014: http://billmoyers.com/2014/02/21/anatomy-of-the-deep-state/.
3. See, for example: Joanne Barkam. "Hired Guns on Astroturf: How to Buy and Sell School Reform." *Dissent: A Quarterly of Politics and Culture,* Spring 2012, http://www.dissentmagazine.org/article/hired-guns-on-astroturfhow-to-buy-and-sell-school-reform; Geoff Decker, "Success Academy Donors Give Big to Cuomo Campaign." *Chalkbeat*, January 17, 2014, http://ny.chalkbeat.org/2014/01/17/success-academy-donors-flood-cuomos-coffers-filings-show/#.U5MbvOhX-uY; Karin Klein. "The Big Special Interests in the Race for California Schools Chief." *Los Angeles Times Opinion*, May 27, 2014, http://www.latimes.com/opinion/opinion-la/la-ol-tuck-torlakson-campaign-20140523-story.html; Brett Chase and Patrick Rehkamp. "School Reform Attracting Billionaires' Money to Illinois Races." *Chicago Sun-Times*, June 1, 2014, http://politics.suntimes.com/article/springfield/school-reform-attracting-billionaires%E2%80%99-money-illinois-races/sun-06012014-114pm.
4. Ravitch, *The Death and Life*, 20–21.
5. "White House Profile: Secretary Arne Duncan" White House Blog, accessed May 15, 2014, http://www.whitehouse.gov/blog/author/Secretary%20Arne%20Duncan.
6. "Meet Your Government: Arne Duncan, Secretary of the Department of Education." AllGov, accessed May 3, 2014, http://www.allgov.com/officials/duncan-arne?officialid=28849.

7. "White House Profile."
8. "Duncan Praised as 'Bona Fide Reformer' of Chicago Education System." *Fox News*, December, 16, 2008, http://www.foxnews.com/politics/2008/12/16/duncan-praised-bona-fide-reformer-chicago-education/.
9. Valerie Strauss. "The Biggest Irony in Chicago's Mass Closing of Schools." *The Washington Post*, May 30, 2013, http://www.washingtonpost.com/blogs/answer-sheet/wp/2013/05/30/the-biggest-irony-in-chicagos-mass-closing-of-schools/.
10. Becky Veveo. "CPS Wants to Close First Renaissance Schools." *WBEZ91.5*. May 8, 2013, http://www.wbez.org/news/education/cps-wants-close-first-renaissance-schools-107072.
11. Ibid.
12. Academy for Urban School Leadership (AUSL), accessed May 13, 2014, http://auslchicago.org.
13. Strauss. "Biggest Irony."
14. "Englewood Parents Protest CPS School Closings." *5 NBC Chicago*, May 21, 2013. http://www.nbcchicago.com/blogs/ward-room/Englewood-Parents-Protest-CPS-School-Closings_Chicago.html.
15. Valerie Strauss. "Chicago Mayor Rahm Emanuel Chooses Private School for Kids." *The Washington Post*, July 12, 2011, http://www.washingtonpost.com/blogs/answer-sheet/post/chicago-mayor-rahm-emanuel-chooses-private-school-for-kids/2011/07/21/gIQAzES7RI_blog.html.
16. "Clear-Cutting Our Schools." *Rethinking Schools* 28, no. 1, Fall 2013, http://www.rethinkingschools.org/archive/28_01/edit281.shtml.
17. Linda Perry. "NYC Public Schools, Co-locations, Charters, Albany." *WBAI Pacifica Radio New York*, March 14, 2014, http://wbai.org/articles.php?article=1824.
18. Jake Grovum. "Lasting Effects from Financial Crash Mean New Normal in States." *Stateline: The Daily News of the Pew Charitable Trust*, September 5, 2013, http://www.pewstates.org/projects/stateline/headlines/lasting-effects-from-financial-crash-mean-new-normal-in-states-85899502664.
19. "Race to the Top Executive Summary." November, 2009. U.S. Department of Education, November, 2009, http://www2.ed.gov/programs/racetothetop/executive-summary.pdf.
20. "The Race to the Top Begins—Remarks by Secretary Arne Duncan." U.S. Department of Education, July 24, 2009, http://www2.ed.gov/news/speeches/2009/07/07242009.html.
21. Ibid.
22. "States Will Lead the Way toward Reform." Secretary Arne Duncan's Remarks at the 2009 Governors Education Symposium, *U.S. Department of Education*, June 14, 2009, http://www2.ed.gov/news/speeches/2009/06/06142009.html.

23. "Race to the Top Begins."
24. "Secretary Duncan Sets Tone for 'Race to the Top' by Naming Innovative New Leader: Joanne Weiss Joins Department of Education from NewSchools Venture Fund to Implement Unprecedented Incentive Program for Bold National Reforms." U.S. Department of Education, May 19, 2009, http://www.ed.gov/news/press-releases/secretary-duncan-sets-tone-race-top-naming-innovative-new-leader.
25. NewSchools Venture Fund, accessed June 1, 2014, http://www.ewschools.org/.
26. "Remarks by the President on Education." The White House, Office of the Press Secretary, July 24, 2009, http://www.whitehouse.gov/the_press_office/Remarks-by-the-President-at-the-Department-of-Education/.
27. Ibid.
28. Ibid.
29. Ibid.
30. "Race to the Top Executive Summary," 10.
31. Ibid., 2.
32. "Remarks by the President on Education."
33. "The Race to the Top Begins."
34. "Race to the Top Application for Initial Funding." U.S. Department of Education, http://www2.ed.gov/programs/racetothetop/phase1-applications/minnesota.pdf, 8.
35. "ESEA Flexibility: Flexibility to Improve Student Academic Achievement and Increase the Quality of Instruction." U.S. Department of Education, September 23, 2011, http://www2.ed.gov/policy/elsec/guid/esea-flexibility/index.html, 2.
36. "Common Core State Standards Initiative: Development Process Timeline."
37. Achieve. "Achieving the Common Core," accessed June 4, 2014, http://www.achieve.org/print/achieving-common-core.
38. Achieve. "Our History."
39. Bill and Melinda Gates Foundation. "Grants," accessed June 4, 2014, http://www.gatesfoundation.org/search#q/k=Achieve%2C%20Inc.&page=2.
40. "Common Core State Standards Initiative: Development Process Timeline."
41. Anthony Cody, "The Secret Sixty Prepare to Write Standards for 50 Million." *Education Week*, July 6, 2009, http://blogs.edweek.org/teachers/living-in-dialogue/2009/07/national_standards_process_ign.html.
42. National Governors Association. "Common Core State Standards Work Group and Feedback Group Announced," July 1, 2009, http://www.nga.org/cms/home/news-room/news-releases/page_2009/col2-content/main-content-list/title_common-core-state-standards-development-work-group-and-feedback-group-announced.html.

43. Cody, 2.
44. "Achieve the Core: Student Achievement Partners," accessed June 3, 2014, http://achievethecore.org/author/2/student-achievement-partners.
45. "GE Foundation Awards $18 Million to Student Achievement Partners," *Philanthropy News Digest*, February 2, 2012, http://www.philanthropynewsdigest.org/news/ge-foundation-awards-18-million-to-student-achievement-partners; Bill and Melinda Gates Foundation. "Awarded Grants," accessed June 12, 2014, http://www.gatesfoundation.org/How-We-Work/Quick-Links/Grants-Database#q/k=student%20achievement%20partners.
46. "America's Choice." National Center on Education and the Economy, accessed June 12, 2014, http://www.ncee.org/programs-affiliates/history/americas-choice/.
47. "Pearson and America's Choice Announce Acquisition Agreement," *Pearson*, August 3, 2010, http://www.pearsoned.com/pearson-and-americas-choice-announce-acquisition-agreement/#.U3edddEU9jo.
48. National Governors Association for Best Practices and the Council of Chief State School Officers. *Reaching Higher: The Common Core State Standards Validation Committee,* June 2010, http://www.corestandards.org/assets/CommonCoreReport_6.10.pdf, 2.
49. National Governors Association. "Common Core State Standards Initiative Validation Committee Announced," September 24, 2009, http://www.nga.org/cms/home/news-room/news-releases/page_2009/col2-content/main-content-list/title_common-core-state-standards-initiative-validation-committee-announced.html.
50. National Governors Association. "Common Core State Standards Available for Comment," September 21, 2009, http://www.corestandards.org/assets/CorePublicFeedback.pdf.
51. National Governors Association. "Common Core State Standards K-12 Work and Feedback Groups Announced," November 10, 2009, http://www.nga.org/cms/home/news-room/news-releases/page_2009/col2-content/main-content-list/title_common-core-state-standards-k-12-work-and-feedback-groups-announced.html.
52. "Common Core State Standards Initiative: Development Timeline."
53. Ibid.
54. "Rahm Emanuel on the Opportunities of Crisis," *WSJ Videos*, November 18, 2008, http://live.wsj.com/video/rahm-emanuel-on-the-opportunities-of-crisis/3F6B9880-D1FD-492B-9A3D-70DBE8EB9E97.html#!3F6B9880-D1FD-492B-9A3D-70DBE8EB9E97.
55. "Common Core State Standards Initiative: Development Timeline."
56. "Reaction to the March 2010 Draft Common Core State Standards: Highlights and Themes from the Public Draft," accessed June 15, 2014, http://www.corestandards.org/assets/k-12-feedback-summary.pdf. See also: "Common Core State Standards Initiative: Development Timeline."

57. "PDK/Gallup Poll of the Public's Attitudes toward the Public Schools," *Phi Delta Kappa International*, August 13, 2013: http://pdkintl.org/programs-resources/poll/.
58. *Reaching Higher: The Common Core State Standards Validation Committee*, 4.
59. Sandra Stotsky. "Common Core's Invalid Validation Committee," Paper presented at a Conference at University of Notre Dame, September 9, 2013, http://www.uaedreform.org/downloads/2013/11/common-cores-invalid-validation-committee.pdf.
60. Michael Petrilli. "Petrilli Testimony on Common Core in Ohio," *Education-next*, November 20, 2013, http://educationnext.org/petrilli-testimony-on-common-core-in-ohio/.
61. Sandra Stotsky, "Testimony in Favor of Wyoming Bill 14LSO.0326.L2" February 12, 2014, http://www.uaedreform.org/downloads/2014/02/testimony-in-favor-of-wyoming-bill-14lso-0326-l2.pdf, 1.
62. Ibid.
63. Ibid.
64. Home School Legal Defense Association. "Building the Machine: The Common Core Documentary," March 31, 2014, https://www.youtube.com/watch?v=zjxBClx01jc. Interestingly, as of September 2014, three states (Indiana, South Carolina, and Oklahoma) have abandoned the CCSS.
65. Ibid.
66. Ibid.
67. Jeff Duncan. "Duncan Introduces Resolution Condemning Common Core," February 12, 2014. http://jeffduncan.house.gov/press-release/duncan-introduces-resolution-condemning-common-core.
68. Achieve the Core, "Our Purpose," accessed June 3, 2014, http://achievethecore.org/about-us.
69. Todd Balf. "The Story Behind the SAT Overhaul," *The New York Times Magazine*, March 6, 2014, http://www.nytimes.com/2014/03/09/magazine/the-story-behind-the-sat-overhaul.html?_r=1.
70. McKinsey and Company, "About Us," accessed June 13, 2014, http://www.mckinsey.com/.
71. Joy Resmovits. "David Coleman, Common Core Writer, Gears Up for SAT Rewrite," *The Huffington Post*, August 30, 2013, http://www.huffingtonpost.com/2013/08/30/david-coleman-common-core-sat_n_3818107.html.
72. "McGraw-Hill Education Forms New Assessment and Reporting Unit to Meet Growing Global Demand, Combines CTB/McGraw-Hill, The Grow Network/McGraw-Hill, and McGraw-Hill Digital Learning." *McGraw-Hill Financial*, December 1, 2005, http://investor.mhfi.com/phoenix.zhtml?c=96562&p=irol-newsArticle&ID=649072&highlight.
73. David Coleman. "What Must Be Done in the Next Two Years," December 8–9, 2011. (Keynote speech, Institute for Learning: 2011

IFL Senior Leadership Meeting, University of Pittsburgh, December 8–9, 2011), http://truthinamericaneducation.com/wp-content/uploads/2013/12/What_must_be_done.pdf.

74. "Jason Zimba." *Achieve the Core: Student Academic Partners*, accessed June 4, 2014, http://achievethecore.org/author/35/jason-zimba.
75. "Massachusetts Board of Elementary and Secondary Education." March 23, 2010, https://www.youtube.com/watch?v=eJZY4mh2rt8.
76. "StandardsWork: Our History." *StandardsWork*, accessed June 13, 2014, http://www.standardswork.org/history.asp. See also, Susan Pimentel." National Assessments Governing Board, accessed June 13, 2014, http://www.nagb.org/newsroom/naep-releases/2011-writing/bio-pimentel.html.

Chapter 9

1. "The Assessment Consortia." *K-12 Center at ETS*, accessed June 20, 2014, http://www.k12center.org/.
2. See, for example: Sean Cavanaugh. "American Institutes for Research Fights Pearson Common-Core Testing Award." *Education Week*, May 6, 2014, http://blogs.edweek.org/edweek/marketplacek12/2014/05/american_institutes_for_research_challenges_pearson_common-core_testing_award_in_court.html; Winnie Hu. "Testing Firm Faces Inquiry on Free Trips for Officials." *The New York Times*, December 21, 2011, http://www.nytimes.com/2011/12/22/education/new-york-attorney-general-is-investigating-pearson-education.html?_r=0.
3. "Special Edition: Testing Resistance and Reform News": April 2–4, 2014. *FairTest: The National Center for Fair and Open Testing*, April 2–4, 2014, http://www.fairtest.org/special-edition-testing-resistance-reform-news-apr.
4. Nancy Thorner and Bonnie O'Neil. "Common Core Dates Back to the Marxist-Socialist Paradigm of UN Charter." *Heartlander Magazine*, April 7, 2014, http://blog.heartland.org/2014/04/common-core-dates-back-to-the-marxist-socialist-paradigm-of-un-charter/; see also, Anthony Cody. "A Progressive and a Conservative Find Common Ground Opposing the Common Core." *Education Week Teacher, Living in Dialogue*, April 15, 2013, http://blogs.edweek.org/teachers/living-in-dialogue/2013/04/a_progressive_and_a_conservati.html; and Valerie Strauss, "Gov. Cuomo May Face Primary Challenge from Progressive Democrat," *The Washington Post*, June 12, 2014; http://www.washingtonpost.com/blogs/answer-sheet/wp/2014/06/12/new-york-gov-cuomo-may-face-primary-challenge-from-progressive-democrat/.
5. "National Testing: Prepare for a Battle. *Education World*, September 15, 1997, http://www.educationworld.com/a_admin/admin/admin020.shtml; Also quoted in: Glenn Gilbert. "State Ready to

Implement Common Core—Finally!" *Morning Sun Opinion*, December 4, 2013, http://www.themorningsun.com/opinion/20131204/gilbert-state-ready-to-implement-common-core-finally.

6. Alexander Russo. "What Is Common Core and Why Is Everyone—Right, Left—so Mad About It?" *Slate*, September 25, 2013, http://www.slate.com/articles/double_x/doublex/2013/09/common_core_either_you_re_against_this_new_push_for_academic_standards_and.html.
7. Jon Campbell. "Education Chief Defends Cancellation of Common Core Forums." *Democrat and Chronicle*. October 15, 2013, http://www.democratandchronicle.com/story/news/local/2013/10/15/education-chief-defends-cancellation-of-common-core-forums/2986771/.
8. Valerie Strauss. "Arne Duncan: 'White Suburban Moms' Upset That Common Core Shows Their Kids Aren't 'Brilliant.'" *The Washington Post*, November 16, 2013, http://www.washingtonpost.com/blogs/answer-sheet/wp/2013/11/16/arne-duncan-white-surburban-moms-upset-that-common-core-shows-their-kids-arent-brilliant/.
9. Achieve. "Race to the Top. Accelerating College and Career Readiness in States: P-20 Longitudinal Data Systems," accessed June 14, 2014, http://www.achieve.org/files/RTTT-P20LongitudinalData.pdf.
10. Institute of Education Sciences (IES). National Center for Education Statistics. "Statewide Longitudinal Data Systems Grant Program: Designing, Developing, Implementing, and Using Longitudinal Data Systems to Improve Student Learning," accessed June 14, 2014, http://nces.ed.gov/programs/slds/about_SLDS.asp.
11. Public Consulting Group (PCG). "Education Analytics," accessed June 17, 2014, http://www.publicconsultinggroup.com/education/EducationAnalytics/index.html.
12. PCG. "Business Partners," accessed June 17, 2014, http://www.publicconsultinggroup.com/about/business_partners/.
13. U.S. Department of Education. "Family Educational Rights and Privacy Act" (FERPA), accessed June 17, 2014, http://www2.ed.gov/policy/gen/guid/fpco/ferpa/index.html.
14. Electronic Privacy Information Center (EPIC). "EPIC v. The U.S. Department of Education: Challenging the Department of Education's Family Educational Rights and Privacy Act (FERPA) 2011 Regulations," accessed June 17, 2014, http://epic.org/apa/ferpa/.
15. Stephanie Simon. "K-12 Student Database Jazzes Tech Startups, Spooks Parents." *Reuters*, March 3, 2013, http://www.reuters.com/article/2013/03/03/us-education-database-idUSBRE92204W20130303.
16. Ibid.
17. Ibid.
18. Ibid.
19. Eric Owens. *Daily Caller*. As reported by Diane Marie. "Bill Gates Crying in His Vault." The Education Action Network. April 28, 2014, http://

teach1776.ning.com/group/the-coalition-against-common-core/forum/topics/inbloom-goes-out-of-business?xg_source=activity.

20. Iwan Streichenberger. Letter posted on inBloom's website April, 2014, https://www.inbloom.org/.
21. Lynn Sweet. "Obama Education Speech in Ohio," *The Chicago Sun-Times*, September 9, 2008, http://blogs.suntimes.com/sweet/2008/09/obama_education_speech_in_ohio.html.
22. Ibid.
23. "Remarks by the President on Education." The White House, Office of the Press Secretary, January 16, 2014, http://www.whitehouse.gov/the_press_office/Remarks-by-the-President-at-the-Department-of-Education/.
24. Alison Damast. "Q&A: Teach for America's Wendy Kopp," *Bloomberg Business Week*, March 26, 2012, http://www.businessweek.com/articles/2012-03-26/q-and-a-teach-for-americas-wendy-kopp; Audrey Cheng. "Teach for America Gains Record Number of Applicants," *Medill on the Hill*, March 11, 2013, http://medillonthehill.net/2013/03/teach-for-america-gains-record-number-of-applicants/.
25. Chad Sommer. "Teach for America's Pro-Corporate, Union-Busting Agenda." *Salon*, January 13, 2014, http://www.salon.com/2014/01/13/teach_for_americas_pro_corporate_union_busting_agenda_partner/.
26. Diane Ravitch. *Reign of Error: The Hoax of the Privatization Movement and the Danger to America's Public Schools*, (New York: Alfred A. Knopf, 2013), 136.
27. Ibid., 133.
28. Wendy Kopp. *One Day, All Children . . .: The Unlikely Triumph of Teach for America and What I Learned along the Way* (New York: PublicAffairs, 2001), xii.
29. Wendy Kopp. *A Chance to Make History: What Works and What Doesn't in Providing Excellent Education for All* (New York: PublicAffairs, 2011), 5. See also, Ravitch, *Reign of Error*, 135.
30. Ravitch, *Reign of Error*, 135.
31. Ibid.
32. Teach for America. "KIPP: Where Great Teachers Become Great School Leaders," accessed June 15, 2014, http://www.teachforamerica.org/assets/documents/08TFA-one_sheetv1r6.pdf.
33. Ravitch, *Reign of Error*, 149–50.
34. Ibid., 138–39.
35. Ibid., 140.
36. Olivia Blanchard. "I Quit Teach for America: Five Weeks of Training Was Not Enough to Prepare Me for a Room of 20 Unruly Elementary Schoolers." *The Atlantic*, September 23, 2013, http://www.theatlantic.com/education/archive/2013/09/i-quit-teach-for-america/279724/.
37. Ravitch, *Reign of Error*, 137.
38. Ibid., 138.
39. Ibid., 134.

40. "Is TFA Undermining the Chicago Public Schools? An Internal TFA Document Shows Plans for a Dramatic Charter Expansion in the Windy City." *Edushyster*, September 9, 2013, http://edushyster.com/?p=3191.
41. Maureen O'Hagan. "Post-Katrina: Will New Orleans Still Be New Orleans? The Institute for Southern Studies." *Facing South*, April 10, 2014, http://www.southernstudies.org/2014/04/post-katrina-will-new-orleans-still-be-new-orleans.html.
42. Jaclyn Zubrzycki. "TFA Alumni Aid New Teachers in New Orleans." *Education Week*, April 19, 2013, http://www.edweek.org/ew/articles/2013/04/19/29neworleans_ep.h32.html.
43. Danielle Dreilinger. "7,000 New Orleans Teachers, Laid Off After Katrina, Win Court Ruling." *The Times-Picayune*, January 16, 2014, http://www.nola.com/crime/index.ssf/2014/01/7000_new_orleans_teachers_laid.html.
44. "Remarks by the President on Education." The White House, Office of the Press Secretary, January 16, 2014, http://www.whitehouse.gov/the_press_office/Remarks-by-the-President-at-the-Department-of-Education/.
45. "Race to the Top Executive Summary." U.S. Department of Education, November, 2009: http://www2.ed.gov/programs/racetothetop/executive-summary.pdf.
46. William L. Sanders and Sandra P. Horn. "Research Findings from the Tennessee Value-Added Assessment System," *Journal of Personnel Evaluation in Education* 12, no. 3, 1998, 247.
47. Ibid.
48. Ibid., 248.
49. Arne Duncan. Letter to Randy Dorn, Superintendent of Public Instruction, State of Washington entitled "Washington Extension Determination Letter," April 24, 2014, http://www2.ed.gov/policy/eseaflex/secretary-letters/wad6.html.
50. "President Obama Announces More Key Administrative Posts." Press Release, May 1, 2014, http://www.ferc.gov/media/headlines/2014/05-01-14-whitehouse.pdf; Robert Gordon, Thomas J. Kane and Douglas O. Staiger. "Identifying Effective Teachers Using Performance on the Job," Discussion Paper 2006–01, The Hamilton Project: Advancing Opportunity, Prosperity and Growth. The Brookings Institution, April, 2006, http://www.brookings.edu/views/papers/200604hamilton_1.pdf.
51. Henry Louis Mencken. *Prejudices: Second Series* (New York: Alfred A. Knopf, 1920), 158.
52. American Statistical Association. "ASA Statement on Using Value-Added Models for Educational Assessment." April 8, 2014, http://www.amstat.org/policy/pdfs/ASA_VAM_Statement.pdf.
53. Linda Darling-Hammond, Audrey Amrein-Beardsley, Edward H. Haertel, Jesse Rothstein. "Getting Teacher Evaluation Right: A Background Paper for Policy Makers. A Research Briefing by the American Educational

Research Association and the National Academy of Education," September 14, 2011, http://www.aera.net/Portals/38/docs/News_Media/AERABriefings/Hill%20Brief%20-%20Teacher%20Eval%202011/GettingTeacherEvaluationRightBackgroundPaper(1).pdf.

54. Los Angeles Teacher Ratings. "*Los Angeles Times*," accessed June 19, 2014, http://projects.latimes.com/value-added.
55. Barbara Jones. "Los Angeles Times Sues LAUSD over Teacher Performance Data." *Los Angeles Daily News*, October 17, 2012, http://www.dailynews.com/social-affairs/20121018/los-angeles-times-sues-lausd-over-teacher-performance-data.
56. Diane Ravitch. "LA Times Plans to Post Teacher VAM Ratings Again," Diane Ravitch's Blog, November 24, 2013, http://dianeravitch.net/2013/11/24/la-times-plans-to-post-teacher-vam-ratings-again/; Alexandra Zavis and Tony Barboza. "Teacher's Suicide Shocks School," *Los Angeles Times*, September 28, 2010, http://articles.latimes.com/2010/sep/28/local/la-me-south-gate-teacher-20100928; In July 2014, the California Court of Appeal overturned a previous court decision that supported the LA Times right to publish teacher rankings according to a VAM model.
57. Tim Walker. "Enough Is Enough: Florida Teachers Sue to Block Flawed Evaluation System," *NEA Today*, April 16, 2013, http://neatoday.org/2013/04/16/enough-is-enough-florida-educators-sue-to-block-flawed-evaluation-system/; Topher Sanders, Steve Patterson, Khristopher J. Brooks, Denise Smith Amos and Christopher Hong. "Florida Releases Controversial Scores on Teacher Effectiveness," accessed June 22, 2014, http://members.jacksonville.com/files/interactives/vam/.
58. Valerie Strauss. "Houston Teachers Sue over Controversial Teacher Evaluation Method." *The Washington Post*, April 30, 2014, http://www.washingtonpost.com/blogs/answer-sheet/wp/2014/04/30/houston-teachers-sue-over-controversial-teacher-evaluation-method/; Carl Wade Gervin. "Tennessee Education Association Sues Knox County Schools over Bonus Plan," *Metro Pulse*, March 10 2014, http://blogs.metropulse.com/the_daily_pulse/2014/03/tennessee-education-associatio.html; "NYSUT: A Union of Professionals. Suit: State Failed to Account for Impact of Poverty in Evaluations," March 10, 2014, http://www.nysut.org/news/2014/march/suit-state-failed-to-account-for-impact-of-poverty-in-evaluations.
59. Department of Education. "Race to the Top Fund," 59688 Federal Register / Vol. 74, No. 221 / Wednesday, November 18, 2009 / Rules and Regulations. 34 CFR Subtitle B, Chapter II; [Docket ID ED–2009–OESE–0006]; RIN 1810–AB07, November 18, 2009, http://www.gpo.gov/fdsys/pkg/FR-2009-11-18/pdf/E9-27426.pdf, 59867.
60. "Race to the Top Executive Summary," 11.

61. "What Is School Choice?" The Friedman Foundation for Educational Choice, accessed March 14, 2014, http://www.edchoice.org/School-Choice/What-is-School-Choice.
62. Nick Gillespie. "The Father of Modern School Reform: Fifty Years Ago, Milton Friedman Introduced the Idea of School Vouchers. Now He Looks Back on His Legacy." *Reason.com*, December 2005, http://reason.com/archives/2005/12/01/the-father-of-modern-school-re.
63. Eric A. Hanushek. "Milton Friedman's Unfinished Business," *Hoover Digest*, Winter 2007, http://hanushek.stanford.edu/publications/milton-friedman%E2%80%99s-unfinished-business.
64. Lindsey Burke. "Remembering Milton Friedman's School Choice Legacy." *The Daily Signal*, July 30, 2012, http://dailysignal.com/2012/07/30/remembering-milton-friedmans-school-choice-legacy/.
65. "The Year of School Choice." *The Wall Street Journal*, July 5, 2011, http://online.wsj.com/news/articles/SB10001424052702304450604576420330972531442.
66. "National Charter School Study 2013. Center for Research on Education Outcomes at Stanford University, accessed June 20, 2014, http://credo.stanford.edu/documents/NCSS%202013%20Final%20Draft.pdf, 57.
67. "KIPP Commitment to Excellence Contract. Sample Student and Family Contract." Published by Teach for America, accessed June 22, 2014, www.kippla.org/sol/commitment-to-excellence.cfm.
68. Ravitch, *Reign of Error*, 175.
69. National Assessment of Educational Progress. "The Nation's Report Card. America's Charter Schools. Results from the NAEP 2003 Pilot Study," U.S. Department of Education, accessed June 22, 2014, http://nces.ed.gov/nationsreportcard/pdf/studies/2005456.pdf, 10.
70. National Assessment of Educational Progress. "A Closer Look at Charter Schools Using Hierarchical Linear Modeling." U.S. Department of Education, August, 2006, http://nces.ed.gov/nationsreportcard/pdf/studies/2006460.pdf, vi.
71. The Civil Rights Project. "Choice Without Equity: Charter School Segregation and the Need for Civil Rights Standards," accessed June 14, 2014, http://civilrightsproject.ucla.edu/news/research/k-12-education/integration-and-diversity/choice-without-equity-2009-report.
72. Joy Resmovits. "Charter School Segregation Target of New Report." The Huffington Post, February 22, 2012, http://www.huffingtonpost.com/2012/02/22/charter-school-education-segregation-equity-race-legislation_n_1295043.html.

Bibliography

"Academic Rankings of World Universities." The Center for World-Class Universities (CWCU) of Shanghai Jiao Tong University, accessed April 29, 2014: http://www.shanghairanking.com/index.html.

Academy for Urban School Leadership (AUSL), accessed May 13, 2014: http://auslchicago.org.

Achieve. "2001 National Education Summit." Achieve, accessed April 14, 2014: http://www.achieve.org/files/2001NationalEducationSummitBriefing%20Book.pdf.

Achieve. "Achieve and the American Diploma Project." Achieve, accessed March 15, 2014: http://www.achieve.org/files/About%20AchieveADP-Apr2012.pdf.

Achieve. "Achieving the Common Core." Achieve, accessed June 4, 2014: http://www.achieve.org/print/achieving-common-core.

Achieve, the Education Trust, and the Thomas B. Fordham Foundation. "Ready or Not: Creating a High School Diploma That Counts." Washington, DC: American Diploma Project, 2004. http://www.achieve.org/ReadyorNot.

Achieve. "Future Ready Project." Achieve, accessed April 14, 2014: http://www.achieve.org/future-ready.

Achieve, the National Governors Association, and the Council of Chief State School Officers. "Benchmarking for Success: Ensuring U.S. Students Receive a World-Class Education." Washington, DC: National Governors Association, 2008, 2.

Achieve. "Our History." Achieve, accessed April 14, 2014: http://www.achieve.org/history-achieve.

Achieve. "Out of Many, One: Toward Rigorous Common Core Standards from the Ground Up" Achieve, July 2008: http://www.achieve.org/files/OutofManyOne.pdf.

Achieve. "Race to the Top. Accelerating College and Career Readiness in States: P-20 Longitudinal Data Systems." Achieve, accessed June 14, 2014: http://www.achieve.org/files/RTTT-P20LongitudinalData.pdf.

Achieve. "A Review of the 1996 National Education Summit." Achieve, accessed March 29, 2014: http://www.achieve.org/summits.

Achieve. "Summits." Achieve, accessed April 14, 2014: http://www.achieve.org/summits.

Achieve the Core. "Our Purpose." Achieve the Core, accessed June 3, 2014: http://achievethecore.org/about-us.

Achieve the Core. "Achieve the Core: Student Achievement Partners." Achieve the Core, accessed June 3, 2014: http://achievethecore.org/author/2/student-achievement-partners.

"America's Choice." National Center on Education and the Economy, accessed June 12, 2014: http://www.ncee.org/programs-affiliates/history/americas-choice/.

American Legislative Exchange Council (ALEC), accessed June 2, 2014: http://www.alec.org/about-alec/history/.

American Statistical Association. "ASA Statement on Using Value-Added Models for Educational Assessment." American Statistical Association, April 8, 2014: http://www.amstat.org/policy/pdfs/ASA_VAM_Statement.pdf.

Anand, Geeta. "India Graduates Millions, but Too Few Are Fit to Hire." *The Wall Street Journal,* April 5, 2011: http://online.wsj.com/news/articles/SB10001424052748703515504576142092863219826.

Anderson, Richard C., Elfrieda H. Hiebert, Judith A. Scott, and Ian A. G. Wilkinson. *Becoming a Nation of Readers: The Report of the Commission on Reading.* Urbana, IL: University of Illinois, 1985.

Andrew, John A. *The Other Side of the Sixties: Young Americans for Freedom and the Rise of Conservative Politics.* New Brunswick, NJ: Rutgers University Press, 1997.

Appleborne, Peter. "Lure of the Education Market Remains Strong for Business." *The New York Times,* January 31, 1996: http://www.nytimes.com/1996/01/31/us/lure-of-the-education-market-remains-strong-for-business.html.

Areen, Judith, and Christopher Jencks. "Education Vouchers: A Proposal for Diversity and Choice." *Teachers College Record* 72, no. 3, 1971, 327–36.

Armstong, S. W. "Illiteracy: An Incurable Disease or Educational Malpractice?" Washington, DC: Senate Republican Policy Committee, 1989.

"The Assessment Consortia." K-12 Center at ETS, accessed June 20, 2014: http://www.k12center.org/.

Bailey, Nancy E. *Misguided Education Reform: Debating the Impact on Students.* Lanham, MD: Rowman and Littlefield Publishers, 2013.

"Baldrige Performance Excellence Program." Baldrige Performance Excellence, accessed March 3, 2014: http://www.baldrigepe.org/.

Balf, Todd. "The Story behind the SAT Overhaul." *The New York Times Magazine,* March 6, 2014: http://www.nytimes.com/2014/03/09/magazine/the-story-behind-the-sat-overhaul.html?_r=1.

Barkham, Joanne. "Hired Guns on Astroturf: How to Buy and Sell School Reform." *Dissent: A Quarterly of Politics and Culture,* Spring 2012: http://www.dissentmagazine.org/article/hired-guns-on-astroturfhow-to-buy-and-sell-school-reform.

Bartlett, Bruce. "Tax Cuts and 'Starving the Beast.'" *Forbes,* May 7, 2010: http://www.forbes.com/2010/05/06/tax-cuts-republicans-starve-the-beast-columnists-bruce-bartlett.html.

Beckham, Joseph, and Barbara Klaymeier Wills. "Duties, Responsibilities, Decision-Making, and Legal Basis for Local School Board Powers." *Education Encyclopedia*, accessed March 20, 2014: http://education.stateuniversity.com/pages/2391/School-Boards.html.

Bell, Terrel H. *The Thirteenth Man: A Reagan Cabinet Memoir.* New York: The Free Press, 1988, 1.

Berliner, David C., and Bruce J. Biddle. *The Manufactured Crisis: Myths, Fraud, and the Attack on America's Public Schools.* Reading, MA: Addison-Wesley Publishing Company, Inc., 1995, 24–26.

Bestor, Arthur. *Educational Wastelands: The Retreat from Learning in Our Public Schools*, 2nd ed. Urbana, IL: University of Illinois Press, 1985.

Bill and Melinda Gates Foundation. "Awarded Grants." Bill and Melinda Gates Foundation, accessed June 12, 2014: http://www.gatesfoundation.org/How-We-Work/Quick-Links/Grants-Database#q/k=student%20achievement%20partners.

Bill and Melinda Gates Foundation. "Bill Gates: Education Commission of the States Annual Conference." Bill and Melinda Gates Foundation, July 11, 2012: http://www.gatesfoundation.org/media-center/speeches/2012/07/bill-gates-education-commission-of-the-states-annual-conference.

Bill and Melinda Gates Foundation. "Grants." Bill and Melinda Gates Foundation, accessed June 4, 2014: http://www.gatesfoundation.org/search#q/k=Achieve%2C%20Inc.&page=2.

Blanchard, Olivia. "I Quit Teach for America: Five Weeks of Training Was Not Enough to Prepare Me for a Room of 20 Unruly Elementary Schoolers." *The Atlantic*, September 23, 2013: http://www.theatlantic.com/education/archive/2013/09/i-quit-teach-for-america/279724/.

"Blue Ribbon Schools Program." Washington DC: U.S. Department of Education: http://www2.ed.gov/programs/nclbbrs/list-1982.pdf.

Bonstingl, John Jay. "The Quality Revolution in Education." *Improving School Quality* 50, no. 3, November 1992, 4–9.

Boyd, James. "Nixon's Southern Strategy: 'It's All in the Charts.'" *The New York Times*, May 17, 1970, 105–108.

Bracey, Gerald. "Righting Wrongs." The Huffington Post, December 3, 2007: http://www.huffingtonpost.com/gerald-bracey/righting-wrongs_b_75189.html.

Bracey, Gerald W. *The War against America's Public Schools: Privatizing Schools, Commercializing Education.* Boston, MA: Allyn and Bacon, 2002, 23–24.

Brady, Tom P. *Black Monday: An Address Made to the Indianola Citizens Council.* Winona, MS: Association of Citizens Council, 1955.

Browne, Beverly, Pamela Kinsey-Barker, and Direka Martin. "Vouchers: An Initiative for School Reform?" *Issues Challenging Education, Horizon Site,* accessed February 20, 2014: http://horizon.unc.edu/projects/issues/papers/Voucher.html.

Buckley, William F., Jr. *God and Man at Yale: The Superstitions of "Academic Freedom."* Washington, DC: Regnery, 1986. (First published in 1951.)

Buckley, William F., Jr., "Mr. Eisenhower's Decision and the Eisenhower Program." *National Review* 1, no. 18, March 21, 1956.

Buckley, William F., Jr. "Our Mission Statement." *The National Review Online,* accessed February 2, 2014: http://www.nationalreview.com/articles/223549/our-mission-statement/william-f-buckley-jr.

Buckley, William F., Jr. "Why the South Must Prevail." *National Review* IV, no. 7, August 24, 1957.

Budowsky, Brent. "Bill Clinton's Rescue Ride." *The Hill,* February 26, 2014: http://thehill.com/opinion/brent-budowsky/199368-brent-budowsky-bill-clintons-rescue-ride.

Burke, Lindsey. "Remembering Milton Friedman's School Choice Legacy." *The Daily Signal,* July 30, 2012: http://dailysignal.com/2012/07/30/remembering-milton-friedmans-school-choice-legacy/.

"Bush Calls Education 'Civil Rights Issue of Our Time.'" *CNN Inside-Politics,* January 19, 2002: http://edition.cnn.com/2002/ALLPOLITICS/01/19/bush.democrats.radio/index.html.

Byrnes, James F. "The Supreme Court Must Be Curbed." Greenwood, MS: Association of Citizens' Councils, 1956. (Originally published in *U.S. News and World Report,* May 18, 1956.)

CNN Online. "Education Chief's 'Terrorist' Remark Ignites Fury: Paige's Apology Does Little to Mollify Teacher's Union." *CNN Online,* February 24, 2004: http://www.cnn.com/2004/EDUCATION/02/24/paige.terrorist.nea/index.html?iref=mpstoryview.

C-SPAN. Complete coverage of the "Reading First Program Oversight" hearings is available on the *C-SPAN* website: http://www.c-span.org/video/?197699-1/reading-first-program-oversight-part-1.

Campbell, Jon. "Education Chief Defends Cancellation of Common Core Forums." *Democrat and Chronicle,* October 15, 2013: http://www.democratandchronicle.com/story/news/local/2013/10/15/education-chief-defends-cancellation-of-common-core-forums/2986771/.

Cannon, Lou. *President Reagan: The Role of a Lifetime.* New York: Public Affairs, 1991.

Carleton, David. *Landmark Congressional Laws on Education: Student's Guide to Landmark Congressional Laws.* Westport, CT: Greenwood Publishing Group, 2001, 193–204.

Carpenter, Dick M., II. "School Choice Signals: Research Review and Survey Experiments." The Friedman Foundation for Educational Choice, January, 2014: http://www.edchoice.org/Research/Reports/School-Choice-Signals--Research-Review-and-Survey-Experiments.aspx.

Carroll, Archie B., and Ann K. Buchholtz. *Business and Society: Ethics and Stakeholder Management,* 7th ed. Mason, OH: South-Western Cengage Learning, 2009.

Carter, Jimmy. "Department of Education Organization Act Statement on Signing S.210 into Law." The American Presidency Project, October 17, 1979: http://www.presidency.ucsb.edu/ws/?pid=31543.

Cavanaugh, Sean. "American Institutes for Research Fights Pearson Common-Core Testing Award." *Education Week*, May 6, 2014: http://blogs.edweek.org/edweek/marketplacek12/2014/05/american_institutes_for_research_challenges_pearson_common-core_testing_award_in_court.html.

Chall, Jeanne S. *Learning to Read: The Great Debate*, 3rd ed. Belmont CA: Wadsworth Publishing Company, 1995.

Chartwell Education Group LLC. "About Us." Chartwell Education Group LLC, accessed April 13, 2014: http://www.chartwelleducation.com/pages/about-us.php.

Chase, Brett, and Patrick Rehkamp. "School Reform Attracting Billionaires' Money to Illinois Races." *The Chicago Sun-Times*, June 1, 2014: http://politics.suntimes.com/article/springfield/school-reform-attracting-billionaires%E2%80%99-money-illinois-races/sun-06012014-114pm.

Cheng, Audrey. "Teach for America Gains Record Number of Applicants." *Medill on the Hill*, March 11, 2013: http://medillonthehill.net/2013/03/teach-for-america-gains-record-number-of-applicants/.

Children's Defense Fund. "Board of Directors Emeriti." Children's Defense Fund, accessed April 4, 2011: http://www.childrensdefense.org/about-us/board-of-directors/emeritus.html.

Children's Defense Fund. "Child Poverty in America 2010." Children's Defense Fund, September 2011: http://www.childrensdefense.org/child-research-data-publications/data/child-poverty-in-america-2010.pdf.

Children's Defense Fund. "Glossary of Terms Frequently Used in Federal Education Discussions." Children's Defense Fund, March 2011: http://www.childrensdefense.org/child-research-data-publications/data/education-glossary-of-terms.pdf.

Children's Defense Fund. "The Poor People's Campaign." Children's Defense Fund, accessed April 4, 2014: http://www.childrensdefense.org/about-us/our-history/poor-peoples-campaign.html.

Chodorov, Frank. *Fugitive Essays: Selected Writings of Frank Chodorov*. Indianapolis, IN: Liberty Press, 1980.

Chodorov, Frank. "A Solution of Our Public School Problem (brought up to date)." *Human Events*, XI, no. 20, May 19, 1954.

Chubb, John E., and Terry M. Moe. *Politics, Markets, and America's Schools*. Washington, DC: The Brookings Institution, 1990.

The Civil Rights Project. "Choice without Equity: Charter School Segregation and the Need for Civil Rights Standards." The Civil Rights Project, accessed June 14, 2014: http://civilrightsproject.ucla.edu/news/research/k-12-education/integration-and-diversity/choice-without-equity-2009-report.

Cobb, James C. *The Most Southern Place on Earth: The Mississippi Delta and the Roots of Regional Identity*. New York: Oxford University Press, 1992.

Cody, Anthony. "A Progressive and a Conservative Find Common Ground Opposing the Common Core." *Education Week Teacher, Living in Dialogue*, April 15, 2013: http://blogs.edweek.org/teachers/living-in-dialogue/2013/04/a_progressive_and_a_conservati.html.

Cody, Anthony. "The Secret Sixty Prepare to Write Standards for 50 Million." *Education Week*, July 6, 2009: http://blogs.edweek.org/teachers/living-in-dialogue/2009/07/national_standards_process_ign.html.

"Clear-Cutting Our Schools." *Rethinking Schools* 28, no. 1 Fall 2013: http://www.rethinkingschools.org/archive/28_01/edit281.shtml.

"The Clinton Years: Improving America's Schools Act." Federal Education Policy and the States, 1945–2009. States' Impact on Federal Education Policy. New York State Education Department, accessed June 3, 2014: http://www.archives.nysed.gov/edpolicy/research/res_essay_clinton_iasa.shtml.

Clinton, William J. "Address before a Joint Session of the Congress of the State of the Union." The American Presidency Project, January 19, 1999: http://www.presidency.ucsb.edu/ws/?pid=57577.

Clinton, William J. "Remarks to the National Governors' Association Education Summit in Palisades, New York." The American Presidency Project, March 27, 1996: http://www.presidency.ucsb.edu/ws/index.php?pid=52594.

Clinton, William J. "Statement on Signing the School-to-Work Opportunities Act of 1994." The American Presidency Project, May 4, 1994: http://www.presidency.ucsb.edu/ws/?pid=50105.

Coleman, David. "What Must Be Done in the Next Two Years." Keynote speech, Institute for Learning: 2011 IFL Senior Leadership Meeting, University of Pittsburgh, December 8–9, 2011: http://truthinamericaneducation.com/wp-content/uploads/2013/12/What_must_be_done.pdf.

College Entrance Examination Board. "On Further Examination: Report of the Advisory Panel on the Scholastic Aptitude Test Score Decline." College Entrance Examination Board. Princeton, NJ: College Board, 1977.

Common Core State Standards Initiative. "Development Process." Common Core State Standards Initiative: Preparing America's Students for College and Career, accessed May 4, 2014: http://www.corestandards.org/about-the-standards/development-process/.

Common Core State Standards Initiative. "Reaction to the March 2010 Draft Common Core State Standards: Highlights and Themes from the Public Draft." Common Core State Standards Initiative, accessed June 15, 2014: http://www.corestandards.org/assets/k-12-feedback-summary.pdf.

Conant, James B. *Education and Liberty*. Cambridge, MA: Harvard University Press, 1953.

Copeland, Larry. "School Cheating Scandal Shakes Up Atlanta." *USA Today*, April 14, 2013: http://www.usatoday.com/story/news/nation/2013/04/13/atlanta-school-cheatring-race/2079327/.

Copperman, Paul. *The Literacy Hoax: The Decline of Reading, Writing, and Learning in the Public Schools and What We Can Do about It.*

New York: William Morrow and Company, 1978. As cited in National Commission on Excellence in Education, 19.

Cremin, Lawrence A. *The Transformation of the School: Progressivism in American Education, 1876–1957.* New York: Alfred A. Knopf, 1961.

Crispino, Joseph. *In Search of Another Country: Mississippi and the Conservative Counterrevolution.* Princeton, NJ: Princeton University Press, 2007.

Cuban, Larry. *The Blackboard and the Bottom Line: Why Schools Can't Be Businesses.* Cambridge, MA: Harvard University Press, 2007.

Curry, Constance. *Silver Rights.* Chapel Hill, NC: Algonquin Books of Chapel Hill, 1995.

Dalheim, Mary. "Shirley Hufstedler—ED's New Head: Who Is She? What Can She Do for Education?" *Instructor* 90, no. 4, August 1980, 42–48.

Damast, Alison. "Q&A: Teach for America's Wendy Kopp," *Bloomberg Business Week*, March 26, 2012: http://www.businessweek.com/articles/2012-03-26/q-and-a-teach-for-americas-wendy-kopp.

Darling-Hammond, Linda, Audrey Amrein-Beardsley, Edward H. Haertel, and Jesse Rothstein. "Getting Teacher Evaluation Right: A Background Paper for Policy Makers. A Research Briefing by the American Educational Research Association and the National Academy of Education." September 14, 2011: http://www.aera.net/Portals/38/docs/News_Media/AERABriefings/Hill%20Brief%20-%20Teacher%20Eval%202011/GettingTeacherEvaluationRightBackgroundPaper(1).pdf.

Decker, Geoff. "Success Academy Donors Give Big to Cuomo Campaign." *Chalkbeat*, January 17, 2014: http://ny.chalkbeat.org/2014/01/17/success-academy-donors-flood-cuomos-coffers-filings-show/#.U5MbvOhX-uY.

Department of Education. "Race to the Top Fund." 59688 Federal Register / Vol. 74, No. 221 / Wednesday, November 18, 2009 / Rules and Regulations. 34 CFR Subtitle B, Chapter II; [Docket ID ED–2009–OESE–0006]; RIN 1810–AB07: http://www.gpo.gov/fdsys/pkg/FR-2009-11-18/pdf/E9-27426.pdf, 59867.

Dewey, Douglas. "How to Separate School and State: A Primer." *The Freeman*, July 1, 1996: http://www.fee.org/the_freeman/detail/how-to-separate-school-and-state-a-primer.

Dewey, John. "Democracy and Education (1916)." In *The Middle Works of John Dewey, 1899–1924*, Vol. 9, edited by Jo Ann Boydston. Carbondale, IL: Southern Illinois University Press, 1985, 93.

"DIBELS Data System. Our History." University of Oregon, accessed April 20, 2014: https://dibels.uoregon.edu/about/#history.

Dillon, Sam. "Schools Chief from Chicago Is Cabinet Pick." *The New York Times*, December 15, 2008: http://www.nytimes.com/2008/12/16/us/politics/16educ.html?_r=0.

Dittmer, John. *Local People: The Struggle for Civil Rights in Mississippi.* Urbana, IL: University of Illinois Press, 1994.

Dougherty, Kevin J,. and Lizabeth Sostre. "Minerva and the Market: The Sources of the Movement for School Choice." In *The Choice Controversy,* edited by Peter W. Cookson. Newbury Park: CA: Corwin Press, 1992, 24–45.

Douglas-Hall, Ayana, and Heather Koball. "The New Poor: Regional Trends in Child Poverty since 2000." *National Center for Child Poverty, Mailman School of Public Health, Columbia University*, August 2006: http://www.nccp.org/publications/pdf/text_672.pdf.

Doyle, Denis P. "A Personal Report from the Education Summit: What Does It Mean for Educational Reform?" The Heritage Lectures, no. 564. Washington DC: The Heritage Foundation, May 21, 1996.

Dreilinger, Danielle. "7,000 New Orleans Teachers, Laid Off After Katrina, Win Court Ruling." *The Times-Picayune*, January 16, 2014: http://www.nola.com/crime/index.ssf/2014/01/7000_new_orleans_teachers_laid.html.

Duncan, Arne. "Washington Extension Determination Letter." Letter to Randy Dorn, Superintendent of Public Instruction, State of Washington, April 24, 2014: http://www2.ed.gov/policy/eseaflex/secretary-letters/wad6.html.

Duncan, Arne. "States Will Lead the Way toward Reform." Secretary Arne Duncan's Remarks at the 2009 Governors Education Symposium, U.S. Department of Education, June 14, 2009: http://www2.ed.gov/news/speeches/2009/06/06142009.html.

Duncan, Garrett Albert. "The Pitfalls of No Child Left Behind." *Viewpoint, Washington University in St. Louis Magazine*, Winter 2005: http://magazine-archives.wustl.edu/winter05/Viewpoint.htm.

Duncan, Jeff. "Duncan Introduces Resolution Condemning Common Core." February 12, 2014: http://jeffduncan.house.gov/press-release/duncan-introduces-resolution-condemning-common-core.

"Duncan Praised as 'Bona Fide Reformer' of Chicago Education System." *Fox News*, December, 16, 2008: http://www.foxnews.com/politics/2008/12/16/duncan-praised-bona-fide-reformer-chicago-education/.

"Duncan Says 82 Percent of America's Schools Could 'Fail' under NCLB This Year." U.S. Department of Education, March 9, 2011: https://www.ed.gov/news/press-releases/duncan-says-82-percent-americas-schools-could-fail-under-nclb-year.

Eakin, Sybil. "Forum: National Education Summit." *Technos Quarterly* 5, no. 2 Summer 1996: http://www.ait.net/technos/tq_05/2eakin.php.

Ebenstein, Lanny. *Milton Friedman: A Biography*. New York: Palgrave Macmillan, 2007, 142–43.

Edelman, Marian Wright. "Revisiting Marks, Mississippi." The Huffington Post, March 25, 2011: http://www.huffingtonpost.com/marian-wright-edelman/revisiting-marks-mississi_b_840786.html.

Edelman, Marian Wright. "The Courage and Vision of Medgar Evers." The Huffington Post, February 8, 2013: http://www.huffingtonpost.com/marian-wright-edelman/the-courage-and-vision-of_b_2649092.html.

Edelman, Peter. *Searching for America's Heart: RFK and the Renewal of Hope*. Boston, MA: Houghton Mifflin Company, 2001.

Edelman, Peter. *So Rich, So Poor: Why It's So Hard to End Poverty in America*. New York: The New Press, 2012.

Edelman, Peter. "The Worst Thing Bill Clinton Has Done." *The Atlantic Monthly* 279, no. 3, 43–58.

Educational Policies Commission, *The Purposes of Education in American Democracy*. Washington DC: National Education Association of the United States, 1938, 39–124.

Electronic Privacy Information Center (EPIC). "EPIC v. The U.S. Department of Education: Challenging the Department of Education's Family Educational Rights and Privacy Act (FERPA) 2011 Regulations," accessed June 17, 2014: http://epic.org/apa/ferpa/.

Emery, Kathy. "The Business Roundtable and Systemic Reform: How Corporate-Engineered High-Stakes Testing Has Eliminated Community Participation in Developing Educational Goals and Policies." Dissertation, University of California, Davis, 2002.

Emery, Kathy, and Susan Ohanian. *Why Is Corporate America Bashing Our Public Schools?* Portsmouth, NH: Heinemann, 2004.

"Englewood Parents Protest CPS School Closings." *5 NBC Chicago*, May 21, 2013: http://www.nbcchicago.com/blogs/ward-room/Englewood-Parents-Protest-CPS-School-Closings_Chicago.html.

"ESEA Flexibility: Flexibility to Improve Student Academic Achievement and Increase the Quality of Instruction." U.S. Department of Education, September 23, 2011: http://www2.ed.gov/policy/elsec/guid/esea-flexibility/index.html.

"The Essential Components of a Successful Education System: Putting Policy into Practice." New York: The Business Roundtable, 1992.

"Fast Facts." National Center for Education Statistics. Institute of Education Sciences, accessed March 21, 2014: http://nces.ed.gov/fastfacts/display.asp?id=372.

"Federal Education Policy and the States, 1945–2009: A Brief Synopsis" *States' Impact on Federal Education Policy Project*. Albany, NY: New York State Archives, January 2006 (revised November 2009).

Finn, Chester. "Speech at a Meeting of the Georgia Policy Foundation." October 8, 1996: https://www.youtube.com/watch?v=v_M_JNOxQ8A.

Finn, Chester E., Jr. *Troublemaker: A Personal History of Education Reform since Sputnik*. Princeton, NJ: Princeton University Press, 2008.

Finn, Chester E., Jr., *We Must Take Charge: Our Schools and Our Future*. New York: The Free press, 1991, 254.

Flesch, Rudolf. *Why Johnny Can't Read and What You Can Do About It*. New York: Harper and Row Publishers, Inc., 1955.

Flynn, John T. *The Road Ahead: America's Creeping Revolution*. New York: Devon-Adair Company, 1949.

Flynn, John T. "Who Owns Your Child's Mind?" In *Public Education under Criticism: Presenting Penetrative Articles from Leading Magazines and Educational Journals Dealing with Criticism of Our Public Schools*, edited by C. Winfield Scott and Clyde M. Hill. New York: Prentice-Hall, 1954, 158–59.

Friedman Foundation for Educational Choice. "What Is School Choice?" The Friedman Foundation for Educational Choice, accessed March 14, 2014: http://www.edchoice.org/School-Choice/What-is-School-Choice.

Friedman, Milton. *Capitalism and Freedom*. Chicago: University of Chicago Press, 1962.

Friedman, Milton. "Fiscal Responsibility." *Newsweek* 7 August 7, 1967: http://0055d26.netsolhost.com/friedman/pdfs/newsweek/NW.08.07.1967.pdf.

Friedman, Milton. "Milton Friedman on Vouchers," CNBC Interview, March 24, 2003. Friedman Foundation for Educational Choice, accessed February 3, 2014: http://www.edchoice.org/The-Friedmans/The-Friedmans-on-School-Choice/Milton-Friedman-on-Vouchers.aspx.

Friedman, Milton. "Selling School Like Groceries: The Voucher Idea," *The New York Times Magazine* September 23, 1975. Friedman Foundation for Educational Choice, accessed February 5, 2014: http://www.edchoice.org/The-Friedmans/The-Friedmans-on-School-Choice/Selling-School-like-Groceries--The-Voucher-Idea.aspx.

Friedman, Milton. "The Promise of Vouchers," *The Wall Street Journal*, December 5, 2005.

Friedman, Milton. "The Role of Government in Education." In *Economics and the Public Interest*. edited by Robert A. Solo. New Brunswick, NJ: Rutgers University Press, 1955. The Friedman Foundation for Educational Choice, accessed February 2, 2014, http://www.edchoice.org/The-Friedmans/The-Friedmans-on-School-Choice/The-Role-of-Government-in-Education.aspx.

Friedman, Milton, and Rose Friedman. *Free to Choose: A Personal Statement*. Orlando, FL: Harcourt Press, 1990.

Friedman, Milton, and Rose Friedman. *Two Lucky People: Memoirs*. Chicago: University of Chicago Press, 1998.

Friedman, Milton, and Anna Jacobson Schwartz. *A Monetary History of the United States, 1867–1960*. Princeton, NJ: Princeton University Press, 1963.

Gamble, Richard, ed. *The Great Traditions: Classic Readings on What It Means to Be an Educated Human Being*. Wilmington DE: ISI Books, 2007.

Gardner, David Pierpont. Interview with Harry Kreisler, "Leadership in Education: Conversation with David Pierpont Gardner." In *Conversations with History*. University of California Berkeley: Institute of International Studies, 1998: http://globetrotter.berkeley.edu/conversations/Gardner/.

Garvin, David A. "How the Baldrige Award Really Works." *Harvard Business Review* 69, no. 6, November–December 1991, 80–96.

"GE Foundation Awards $18 Million to Student Achievement Partners," *Philanthropy News Digest*, February 2, 2012: http://www.philanthropynewsdigest.org/news/ge-foundation-awards-18-million-to-student-achievement-partners.

Gerstner, Louis V. "Lessons from 40 Years of Education 'Reform': Let's Abolish Local School Districts and Finally Adopt National Standards." *The Wall Street Journal*, December 1, 2008: http://online.wsj.com/news/articles/SB122809533452168067.

Gerstner, Louis V., Jr. "Remarks of Louis V. Gerstner, Jr., Chairman and CEO—IBM Corporation at the National Governors' Association Annual Meeting." National Governors Association Annual Meeting, Burlington, VT, July 30, 1995.

Gerstner, Louis V., Jr., with Roger D. Semerad, Denis Philip Doyle, and William B. Johnston. *Reinventing Education: Entrepreneurship in America's Public Schools*. New York: The Penguin Group, 1994.

Gervin, Carl Wade. "Tennessee Education Association Sues Knox County Schools over Bonus Plan." *Metro Pulse*, March 10, 2014: http://blogs.metropulse.com/the_daily_pulse/2014/03/tennessee-education-associatio.html.

Gilbert, Glenn. "State Ready to Implement Common Core—Finally!" *Morning Sun Opinion*, December 4, 2013: http://www.themorningsun.com/opinion/20131204/gilbert-state-ready-to-implement-common-core-finally.

Gillespie, Nick. "The Father of Modern School Reform: Fifty Years Ago, Milton Friedman Introduced the Idea of School Vouchers. Now He Looks Back on His Legacy." *Reason.com*, December 2005: http://reason.com/archives/2005/12/01/the-father-of-modern-school-re.

Goals 2000: Educate America Act: http://www2.ed.gov/legislation/GOALS2000/TheAct/index.html.

Good, Curtis. "A Nation at Risk: Committee Members Speak Their Mind." In *American Educational History Journal*, edited by J. Wesley Null, 37, no. 1 and 2, 2010, 373.

Goodman, Ken. "Comments on the Reading Excellence Act (U.S.) (HR 2614, Senate passed version). An Invited Contribution." International Reading Association, December 1998. Reading Online: http://www.readingonline.org/critical/act.html.

Gordon, Robert, Thomas J. Kane, and Douglas O. Staiger. "Identifying Effective Teachers Using Performance on the Job." Discussion Paper 2006–01, the Hamilton Project: Advancing Opportunity, Prosperity and Growth. The Brookings Institution, April 2006: http://www.brookings.edu/views/papers/200604hamilton_1.pdf.

Graham Patricia Albjerg. *Schooling America: How the Public Schools Meet the Nation's Changing Needs*. New York: Oxford University Press, 2005.

Grossman, Tabitha, Ryan Reyna, and Stephanie Shipton. "Realizing the Potential: How Governors Can Lead Effective Implementation of the Common Core State Standards." National Governors Association, October 2011: http://www.nga.org/files/live/sites/NGA/files/pdf/1110CCSSIIMPLEMENTATIONGUIDE.PDF, 4.

Grovum, Jake. "Lasting Effects from Financial Crash Mean New Normal in States." *Stateline: The Daily News of the Pew Charitable Trust*,

September 5, 2013: http://www.pewstates.org/projects/stateline/headlines/lasting-effects-from-financial-crash-mean-new-normal-in-states-85899502664.

Gschwandtner, Gerhard. "David T. Kearns." *Selling Power Magazine*, accessed March 3, 2014: http://www.sellingpower.com/content/article/?a=3395/david-t-kearns&page=5.

Hanushek, Eric A. "Milton Friedman's Unfinished Business." *Hoover Digest*, Winter 2007: http://hanushek.stanford.edu/publications/milton-friedman%E2%80%99s-unfinished-business.

Harrigan, Anthony. "The South Is Different." *National Review*, March 8, 1958, 1.

Harris, Gardiner. "Medicines Made in India Set Off Safety Worries." *The New York Times*, February 14, 2014: http://www.nytimes.com/2014/02/15/world/asia/medicines-made-in-india-set-off-safety-worries.html?_r=0.

Hartman, Andrew. *Education and the Cold War: The Battle for the American School.* New York: Palgrave Macmillan, 2008, 96, 142.

Harvey, David. *A Brief History of Neoliberalism.* New York: Oxford University Press, 2005.

Hayek, F. A. *The Road to Serfdom Text and Documents; the Definitive Edition*, edited by Bruce Caldwell. London: University of Chicago Press, 2007.

Heath, Thomas. "Louis V. Gerstner Jr. Lays Out His Post-IBM Life." *The Washington Post*, June 7, 2013: http://www.washingtonpost.com/business/economy/louis-v-gerstner-jr-lays-out-his-post-ibm-life/2013/06/07/04e9da2a-cd42-11e2-8845-d970ccb04497_story.html.

Heilig, Julian Vasquez. "Billionaires Co-Opt Minority Groups into Campaign for Education Reform." *Cloaking Inequity*, March 7, 2014: http://cloakinginequity.com/2014/03/07/billionaires-co-opt-minority-groups-into-campaign-for-education-reform/.

Heilig, Julian Vasquez, and Linda Darling-Hammond. "Accountability Texas-Style: The Progress and Learning of Urban Minority Students in a High-Stakes Testing Context." *Educational Evaluation and Policy Analysis* 30, no. 2, 2008, 75–110.

Heise, Michael M. "Goals 2000: Educate America Act: The Federalization and Legalization of Educational Policy." *Fordham Law Review* 63, 1994, 345: http://ir.lawnet.fordham.edu/flr/vol63/iss2/2.

"History of Business Roundtable." Business Roundtable, accessed March 20, 2014: http://www.businessroundtable.org/about/history.

Home School Legal Defense Association. "Building the Machine: The Common Core Documentary." March 31, 2014: https://www.youtube.com/watch?v=zjxBClx01jc.

Hu, Winnie. "Testing Firm Faces Inquiry on Free Trips for Officials." *The New York Times*, December 21, 2011: http://www.nytimes.com/2011/12/22/education/new-york-attorney-general-is-investigating-pearson-education.html?_r=0.

Hubbard, David. *This Happened in Pasadena*. New York: Macmillan, 1951.

The Hunt Institute. "2002 Governors Education Symposium Report." The Hunt Institute, December 1, 2002: http://www.hunt-institute.org/knowledge-library/articles/2002-12-1/2002-governors-education-symposium-report/.

Hursh, David. "Dr. David Hursh on Neoliberalism and 'Reform.'" Diane Ravitch's Blog, March 13, 2014: http://dianeravitch.net/2014/03/13/full-youtube-video-for-dr-david-hursh-on-neoliberalim-and-reform/.

IBM. "About IBM." IBM, accessed March 14, 2014: http://www.ibm.com/ibm/us/en/.

Improving America's Schools Act of 1994 (IASA), Part C, Sec. 10301. http://www2.ed.gov/legislation/ESEA/toc.html.

Institute of Education Sciences (IES). "Statewide Longitudinal Data Systems Grant Program: Designing, Developing, Implementing, and Using Longitudinal Data Systems to Improve Student Learning." National Center for Education Statistics, accessed June 14, 2014: http://nces.ed.gov/programs/slds/about_SLDS.asp.

"Is TFA Undermining the Chicago Public Schools? An Internal TFA Document Shows Plans for a Dramatic Charter Expansion in the Windy City." *Edushyster*, September 9, 2013: http://edushyster.com/?p=3191.

"Jason Zimba." Achieve the Core: Student Academic Partners, accessed June 4, 2014, http://achievethecore.org/author/35/jason-zimba.

Jehlen, Alain. "ESEA at 45." National Education Association, accessed March 24, 2014: http://www.nea.org/home/38860.htm.

Jones, Barbara. "Los Angeles Times Sues LAUSD over Teacher Performance Data." *Los Angeles Daily News,* October 17, 2012: http://www.dailynews.com/social-affairs/20121018/los-angeles-times-sues-lausd-over-teacher-performance-data.

Jones, Denisha. "Beware of Education Reformers Who Co-Opt the Language of the Civil Rights Movement. *emPower*, February 27, 2014: http://www.empowermagazine.com/beware-education-reformers-co-opt-language-civil-rights-movement/.

Karier, Clarence J. *The Individual, Society, and Education: A History of American Educational Ideas,* 2nd ed. Urbana, IL: University of Illinois Press, 1986, 278.

Kearns, David T., and David A. Nadler. *Prophets in the Dark: How Xerox Reinvented Itself and Beat Back the Japanese.* New York: HarperCollins Publishers, 1992.

Keynes, John Maynard. *Activities 1940–46. Shaping the Post-War World: Employment and Commodities,* vol. 27. In *The Collected Writings of John Maynard Keynes,* edited by Donald Moggridge, London: Macmillan [for the Royal Economic Society], 1980..

"KIPP Commitment to Excellence Contract. Sample Student and Family Contract." Published by Teach for America, accessed June 22, 2014: www.kippla.org/sol/commitment-to-excellence.cfm.

Kirk, Annette Y. "Annette Kirk on Leadership." *The Russell Kirk Center for Cultural Renewal*, Grand Valley State University, Allendale Charter Township, MI, March 3, 2010.

Kirk, Russell. *The Conservative Mind: from Burke to Eliot*, 7th revised edition. Washington DC: Regency, 1985.Klein, Karin. "The Big Special Interests in the Race for California Schools Chief." *Los Angeles Times Opinion*, May 27, 2014: http://www.latimes.com/opinion/opinion-la/la-ol-tuck-torlakson-campaign-20140523-story.html.

Klein, Naomi. *The Shock Doctrine: The Rise of Disaster Capitalism.* New York: Picador, 2007.

Koerner, James D. *Who Controls American Schools?—A Guide for Layman.* Boston, MA: Beacon Press, 1968.

Kolb, Ruth F., and Robert P. Strauss. "State Laws Governing School Board Ethics." Presentation at the American Education Finance Association Conference 1999 Research Conference, Seattle, Washington, March 19, 1999.

Kopp, Wendy. *A Chance to Make History: What Works and What Doesn't in Providing Excellent Education for All.* New York: PublicAffairs, 2011.

Kopp, Wendy. *One Day, All Children . . .: The Unlikely Triumph of Teach for America and What I Learned along the Way.* New York: PublicAffairs, 2001.

Kozol, Jonathan. *Death at an Early Age: The Destruction of the Hearts and Minds of Negro Children in the Boston Public Schools.* Boston, MA: Houghton Mifflin, 1967.Landsmann, Leanna, and Mary Harbaugh. "Education's Entrepreneurs (includes comments by chief executive officers on education) (Educating America: An Entrepreneurial Approach). *Forbes,* October 14, 1991." *Highbeam Business*, accessed March 5, 2014: http://business.highbeam.com/392705/article-1G1-11303756/education-entrepreneurs.

Larson, Leslie. "Former First Lady Barbara Bush: Bill Clinton Thinks of George H. W. Bush Like the Father He Didn't Have." *Daily News*, January 21, 2014: http://www.nydailynews.com/news/politics/lady-barbara-bush-love-bill-clinton-article-1.1586676.

Layton, Lyndsey. "How Bill Gates Pulled Off the Swift Common Core Revolution." *The Washington Post*, June 7, 2014: http://www.washingtonpost.com/politics/how-bill-gates-pulled-off-the-swift-common-core-revolution/2014/06/07/a830e32e-ec34-11e3-9f5c-9075d5508f0a_story.html.

Layton, Lyndsey. "New Orleans Leads Nation in Public Charter School Enrollment." *The Washington Post*, December 10, 2013: http://www.washingtonpost.com/local/education/new-orleans-leads-nation-in-percentage-of-public-charter-school-enrollment/2013/12/10/cb9c4ca6-61d6-11e3-bf45-61f69f54fc5f_story.html.

Leung, Rebecca. "The Texas Miracle: 60 Minutes Investigates Claims That Houston Schools Falsified Dropout Rates." *CBS News*, January 6, 2004: http://www.cbsnews.com/news/the-texas-miracle/.

Lichtman, Allan J. *White Protestant Nation: The Rise of the American Conservative Movement.* New York: Atlantic Monthly Press, 2008.

Lofren, Mike. "Anatomy of the Deep State." *Moyers and Company*, February 21, 2014: http://billmoyers.com/2014/02/21/anatomy-of-the-deep-state/.

Los Angeles Teacher Ratings. "*Los Angeles Times*," accessed June 19, 2014: http://projects.latimes.com/value-added.

Martin, Douglas. "William F. Buckley Is Dead at 82." *The New York Times*, February 27, 2008.

Martin, J. B. "The Deep South Says Never." *Saturday Evening Post*, CCXIX, June 15, 1957, 23.

Martin, Jonathan, "Republican See Wedge in Common Core." *The New York Times*, April 19, 2014: http://www.nytimes.com/2014/04/20/us/politics/republicans-see-political-wedge-in-common-core.html?_r=1.

"Massachusetts Board of Elementary and Secondary Education." March 23, 2010, https://www.youtube.com/watch?v=eJZY4mh2rt8.

Maylahn, Paula, and Pat Walkington. "Six Steps to Plan for Success in the K-12 Education Market." *Selling to Our Schools. Our Expertise. Your Success*, accessed June 13, 2014: http://www.sellingtoschools.com/articles/plan-sales-success-k-12-sales-education-market.

McCandless, Glenn. "Positioning Your Company for Ed-Tech Platform Leadership." *Selling to Schools. Our Expertise. Your Success*, accessed June 13, 2014: http://www.sellingtoschools.com/education-marketing-strategies-for-platform-leadership.

McDonough, Patricia M. "The School-to-College Transition: Challenges and Prospects." National Association of State Student Grant and Aid Programs, 2004: http://www.nassgap.org/index.aspx.

"McGraw-Hill Education Forms New Assessment and Reporting Unit to Meet Growing Global Demand, Combines CTB/McGraw-Hill, The Grow Network/McGraw-Hill, and McGraw-Hill Digital Learning." *McGraw Hill Financial*, December 1, 2005: http://investor.mhfi.com/phoenix.zhtml?c=96562&p=irol-newsArticle&ID=649072&highlight.

McGuigan, Patrick B., and Stacy Martin. "Schools approach No Child Left Behind Deadline; Feds Say Nation's Schools Cannot Meet It." *CapitolBeatOK*, April 3, 2011: http://capitolbeatok.com/reports/schools-approach-no-child-left-behind-deadline-feds-say-nations-schools-cannot-meet-it.

McKinsey and Company. "About Us." McKinsey and Company, accessed June 13, 2014: http://www.mckinsey.com/.

McMillen, Neil R. *The Citizens' Council: Organized Resistance to the Second Reconstruction, 1954–64.* Chicago: University of Illinois Press, 1971."Meet Your Government: Arne Duncan, Secretary of the Department of Education." AllGov, accessed May 3, 2014: http://www.allgov.com/officials/duncan-arne?officialid=28849.

Mencken, Henry Louis. *Prejudices: Second Series.* New York: Alfred A. Knopf, 1920, 158.

Milkis, Sidney, and Michael Nelson. *The American Presidency: Origins and Development, 1776–2011,* 6th ed. Thousand Oaks, CA: CQ Press, 2011, 396.

Miller, Julie A. "Report Questioning 'Crisis' in Education Triggers an Uproar." *Education Week*, October 9, 1991: http://www.edweek.org/ew/articles/1991/10/09/06crisis.h11.html.

Miller, Matt. "First, Kill All the School Boards: A Modest Proposal to Fix the Schools." *The Atlantic*, January 1, 2008: http://www.theatlantic.com/magazine/archive/2008/01/first-kill-all-the-school-boards/306579/.

Mintrom, Michael. *Policy Entrepreneurs and School Choice, American Governance and Public Policy Series.* Washington D.C.: Georgetown University Press, 2000.

Molnar, Alex. "School Vouchers: The Law, the Research, and Public Policy Implications." Center for Education Research, Analysis, and Innovation. Milwaukee, WI: University of Wisconsin–Milwaukee, 2001, 3.Moore, Darrin. "The Prophet of Conservatism: Russell Kirk." *The Imaginative Conservative*, 2012: http://www.theimaginativeconservative.org/2012/02/prophet-of-conservatism-russell-kirk.html.

Moser, John E. "The Ideological Odyssey of John T. Flynn" John Moser's Home Page at Ashland University: http://personal.ashland.edu/~jmoser1/flynn.html.

Moser, John E. *Right Turn: John T. Flynn and the Transformation of American Liberalism.* New York: New York University Press, 2005.

Munday, L. A. "Declining Admissions Test Scores," ACT Research Report No. 71. Iowa City, IA: The Research and Development Division of the American College Testing Program, February 1976.

Murdock, Deroy. "Friedman: Call Them Government Schools," *National Review Online*, August 1, 2012: http://www.nationalreview.com/corner/312879/friedman-call-them-government-schools-deroy-murdock.

Nash, George H. *The Conservative Intellectual Movement since 1945.* New York: Basic Books, 1976, 15.

National Assessment of Educational Progress. "A Closer Look at Charter Schools Using Hierarchical Linear Modeling." U.S. Department of Education, August 2006: http://nces.ed.gov/nationsreportcard/pdf/studies/2006460.pdf.

National Assessment of Educational Progress. "The Nation's Report Card. America's Charter Schools. Results from the NAEP 2003 Pilot Study," U.S. Department of Education, accessed June 22, 2014: http://nces.ed.gov/nationsreportcard/pdf/studies/2005456.pdf.

National Association for the Advancement of Colored People (NAACP). "Resolution on Charter Schools." National Association for the Advancement of Colored People: http://naacp.3cdn.net/ec6459eda5247ea257_d1m6bxsf6.pdf.

"National Charter School Study 2013," p. 57. Center for Research on Education Outcomes at Stanford University, accessed June 20, 2014: http://credo.stanford.edu/documents/NCSS%202013%20Final%20Draft.pdf.

National Commission on Excellence in Education (NCEE), "A Nation at Risk: The Imperative for Educational Reform," April 1983.

National Education Association, *The Pasadena Story: An Analysis of Some Forces and Factors That Injured a Superior School System: Report of an Investigation by the National Commission for the Defense of Democracy through Education of the National Education Association of the United States.* Washington, DC: National Association of the United States, 1951.

National Governors Association. "Common Core State Standards Available for Comment." National Governors Association, September 21, 2009: http://www.corestandards.org/assets/CorePublicFeedback.pdf.

National Governors Association. "Common Core State Standards Initiative Validation Committee Announced." National Governors Association, September 24, 2009: http://www.nga.org/cms/home/news-room/news-releases/page_2009/col2-content/main-content-list/title_common-core-state-standards-initiative-validation-committee-announced.html.

National Governors Association. "Common Core State Standards K-12 Work and Feedback Groups Announced." National Governors Association, November 10, 2009: http://www.nga.org/cms/home/news-room/news-releases/page_2009/col2-content/main-content-list/title_common-core-state-standards-k-12-work-and-feedback-groups-announced.html.

National Governors Association. "Common Core State Standards Work Group and Feedback Group Announced." National Governors Association, July 1, 2009: http://www.nga.org/cms/home/news-room/news-releases/page_2009/col2-content/main-content-list/title_common-core-state-standards-development-work-group-and-feedback-group-announced.html.National Governors Association for Best Practices and the Council of Chief State School Officers. "Reaching Higher: The Common Core State Standards Validation Committee," June 2010: http://www.corestandards.org/assets/CommonCoreReport_6.10.pdf.

National Institute of Child Health and Human Development. *Report of the National Reading Panel. Teaching Children to Read: An Evidence-Based Assessment of the Scientific Research Literature on Reading and Its Implications for Reading Instruction* (NIH Publication No. 00-4769). Washington, DC: U.S. Government Printing Office, 2000.

National Research Council. *Preventing Reading Difficulties in Young Children.* Washington, DC: National Academy Press, 1998.

"National Testing: Prepare for a Battle." *Education World*, September 15, 1997: http://www.educationworld.com/a_admin/admin/admin020.shtml.

NewSchools Venture Fund, accessed June 1, 2014: http://www.newschools.org/.

Newton, Michael *The Ku Klux Klan in Mississippi: A History.* Jefferson, NC: McFarland and Company, 2010.

Nixon, Richard. "Special Message to the Congress on Education Reform" (speech before Congress, Washington DC, March 3, 1970). The American Presidency Project: http://www.presidency.ucsb.edu/ws/?pid=2895.

Nock, Albert Jay. *The Theory of Education in the United States.* Auburn, AL: The Ludwig von Mises Institute, 2007, 31.

"NYSUT: A Union of Professionals. Suit: State Failed to Account for Impact of Poverty in Evaluations," March 10, 2014: http://www.nysut.org/news/2014/march/suit-state-failed-to-account-for-impact-of-poverty-in-evaluations.

Obama, Barack. "Remarks by the President on Education." The White House, Office of the Press Secretary, January 16, 2014: http://www.whitehouse.gov/the_press_office/Remarks-by-the-President-at-the-Department-of-Education/.

"Occupational Outlook Handbook." Bureau of Labor Statistics, accessed March 21, 2014: http://www.bls.gov/ooh/management/elementary-middle-and-high-school-principals.htm.

O'Hagan, Maureen. "Post-Katrina: Will New Orleans Still Be New Orleans? The Institute for Southern Studies." *Facing South,* April 10, 2014: http://www.southernstudies.org/2014/04/post-katrina-will-new-orleans-still-be-new-orleans.html.

Ordover, Nancy. *American Eugenics: Race, Queer Anatomy, and the Science of Nationalism.* Minneapolis, MN: University of Minnesota Press, 2003.

Orfield, Gary, Susan E. Eaton, and the Harvard Project on School Desegregation. *Dismantling Desegregation: The Quiet Reversal of Brown v. Board of Education.* New York: The New Press, 1996.

Osborne, David, and Ted Gaebler. *Reinventing Government: How the Entrepreneurial Spirit Is Transforming the Public Sector from Schoolhouse to Statehouse, City Hall to the Pentagon.* Reading, MA: Addison-Wesley Publishing Company, Inc., 1993.

Owens, Eric. *Daily Caller.* As Reported by Diane Marie. "Bill Gates Crying in His Vault." The Education Action Network, April 28, 2014: http://teach1776.ning.com/group/the-coalition-against-common-core/forum/topics/inbloom-goes-out-of-business?xg_source=activity.

Paige, Rod. *The War against Hope: How Teachers' Unions Hurt Children, Hinder Teachers, and Endanger Public Education.* Nashville, TN: Thomas Nelson, 2006.

Parker, Jonathan. "No Child Left Behind: The Politics and Policy of Education Reform." In *Assessing the George W. Bush Presidency: A Tale of Two Terms,* edited by Andrew Wroe and Jon Herbert. Edinburgh, UK: Edinburgh University Press, 2009.

"Pasadena Revisited." *Time Magazine,* May 7, 1951.

Patterson, James T. *Brown v. Board of Education: A Civil Rights Milestone and Its Troubled Legacy (Pivotal Moments in American History Edition)*. New York: Oxford University Press, 2002.

"PDK/Gallup Poll of the Public's Attitudes toward the Public Schools," *Phi Delta Kappa International*, August 13, 2013: http://pdkintl.org/programs-resources/poll/.

Pear, Robert. "Education Chief Calls Union 'Terrorist,' Then Recants." *The New York Times*, February 24, 2004: http://www.nytimes.com/2004/02/24/us/education-chief-calls-union-terrorist-then-recants.html.

"Pearson and America's Choice Announce Acquisition Agreement," *Pearson*, August 3, 2010: http://www.pearsoned.com/pearson-and-americas-choice-announce-acquisition-agreement/#.U3edddEU9jo.

Perry, George L., ed. *Economic Events, Ideas, and Policies: The 1960s and After.* Washington DC: Brookings Institution Press, 2000.

Perry, Linda "NYC Public Schools, Co-locations, Charters, Albany."

"Perspectives on Education in America." *Journal of Educational Research* 86, no. 5, May–June 1993, 269.

Philips-Fein, Kim. *Invisible Hands: The Making of the Conservative Movement from the New Deal to Reagan.* New York: W. W. Norton and Company, Inc., 2009, 261–62.

Petrilli, Michael. "Petrilli Testimony on Common Core in Ohio," *Education-Next,* November 20, 2013: http://educationnext.org/petrilli-testimony-on-common-core-in-ohio/.

"President Obama Announces More Key Administrative Posts." Press Release, May 1, 2014: http://www.ferc.gov/media/headlines/2014/05-01-14-whitehouse.pdf.

Public Consulting Group (PCG). "Business Partners." Public Consulting Group, accessed June 17, 2014: http://www.publicconsultinggroup.com/about/business_partners/.

Public Consulting Group (PCG). "Education Analytics." Public Consulting Group, accessed June 17, 2014: http://www.publicconsultinggroup.com/education/EducationAnalytics/index.html.

"Race to the Top Application for Initial Funding." U.S. Department of Education, 2010, accessed August 22, 2014: http://www2.ed.gov/programs/racetothetop/phase1-applications/minnesota.pdf.

"Race to the Top Executive Summary." U.S. Department of Education, November, 2009: http://www2.ed.gov/programs/racetothetop/executive-summary.pdf.

Raffel, Jeffrey. *Historical Dictionary of School Segregation and Desegregation: The American Experience.* Westport, CT: Greenwood, 1998.

"Rahm Emanuel on the Opportunities of Crisis," *WSJ Videos*, November 18, 2008: http://live.wsj.com/video/rahm-emanuel-on-the-opportunities-of-crisis/3F6B9880-D1FD-492B-9A3D-70DBE8EB9E97.html#!3F6B9880-D1FD-492B-9A3D-70DBE8EB9E97.

Ravitch, Diane. "50 States, 50 Standards: The Continuing Need for National Voluntary Standards in Education." The Brookings Institution, Summer 1996: http://www.brookings.edu/research/articles/1996/06/summer-education-ravitch.

Ravitch, Diane. *The Death and Life of the Great American School System: How Testing and Choice Are Undermining Education.* New York: Basic Books, 2011.

Ravitch, Diane. "How Embarrassing for the Friedman Foundation." Diane Ravitch's Blog, January 9, 2014: http://dianeravitch.net/2014/01/09/how-embarrassing-for-the-friedman-foundation/.

Ravitch, Diane. "LA Times Plans to Post Teacher VAM Ratings Again." Diane Ravitch's Blog, November 24, 2013: http://dianeravitch.net/2013/11/24/la-times-plans-to-post-teacher-vam-ratings-again/.

Ravitch, Diane. *Reign of Error: The Hoax of the Privatization Movement and the Danger to America's Public Schools.* New York: Alfred A. Knopf, 2013.

Ravitch, Diane. "Why We Will Win!" Keynote Speech. Network for Public Education First Annual Conference, Houston, TX, March 2, 2014: http://dianeravitch.net/2014/03/06/my-speech-at-the-network-for-public-education-why-we-will-win/.

Reagan, Ronald. "First Inaugural Address." Ronald Reagan Presidential Library and Museum, January 20, 1981: http://www.reagan.utexas.edu/archives/speeches/publicpapers.html.

Reagan, Ronald. "Remarks on Receiving the Final Report of the National Commission on Excellence in Education." Ronald Reagan Presidential Library and Museum, April 26, 1983: http://www.reagan.utexas.edu/archives/speeches/1983/42683d.htm.

Reagan, Ronald. "Republican National Convention Acceptance Speech." Ronald Reagan Presidential Library and Museum, July 17, 1980: http://www.reagan.utexas.edu/archives/speeches/publicpapers.html.

Reed, Adolph, Jr., "Nothing Left: The Long Slow Surrender of American Liberals." *Harper's Magazine,* 328, no. 1966, March 2014, 29.

"Remarks by the President on Education." The White House, Office of the Press Secretary, July 24, 2009: http://www.whitehouse.gov/the_press_office/Remarks-by-the-President-at-the-Department-of-Education/.

Resmovits, Joy. "Charter School Segregation Target of New Report." The Huffington Post, February 22, 2012: http://www.huffingtonpost.com/2012/02/22/charter-school-education-segregation-equity-race-legislation_n_1295043.html.

Resmovits, Joy. "David Coleman, Common Core Writer, Gears Up for SAT Rewrite." The Huffington Post, August 30, 2013: http://www.huffingtonpost.com/2013/08/30/david-coleman-common-core-sat_n_3818107.html.

Rhodes, Jesse H. *An Education in Politics: The Origin and Evolution of No Child Left Behind.* Ithaca, NY: Cornell University Press, 2012.

Rickover, Hyman G. *Education and Freedom.* New York: E. P. Dutton, 1959.

"RIP Irving Louis Horowitz." The Russell Kirk Center for Cultural Renewel: http://www.kirkcenter.org/index.php/news/.

Robertson, Joe. "Scores on ACT Point to Many Disparities." *Kansas City Star*, August 21, 2013: http://www.kansascity.com/2013/08/21/4424263/scores-on-act-point-to-many-disparities.html.

"Rod Paige Joins Board of Fordham Foundation." *Education Week*, May 3, 2005: http://www.edweek.org/ew/articles/2005/05/04/34fed-3.h24.html.

Rothbard, Murray N. *Education: Free and Compulsory.* Auburn, AL: Ludwig von Mises Institute, 1999.

Rubio, Phillip F. *A History of Affirmative Action, 1619–2000.* Jackson, MS: The University of Mississippi Press, 2001, 75.

The Russell Kirk Center for Cultural Renewel. "About Russell Kirk." The Russell Kirk Center for Cultural Renewal, accessed May 20, 2014: http://www.kirkcenter.org/index.php/about-kirk/.

The Russell Kirk Center for Cultural Renewel. "Ten Conservative Principles," The Russell Kirk Center for Cultural Renewel, accessed May 20, 2014 http://www.kirkcenter.org/index.php/detail.

Russo, Alexander. "What Is Common Core and Why Is Everyone—Right, Left—so Mad About It?" *Slate*, September 25, 2013: http://www.slate.com/articles/double_x/doublex/2013/09/common_core_either_you_re_against_this_new_push_for_academic_standards_and.html.

Sanders, Topher, Steve Patterson, Khristopher J. Brooks, Denise Smith Amos, and Christopher Hong. "Florida Releases Controversial Scores on Teacher Effectiveness," accessed June 22, 2014: http://members.jacksonville.com/files/interactives/vam/.

Sanders, William, and Sandra P. Horn, "Research Findings from the Tennessee Value-Added Assessment System." *Journal of Personnel Evaluation in Education* 12, no. 3, 1998,. .

Sandia National Laboratories. "About Sandia." Sandia National Laboratories, accessed March 12, 2014: www.Sandia.gov.

Schaefer, H. Luke, and Kathryn Edin. "Extreme Poverty in the United States, 1996 to 2011." Policy Brief #28. National Poverty Center, University of Michigan. Gerald R. Ford School of Public Policy, accessed April 12, 2014: http://www.npc.umich.edu/publications/policy_briefs/brief28/.

Schemo, Diana Jean. "Justice Dept. Is Asked to Investigate Reading Plan." *The New York Times*, April 21, 2007: http://www.nytimes.com/2007/04/21/us/21reading.html?_r=0.

Scherer, Marge. "On Savage Inequalities: A Conversation with Jonathan Kozol." *Educational Leadership* 50, no. 4 (December 1992–January 1993), 4–9.

"The Science of Reading Instruction and No Child Left Behind." Civic Bulletin, No. 49, September 2007. Bulletin Adapted from a Transcript of a Manhattan Institute Forum in New York City, May 22, 2007: http://www.manhattan-institute.org/html/cb_49.htm.

Seaborg, Glenn. "A Nation at Risk Revisited." *Glenn Seaborg: His Life and Contributions, Part I.* Berkeley, CA: University of California, Lawrence Berkeley National Laboratory: http://www2.lbl.gov/Publications/Seaborg/risk.htm.

"Secretary Duncan Sets Tone for 'Race to the Top' by Naming Innovative New Leader: Joanne Weiss Joins Department of Education from NewSchools Venture Fund to Implement Unprecedented Incentive Program for Bold National Reforms." U.S. Department of Education, May 19, 2009: http://www.ed.gov/news/press-releases/secretary-duncan-sets-tone-race-top-naming-innovative-new-leader

Simon, Stephanie. "K-12 Student Database Jazzes Tech Startups, Spooks Parents." *Reuters*, March 3, 2013: http://www.reuters.com/article/2013/03/03/us-education-database-idUSBRE92204W20130303.

Smith, Mortimer. *And Madly Teach: A Layman Looks at Public School Education.* Chicago: Henry Regnery Company, 1949.

Sommer, Chad. "Teach for America's Pro-Corporate, Union-Busting Agenda." *Salon*, January 13, 2014: http://www.salon.com/2014/01/13/teach_for_americas_pro_corporate_union_busting_agenda_partner/.

Sommer, Jay M. "The Excellence Commission and the Humanities." In *Challenges to the Humanities*, edited by Chester E. Finn, Jr., Diane Ravitch and P. Holley Roberts. New York, Holmes and Meier Publishers, Inc., 1985, 174–186.

"Special Edition: Testing Resistance and Reform News." *FairTest: The National Center for Fair and Open Testing*, April 2–4, 2014: http://www.fairtest.org/special-edition-testing-resistance-reform-news-apr

Stallings, D. T. "A Brief History of the United States Department of Education: 1979–2002." Center for Child and Family Policy, Duke University, 2002, 3.

"StandardsWork: Our History." *StandardsWork*, accessed June 13, 2014: http://www.standardswork.org/history.asp.

Stedman, Lawrence C. "The NAEP Long-Term Trend Assessment: A Review of Its Transformation, Use, and Findings." A Paper Commissioned for the 20th Anniversary of the National Assessment Governing Board: 1988–2008. Washington DC: National Assessment Governing Board, March, 2009, 2.

Stedman, Lawrence C. "The Sandia Report and U.S. Achievement: An Assessment. *Journal of Educational Research* 87, no. 3, January–February 1994.

Stiglitz, Joseph E. *Globalization and Its Discontents.* New York: W. W. Norton and Company, 2003.

Stillman, Jessica, "A Lesson in Hustle: How an Edtec Startup Got Their Product into 3000 Schools in a Year." *Women 2.0*, October 28, 2013: http://women2.com/lesson-hustle-edtech-startup-got-product-3000-schools-year/.

Strauss, Valerie. "Arne Duncan: 'White Suburban Moms' Upset That Common Core Shows Their Kids Aren't 'Brilliant.'" *The Washington Post*, November 16, 2013: http://www.washingtonpost.com/blogs/answer-sheet/wp/2013/11/16/arne-duncan-white-surburban-moms-upset-that-common-core-shows-their-kids-arent-brilliant/.

Strauss, Valerie. "The Biggest Irony in Chicago's Mass Closing of Schools." *The Washington Post*, May 30, 2013: http://www.washingtonpost.com/blogs/answer-sheet/wp/2013/05/30/the-biggest-irony-in-chicagos-mass-closing-of-schools/.

Strauss, Valerie. "Chicago Mayor Rahm Emanuel Chooses Private School for Kids." *The Washington Post*, July 12, 2011: http://www.washingtonpost.com/blogs/answer-sheet/post/chicago-mayor-rahm-emanuel-chooses-private-school-for-kids/2011/07/21/gIQAzES7RI_blog.html.

Strauss, Valerie. "Gov. Cuomo May Face Primary Challenge from Progressive Democrat." *The Washington Post*, June 12, 2014: http://www.washingtonpost.com/blogs/answer-sheet/wp/2014/06/12/new-york-gov-cuomo-may-face-primary-challenge-from-progressive-democrat/.

Strauss, Valerie. "Houston Teachers Sue over Controversial Teacher Evaluation Method." *The Washington Post*, April 30, 2014: http://www.washingtonpost.com/blogs/answer-sheet/wp/2014/04/30/houston-teachers-sue-over-controversial-teacher-evaluation-method/.

Strauss, Valerie. "Key Flaw in Market-Based School Reform: A Misunderstanding of the Civil Rights Struggle." *The Washington Post*, August 5, 2013: http://www.washingtonpost.com/blogs/answer-sheet/wp/2013/08/05/key-flaw-in-market-based-school-reform-a-misunderstanding-of-the-civil-rights-struggle/.

Streichenberger, Iwan. Letter posted on inBloom's website April, 2014, https://www.inbloom.org/.

Stotsky, Sandra. "Common Core's Invalid Validation Committee." Paper Presented at a Conference at University of Notre Dame, September 9, 2013: http://www.uaedreform.org/downloads/2013/11/common-cores-invalid-validation-committee.pdf.

Stotsky, Sandra. "Testimony in Favor of Wyoming Bill 14LSO.0326.L2." February 12, 2014: http://www.uaedreform.org/downloads/2014/02/testimony-in-favor-of-wyoming-bill-14lso-0326-l2.pdf.Stuart, Foster. *Red Alert: Educators Confront the Red Scare in American Public Schools, 1947–1954.* New York: Peter Lang, 2000.

Superfine, Benjamin M. *Equality in Education Law and Policy, 1954–2010.* Cambridge, UK: Cambridge University Press, 2013, 37–67.

"Susan Pimentel." GE Foundation, accessed April 23, 2014: https://sites.google.com/site/gefoundation2011a/sue- pimentel.

"Susan Pimentel." National Assessments Governing Board, accessed June 13, 2014, http://www.nagb.org/newsroom/naep-releases/2011-writing/bio-pimentel.html.

Sutton, Matthew Avery. *Jerry Falwell and the Rise of the Christian Right: A Brief History and Documents*. Bedford, NY: St. Martin's Press, 2012.

Sweet, Lynn. "Obama Education Speech in Ohio." *The Chicago Sun-Times*, September 9, 2008: http://blogs.suntimes.com/sweet/2008/09/obama_education_speech_in_ohio.html.

Sweet, Robert W., Jr. "Illiteracy: An Incurable Disease or Education Malpractice?" The National Right to Read Foundation, 1996: http://www.nrrf.org/essay_Illiteracy.html.

Tanner, Daniel. "A Nation 'Truly' at Risk." *Phi Delta Kappan* 75, no. 4, December 1993, 288–97.

Teach for America. "KIPP: Where Great Teachers Become Great School Leaders." Teach for America, accessed June 15, 2014, http://www.teachforamerica.org/assets/documents/08TFA-one_sheetv1r6.pdf.

"Themes and Discussion Points from A Nation at Risk Summit," Washington DC: The Center for Education Reform, April 3, 1998: http://www.edreform.com/edreform-university/resource/themes-discussion-points-from-a-nation-at-risk-summit-1998/.

The Thomas B. Fordham Institute. "About Us." Thomas B. Fordham Institute, accessed May 1, 2014: http://www.edexcellence.net/about-us.

Thorner, Nancy and O'Neil, Bonniel. "Common Core Dates Back to the Marxist-Socialist Paradigm of UN Charter." *Heartlander Magazine*, April 7, 2014: http://blog.heartland.org/2014/04/common-core-dates-back-to-the-marxist-socialist-paradigm-of-un-charter/.

Toppo, Greg. "Memo Warns of Rampant Cheating in DC Public Schools." *USA Today*, April 11, 2013: http://www.usatoday.com/story/news/nation/2013/04/11/memo-washington-dc-schools-cheating/2074473/.

Tozer, Steven, Guy Senese, and Paul C. Violas. *School and Society: Historical and Contemporary Perspectives*, 7th ed. New York: McGraw Hill, 2013.

Truman, Harry S. "Education Our First Line of Defense: Learning Alone Can Combat the Tenets of Communism." *Public Papers of Truman, 1945–53*. Harry S. Truman Library and Museum, March 8, 1949: http://trumanlibrary.org/publicpapers/viewpapers.php?pid=1067.

Turnbull, William A. "Student Change, Program Change: Why the SAT Scores Kept Falling." Educational Testing Service. College Board Report No. 85–2, ETS RR No. 85–28. New York: College Entrance Examination Board, 1985.

U.S. Department of Education. "Family Educational Rights and Privacy Act" (FERPA), accessed June 17, 2014: http://www2.ed.gov/policy/gen/guid/fpco/ferpa/index.html.

"U.S. Pharmaceutical Companies Testing Drugs on India's Poor." *New America Media*, August 1, 2011: http://www.independent.co.uk/news/world/asia/without-consent-how-drugs-companies-exploit-indian-guinea-pigs-6261919.html.

Vinovskis, Maris A. *From A Nation at Risk to No Child Left Behind: National Education Goals and the Creation of Federal Education Policy*. New York: Teachers College Press, 2009.

Viveo, Becky. "CPS Wants to Close First Renaissance Schools." *WBEZ91.5.* May 8, 2013: http://www.wbez.org/news/education/cps-wants-close-first-renaissance-schools-107072.

Vobejda, Barbara, and Judith Havemann. "2 HHS Officials Quit over Welfare Changes." *The Washington Post*, September 12, 1996: http://www.washingtonpost.com/wp-srv/national/longterm/welfare/quit.htm.

"The von Mises Institute:" http://mises.org/Literature/Author/731.

Walker, Tim. "Enough Is Enough: Florida Teachers Sue to Block Flawed Evaluation System." *NEA Today*, April 16, 2013: http://neatoday.org/2013/04/16/enough-is-enough-florida-educators-sue-to-block-flawed-evaluation-system/.

Wall Street Journal. "The Year of School Choice." *The Wall Street Journal*, July 5, 2011: http://online.wsj.com/news/articles/SB10001424052702304450604576420330972531442

Washington Post Foreign Staff. "How 35 Countries Compare on Poverty (The U.S. Is Ranked 34th)." *The Washington Post*, April 15, 2013: http://www.washingtonpost.com/blogs/worldviews/wp/2013/04/15/map-how-35-countries-compare-on-child-poverty-the-u-s-is-ranked-34th/.

WBAI Pacifica Radio New York, March 14, 2014: http://wbai.org/articles.php?article=1824.

Westbrook, Robert B. *John Dewey and American Democracy.* Ithaca NY: Cornell University Press, 1991, 339–41.

White, John J. "College Boards." In *Encyclopedia of Education Reform and Dissent*, edited by Thomas C. Hunt, James C. Carper, Thomas J. Lasley II, and C. Daniel Raisch. Thousand Oaks, CA: Sage Publications, 2010, 181.

"White House Profile: Secretary Arne Duncan." White House Blog, accessed May 15, 2014: http://www.whitehouse.gov/blog/author/Secretary%20Arne%20Duncan.

"Without Consent: How Drug Companies Exploit Indian 'Guinea Pigs.'" *The Independent*, May 6, 2014: http://newamericamedia.org/2011/08/us-pharmaceutical-companies-testing-drugs-on-indias-poor.php.

"World University Rankings, 2013–14" (Sponsored by Reuters) *Times Higher Education,* accessed April 29, 2014: http://www.timeshighereducation.co.uk/world-university-rankings/2013-14/world-ranking.

Yanrong, Zhao. "Chinese Pharmaceuticals Testing the U.S. Drug Market." *The China Daily/USA,* October 28, 2011: http://usa.chinadaily.com.cn/business/2011-10/28/content_13997107.htm.

Zancanella, Donald and Moore, Michael. "The Origins of the Common Core: Untold Stories." *Language Arts* 91, no. 4, March.

Zavis, Alexandra and Barboza, Tony. "Teacher's Suicide Shocks School," *The Los Angeles Times*, September 28, 2010: http://articles.latimes.com/2010/sep/28/local/la-me-south-gate-teacher-20100928.

Zubrzycki, Jaclyn. "TFA Alumni Aid New Teachers in New Orleans." *Education Week*, April 19, 2013: http://www.edweek.org/ew/articles/2013/04/19/29neworleans_ep.h32.html.

Index

CPSIA information can be obtained
at www.ICGtesting.com
Printed in the USA
LVOW01*0316200417
531464LV00022B/650/P

9 781137 482679